MW00389548

ROCK 'N' ROLL ROAD TRIP

ROCK 'N' ROLL ROAD TRIP

The Ultimate Guide to the Sites,
the Shrines, and the Legends
Across America

A. M. Nolan

PHAROS BOOKS
A SCRIPPS HOWARD COMPANY
NEW YORK

To Michael, who put up with me and
my boxes of pop music trivia.

Cover art: map courtesy of H. M. Gousha/
Simon & Schuster;
photograph of Hollywood and Vine
courtesy of Photofest;
all other photographs courtesy of Jerry Ohlinger.
Interior design by Sara Stemen
Maps by Abira Ali and Pat Redding

Copyright © 1992 by Abigail McGanney Nolan

All rights reserved. No part of this book may be
reproduced in any form or by any means without
permission in writing from the publisher.

First published in 1992

Library of Congress Cataloging-in-Publication Data

Nolan, A. M. (Abigail McGanney)
Rock 'n' roll road trip : the ultimate guide to the sites,
the shrines, and the legends across America /
A.M. Nolan.
p.   cm.
Includes index.
1. Rock music—United States—History and
criticism.   2. Musical landmarks—United States—
Guidebooks.   3. Music-halls (Variety-theaters, cabarets,
etc.)—United States—Guidebooks.   4. United States—
Guidebooks.   I. Title.   II. Title: Rock and roll road trip.
ML3534.N64   1992
781.66'0973—dc20   92-20229   CIP   MN

Printed in the United States of America

Pharos Books are available at special discounts on bulk
purchases for sales promotions, premiums, fundraising,
or educational use. For details contact the Special Sales
Department, Pharos Books, 200 Park Avenue, New York,
NY 10166

Pharos Books
A Scripps Howard Company
200 Park Avenue
New York, NY 10166

10 9 8 7 6 5 4 3 2 1

CONTENTS

INTRODUCTION

This is a book about a cold lake in Wisconsin, a poultry store in Philadelphia, a warehouse in New Orleans, a dank basement in Los Angeles. Landmarks of rock and roll are rarely of the glamourous sort.

Rock and roll certainly wasn't glamourous at its outset. It was loud, new, thrilling, neither smooth nor polite. The music was made by accident—a crossbreeding of a half-dozen styles. (Someone once called jazz the sound of surprise, but the pioneering rock and roll performers still sound a little shocked that they're being allowed to sing and play that way.) The first studios and clubs were likewise created without much premeditation. The Dew Drop Inn in New Orleans, for instance, evolved from a barbershop—and the city's most durable studio was initially an appliance store. Who could have known that they would become legendary?

And so it went through the years. The psychedelic ballroom era in the late '60s started in San Francisco not as a trend but as a big party in an acoustically unsound union hall. Flagship punk clubs of the '70s—CBGB in New York, Raul's in Austin, the Longhorn in Minneapolis—were born out of not only the need of musicians to perform, but also the skeptical willingness of club owners to give them a chance. These places, and others in many other cities, generated a sense of community—a scene, if you will.

It's the very randomness of these scenes and successes—the fact that all of the elements were thrown together so quickly—that makes the pop music histories of these sixteen cities so fascinating to trace. Who could have guessed that great R&B records would emerge from a Scandinavian stronghold like Minneapolis, that the wild parties of a college town in Georgia would produce so many good bands, that a big hall in Austin would become a home for so many different musical styles and fans? It only begins to make sense when you unravel the musical chain of events.

But the seeming randomness of successful clubs and scenes is also a clue to how fragile—and how easily squelched—they can be. As influential as it was, the Masque, L.A.'s punk mecca, lasted only about six months, unable to meet city safety regulations. Legendary venues have fallen victim to fire codes and fires, landlord disputes and redevelopment plans, and—maybe most of all—pure, simple changes of taste. The squeaky-clean teen clubs of the early to mid-'60s, for instance, quickly lost their appeal once the psychedelic ballrooms started offering big-name acts and a groovy, drugged-out atmosphere.

This book is a guide both to the clubs, studios, and record stores that have managed to survive, and to the historic spots that are still talked about, long after they have made way for parking lots and condos. For each city, we've supplied a map that shows some of the key sites, past and present. Don't forget the tapes on this trip, and always call ahead. See you in Tupelo.

Although space limits the number of sites included here, all suggestions for a future edition are welcome. Please send them to ROCK 'N' ROLL ROAD TRIP, c/o Pharos Books, 200 Park Avenue, New York, NY 10166.

ACKNOWLEDGMENTS

Many thanks are due to the following people, who helped me in many ways. Personal tours were particularly appreciated.

David Anthony, Jon Hafter and B. George of the ARChive of Contemporary Music, Greg Baker, Danny Beard, William Bell, David Bieber, Art Black, Jess Bravin, Jerry Brock, Franklin Brooks, Jeff Calder, Mark Caro, John Carroll, Curtis Casella, the folks at the Center for Southern Folklore in Memphis, Stephanie Chernikowski, Ruth Clenott, Jim Clevo, Jim Cole, Art Collins, Sylvia Colwell, Cynthia Connolly, Alex Cooley, Olivia Cottrell, Jan Crawford, Randy Crittendon, Dave Daniels, Joel Davis, Jimmy Denson, Jim Dickinson, Steve Dollar, Michael Dorf, Karen Durbin, Steve Fallon, Clayton Faught, Sharyn Felder, Brad First, Don Fox, Gilbert Fuchsberg (who came to the rescue with a working computer), Cam Garrett, Richard Gehr, Russ Gibb, Joseph Gonzalez, Jr., William Griggs, Peter Guralnick, Joyce Halasa, Bill Hamann, Jeff Hannusch, Jim Harold, Rick Harte, Cathy Hendrix, Barbara Hoover, Mike Jann, James Jenkins, Margaret Jerrido, Peter Jesperson, Carl Jones, Ken Jones, Terry Katzman, Tim Kerr, Paul Kolderie, Kenn Kweder, Ruth Leitman, Jeffrey Lemlich, Vicki Gold Levi, Bruce Licher, Mary Kay Linge, Henry LoConti, Kathei Logue, Tristram Lozaw, Tom Lyle, Ian MacKaye, Ray Manzarek, Steve Marker, Cosimo Matassa, Mary Lou McGanney, Thomas McGanney, D. Joseph Menn, Bob Meyer, Casey Monahan, Scott Morgan, Margaret Moser, Brendan Mullen, John Navarese, Charles Neville, Don Nix, Doris and Paul Nolan, Michael Oberman, Pat O'Day, Tom and Ellen Oglivy, Yvonne Olivier, Herbie O'Mell, Buck Ormsby, Chris Osgood, Tary Owens, Anastasia Pantsios, Tony Paris, Larry Parypa, Bruce Pavitt, Cutts Peaslee, Allan Pepper, Glenn Phillips, Jonathan Poneman, Martha Proctor, Jeff Rankin, Paul Ray, Valerie Riles, Bobby Robinson, Mike Rubin, Corey Rusk, Dan Sause, Thomas Schoenith, Michael Schreibman, Chris and Swannie Schuba, Marshall Sehorn, Ken Settle, Tom Sheehy, Bonnie Simmons, John Slate, Charles Stevenson, Henry Stone, Ken Stringfellow, Jim Sutcliffe, Joseph "Butterball" Tambora, Joseph Tarsia, Queenie Taylor, Allen Toussaint, Conrad Uno, Jim Walsh, Ed Ward, Kim Warnick, Brad Wernle, John Wheat, Chuck White, Burton Wilson, Don Wilson, and Leslie Wimmer.

I want to single out my editor Eileen Schlesinger for her patience and wise advice, and my friend and agent Jeremy Solomon for his support and good humor. Thanks also to mapmakers Abira Ali and Pat Redding, and to the many photographers whose work appears here.

The Northeast

BOSTON

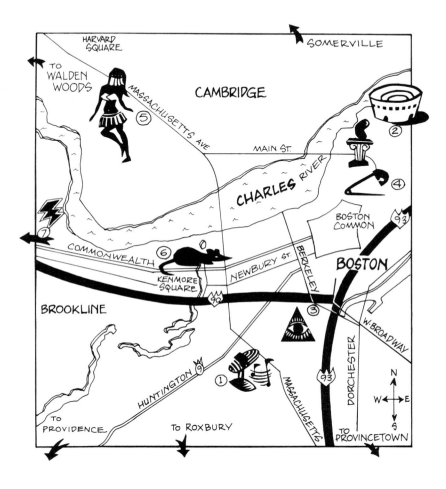

Now saddled with a hip reputation, this Massachusetts city was not a rock and roll stronghold in the '50s. "Risqué" pop hits were often banned from the airwaves, and all rock and roll shows were prohibited from 1956 to 1958. Not surprisingly, the area's very first bona fide rock and roll singer, Freddie "Boom Boom" Cannon, had to leave for Philadelphia to get his career going.

From the '60s to the present, however, Boston has unleashed a steady stream of talented solo artists and original, eccentric bands. The most famous solo artists have been female folkies from area colleges: Joan Baez (Boston University), Bonnie Raitt (Radcliffe), and Tracy Chapman (Tufts). But then there is Donna Summer, who hails from Roxbury, Boston's biggest black neighborhood, and was never a folksinger. She went to Germany to get her record contract.

Boston's garage-band tradition started off with groups like the Remains and the Barbarians, gained national attention when the J. Geils Band and Aerosmith hit big, and is still strong as so-called "alternative" groups like the Pixies, the Lemonheads, the Breeders, and Bullet LaVolta slide their way into pop culture. (The Standells' hit "Dirty Water," which refers to the Charles River, would be a perfect example of the Beantown sound— if the band was from Boston and not from Los Angeles.) But although the city is best known for ragged and raucous bands, it has also done well with clean, slick sounds; witness the gold records of the Cars, New Edition, and New Kids on the Block.

Boston has also been the site of legendary shows and infamous incidents. In 1958, for instance, one of Alan Freed's all-star tours was implicated in causing a riot (*see* **Boston Arena**). And in 1968, James Brown may have helped to prevent one (*see* **Boston Garden**). One of the oddest footnotes in Boston's pop music history occurred that same year: In the hopes of duplicating the hoopla and sales surrounding "the Sound of San Francisco," the MGM record label (and then copycat companies) signed up Boston bands like Ultimate Spinach, the Beacon Street Union, and the Apple Pie Motherhood Band. The names might sound like San Francisco bands, but record buyers didn't fall for the "Bosstown sound" marketing hype. Their hopes raised high, the bands subsequently sank without a trace, and the local music scene didn't recover its dignity for several years.

Aerosmith Apartment   *1325 Commonwealth Ave., #2B*

All five members of the band lived together in this apartment from 1970 to 1972. They acquired separate abodes after Clive Davis saw them perform at Max's Kansas City and signed them to Columbia Records. (Aerosmith's 1991 video for "Sweet Emotion" opens with a shot of this building.)

Atlantis Sound   *1092 Commonwealth Ave.*

Rick Harte helped get Boston's independent rock and roll scene off the ground when he recorded a local band called the Infliktors at this hi-fi store in October 1978. With the help of a store employee, they took over the place after it had closed, using a Crown two-track recorder for the sessions. Harte admits now that "we really didn't know what we were doing." But he learned—and started his Ace of Hearts label, which released records by quintessential Boston bands such as the Neighborhoods,

The Aerosmith Abode, as it looks today. (Photo by Diane Bergamasco.)

the Lyres, the Neats, the Nervous Eaters, Mission of Burma, and Birdsongs of the Mesozoic.

❶ Boston Arena   *238 St. Botolph St.*

This 7,200-seat arena in downtown Boston has been host to a number of important shows. On May 3, 1958, Alan Freed promoted a concert here that helped to destroy his career. On the bill of his "Big Beat" road show were stars such as Chuck Berry, Jerry Lee Lewis, Buddy Holly, the Chantels, the Diamonds, and Screamin' Jay Hawkins. Unfortunately for Freed and some members of the audience, there was a high level of tension throughout most of the show and gang violence ensued afterward. Newspaper accounts of a full-scale riot may have been exaggerated— according to one Freed associate, police connected unrelated crimes in the area to the Boston Arena show—but that didn't help Freed's reputation. Freed was indicted under an old antianarchy statute and "Big Beat" shows were canceled by officials in four Northeastern cities. Other Arena shows here have gone better: the first Motortown Revue, for instance, was kicked off here in 1963. It's now the Matthews Arena, Northeastern University's ice hockey rink.

❷ Boston Garden   *150 Causeway St.*

The home of the Bruins and the Celtics has hosted its share of rock and roll concerts, including the Beatles' first Boston show and the infamous Monkees/Jimi Hendrix double bill. In 1972, then-mayor Kevin White bailed the Rolling Stones out of jail in order to ensure that their concert date here would proceed. (White mainly wanted to avoid a riot.)

Perhaps the most notable night occurred when James Brown was scheduled to perform two days after Martin Luther King, Jr.'s assassination.
City officials, who feared looting and racial violence, arranged with
Brown for his show to be televised live and twice more over the weekend.
Brown made a public entreaty to blacks to contain their grief, which
was later entered into the congressional record. As Brown writes in his
autobiography, "Boston got through the weekend almost without any
trouble at all." Not so 197 other towns and cities. In Washington eleven
were killed, and in Chicago, nine were killed. The Garden continues to
host rock shows.

❸ The Boston Tea Party   *53 Berkeley St., then 15 Lansdowne St.*
During the late '60s, a Kansas City lawyer named Ray Riepen transformed
an old church into the Tea Party, Boston's "psychedelic ballroom." Mod-
eled after the wild venues Riepen had seen during a recent visit to San
Francisco, the Tea Party soon became the center of the local music world.
It featured the top local bands and touring acts ranging from the Allman
Brothers to Led Zeppelin, who made a big splash here on their first
American tour. (The audience demanded seven encores, and got a four-
hour show.)

In the summer of 1967, the Velvet Underground—minus Nico and the
rest of Andy Warhol's Exploding Plastic Inevitable—was the house band.

*Tea Party patrons gather at back for a sunrise Easter service, 1970. (Photo by
Clif Garboden.)*

Cantone's in its heyday, 1978. (Photo collage by Phil in Phlash.)

The group took on the Tea Party's booking agent as manager and soon lost the cultural cachet Warhol's connection had given them. John Cale left the group in the fall, and was replaced by Doug Yule, a Boston-area bassist.

Ray Riepen also had a hand in turning WBCN, a classical music radio station, into an "underground" rock and roll station. He persuaded the station owners to broadcast live from the hall from midnight to 4 A.M. With DJs like Mississippi Harold Wilson and Peter Wolf (whose on-air name was Woofuh Goofuh), the show was a huge success. By the end of the year, the progressive rock format was running twenty-four hours a day. The Tea Party also gave Don Law, now the city's most powerful promoter, his start in the booking business. The hall closed in January 1970, less than three years after it opened.

Cambridge Common   *north of Harvard Sq.*

Boston-born Jonathan Richman often played here for change—and attention—when he was starting out as a solo performer. By 1971, having moved up in the world, he and the Modern Lovers returned to play a free concert with the Allman Brothers Band.

❹ Cantone's   *69 Broad St.*

In the late '70s and early '80s, this Italian restaurant/rock dive served lunch to businessmen and rock and roll music to punks. Located in the financial district, it didn't survive the '80s real estate boom. Memorable shows include sets by local legends Mission of Burma, the Neighborhoods, Someone and the Somebodies, and DMZ.

Club 47   *47 Mt. Auburn, then 47 Palmer, Cambridge*
Founded by Paula Kelley in 1958, this small coffeehouse was a pioneering outpost for folk music. Joan Baez played here often, and Maria Muldaur made her debut here in July 1962. And, as the legend goes, Arlo Guthrie was discovered here.

The first location was a storefront, packing people in for urban bluesmen like Howlin' Wolf. At times the room was just too small—when local legend Jackie Washington played, the front window would break from the pressure of the crowd. In 1964, the club moved to Palmer Street (and got permission from the city to use the number 47 as its address). It closed in 1969, but the folk tradition was maintained at 47 Palmer under new ownership and the name of **Passim**. Singer/songwriters like Shawn Colvin, Tom Waits, Bonnie Raitt, Tracy Chapman, and Suzanne Vega have all been frequent visitors.

Donnelly Memorial Theatre   *209 Massachusetts Ave.*
In the early '60s, this theater booked many of the big touring soul shows that featured stars such as Solomon Burke, Garnett Mimms, Joe Tex, Rufus Thomas, and Otis Redding. Writer Peter Guralnick was lucky enough to be an usher then, getting good seats and some glimpses backstage.

Fort Apache   *1 Camp St., Cambridge*
A real alternative rock landmark, this studio—in its three different incarnations—has been used by all the local stars, including the Pixies, Dinosaur Jr., Bullet LaVolta, the Blake Babies, Throwing Muses, and the Lemonheads. Owner Gary Smith is also active in searching out bands to record here; for instance, he found the Pixies performing at the Rat and worked with them on their first album. (Rounder Records shares Fort Apache's address.)

Harvard Square Theater   *10 Church St., Cambridge*
Boston has the perhaps dubious distinction of being the original bastion of rock criticism. And a May 9, 1975 performance at this theater inspired the most famous line of rock writing ever: "I saw rock & roll's future and its name is Bruce Springsteen." Jon Landau (who certainly found *his* future with Springsteen) caught the Boss's show (which included the first live performance of "Born to Run") and was inspired to include the line in the resulting lengthy essay in Boston's *Real Paper*. Springsteen had opened for Bonnie Raitt, who let him play his full two-hour show. He concluded to a thunderous ovation, and unfortunately for headliner Bonnie, a good portion of the crowd left when he did.

Other performers at this theater include Iggy Pop and the Stooges, Bob

Dylan, and the Clash, who made their local debut here in 1978. The space is now occupied by a multiplex.

Jack's   *952 Massachusetts Ave., Cambridge*

Opened in 1969, this establishment was the longest running pop music club in the Boston area before it burned down in a very suspicious fire in 1986. The J. Geils Band played here all the time in the early '70s. After the "Bosstown sound" fiasco, J. Geils restored some credibility to the local scene. Their 1971 self-titled debut album produced the hit "Looking for a Love."

⑤ The Middle East Restaurant   *472 Massachusetts Ave., Cambridge*

After the mid-'80s reign of a club called Green St. Station, located in Jamaica Plain, this accessible Central Square venue became an obligatory stop for upcoming local bands as well as for the top touring alternative acts. Thurston Moore, Mike Watt and Kira Roessler, the Unsane, and the Fluid have all put on shows in the back room of this functioning restaurant.

Newbury Comics   *332 Newbury St.*

In 1978, Mike Dreese and John Brusger opened a store at 268 Newbury St. that sold comics and comics only. In late 1979, a friend wanted to get rid of some of his record collection. Dreese and Brusger obliged by selling the records from the comic store and a record retail chain was born. Newbury Comics soon had the city's best selection of imports and local releases, and since 1980, they've launched a record label (Modern Method), a magazine (*Boston Rock*, which is now independent) and seven other stores.

The Middle East Restaurant, 1992.
(Photo by Diane Bergamasco.)

Orchard Park Projects *around Dearborn and Ziegler, Roxbury*

This public housing project was home to four members of New Edition before they became superstars. In 1982, they were heard singing together by Maurice Starr, the future svengali to New Kids on the Block, who added another member and got them a recording contract. After many hit records, New Edition splintered off, no less successfully, into solo acts (Bobby Brown, Brown's replacement Johnny Gill, and Ralph Tresvant) and a trio called Bell Biv Devoe. But in 1990, they reunited for a remix of the tersely titled "Ronnie, Bobby, Ricky, Mike, Ralph, and Johnny (Word to the Mutha)!" and filmed a video in the area.

The Paradise *967 Commonwealth Ave.*

Since opening in 1977, this has been one of the top clubs in Boston, making a specialty of booking upcoming acts from England. In 1980, U2 played one of their first U.S. shows here, opening for a now-forgotten band named Barooga. The next year, U2 recorded their live single of "11 O'Clock Tick Tock" here. The Psychedelic Furs, Sinéad O'Connor, and Billy Bragg also stopped here on their way up. Local bands like O-Positive, the Cave Dogs, and the Heretics have also regularly played the Paradise. Even Aerosmith has put on a few shows here, under a different name of course.

Paul's Mall *733 Boylston St.*

This long-lived basement club (1964–1978) featured soul, comedy, and rock acts in week-long engagements. High points include shows by Earth, Wind, and Fire; Harold Melvin and the Blue Notes; Randy Newman; and Bruce Springsteen (opening for David Bromberg). An adjoining club, the Jazz Workshop, was run by the same team. It featured genius types like John Coltrane, Cannonball Adderly, and Keith Jarrett, who was the house pianist for a while.

Psychedelic Supermarket *590 Commonwealth Ave.*

Donna Summer made her professional debut at this club in 1967. She was the lead singer of an otherwise all-white rock band; they called themselves Crow. The next year, she moved to Germany to star in a production of *Hair*. The Supermarket has since been torn down and replaced by the Nickelodeon Cinema.

⑥ The Rat *528 Commonwealth Ave., Kenmore Sq.*

This club has operated under many names and owners, but its most famous incarnation has been around since August '74. Jim Harold took over a club called TJ's, renamed it the Rathskeller, and started booking bands with original material. The first band was Mickey Clean and the Mezz. Harold recalls: "They were horrible but they were doing their own thing."

Local legend Willie Alexander gave the club its nickname when he introduced his "Let's Go to the Rat" anthem, to the tune of the Danny

Mission of Burma at the Rat, 1981. (Photo by Diane Bergamasco.)

and the Juniors classic. The nickname became official when the 1976 *Live at the Rat* double album was released. The Real Kids, DMZ, and the Boize were a few of the bands featured. Harold also booked out-of-town legends just as they were starting out: Blondie, Talking Heads, R.E.M., the Police. And the Romantics from Detroit ended up playing an entire weekend when they were stuck in town during the 1978 blizzard.

Approaching its twentieth anniversary, The Rat continues as an important club for rising local bands. Harold hasn't changed its looks or his adventurous booking policy.

Skippy White's Records   *former location: 1763 Washington*
Skippy White, whose real name is Fred LeBlanc, opened his first R&B record store in early 1961. Since then he and his stores have become institutions. He remained on the edge of Roxbury for over twenty-five years, serving the neighborhood as well as collectors.

His was one of the few businesses that wasn't harmed during the riots of 1967 and 1968. Cars were being turned over and torched, but kids would come running into his store—with bricks in their hands—to ask about the new Otis Redding release. "And I can remember," LeBlanc said recently, "a big helmeted policeman coming in with his big riot stick, asking "Do you have 'The Happening' by Diana Ross and the Supremes?'" And I sold him a record." Today his main outlet is located in Jamaica Plain.

Synchro Sound   *331 Newbury St.*

This Boston recording studio has had several incarnations—as well as its share of hits—since opening in the early '70s. For starters, Aerosmith recorded their first hit single, "Dream On," here. In the late '70s, a local DJ named Arthur Baker took an engineering course here, and immediately started producing dance records. After moving to New York City, he became one of the most sought-after producer/remixers of the '80s.

The Cars bought Intermedia in 1980 and remodeled it as Synchro Sound. They recorded parts of the *Shake It Up* album here, as well as a score of outside projects. Ric Ocasek, for instance, produced the Romeo Void single, "Never Say Never," here. The Cars sold the studio in 1988 but a partnership of five is continuing the facility as Synchro Sound.

❼ The Underground   *1110 Commonwealth Ave.*

Widely hailed as Boston's "most amazing club ever," it had a short life; it opened in 1980 but was closed and turned into a laundromat by evil landlords (Boston University) in 1983. This small, L-shaped room was located under a B.U. dorm and worked as a catalyst in getting local bands formed. It was the site, for instance, of the debut performance by local group Someone and the Somebodies.

Where It's At   *660 Beacon, then 1101 Commonwealth Ave.*

This teen club was at the center of the Boston scene in the mid-'60s. Like the Boston Tea Party, it booked local bands as well as the big touring acts. A popular mid-'60s Boston band, the Remains, made a live album here.

Blurt at the Underground, 1980. (Photo by Diane Bergamasco.)

Mitch Ryder and the Detroit Wheels on the stage of Where It's At, 1968. (Photo by Kathei Logue.)

👫 Schools

Berklee College of Music   *1140 Boylston St.*

Quincy Jones went here for about a year, taking ten classes a day, but left for an arranging job in New York City while still a teenager. Other famous attendees (they didn't all graduate) include Bruce Cockburn, Melissa Etheridge, producer Arif Mardin, Billy Squier, Elliot Easton of the Cars, Aimee Mann of 'Til Tuesday, and Kurt Ralske of New York's Ultra Vivid Scene.

Boston University

Joan Baez's alma mater. Aerosmith played free shows there in exchange for practice space.

Harvard University

Gram Parsons went here for one semester, Bonnie Raitt spent two years at Radcliffe, and Jerry Harrison graduated in 1971. In the mid-to-late '80s, members of Galaxie 500, the Lemonheads, Bullet LaVolta, and Trip Shakespeare were students here and played at parties around campus. The rap magazine *The Source* was started in a dorm room by two students. And, as if that weren't enough, the Cars played the 1977 Freshman Mixer.

WHRB   *45 Quincy St.*

This campus radio station, located in the basement of Memorial Hall, has been the site of several beginnings. Tom Rush became known for his

folk show here and then gained fame as a performer. The first release by Rounder Records was taped here in 1973. Most recently, two Harvard students founded *The Source* as an outgrowth of their WHRB rap show.
Harvard Stadium   *North Harvard St.*
Janis Joplin's last performance ever was held here on August 12, 1970. Forty thousand people attended—half bought tickets, half vaulted the walls. She died less than two months later in Los Angeles.

New England Conservatory of Music   *290 Huntington Ave.*
Legendary funk keyboardist Bernie Worrell went here for three years but had to drop out when his father died.

🦅 DETOURS

Concord, MA   *20 miles NW of Boston*
The preservation of Walden Woods, the inspiration for Henry David Thoreau's great work, *Walden,* has been made a cause celebre for celebrities ranging from rock star Don Henley to Senator Edward M. Kennedy. In a well-publicized effort to keep nasty developers and ignorant town officials from further spoiling Thoreau's retreat, members of the Walden Woods Project have put on concerts, given lectures, and even published a coffee-table book for the cause.

Providence, RI   *51 miles SW of Boston*
Rhode Island School of Design
Chris Frantz, Tina Weymouth, and David Byrne of Talking Heads met on this campus in the early '70s. Frantz and Byrne were in a band together called the Artistics, which had a few shows at the RISD Tap Room. It was only after moving to New York City, however, that the trio formed Talking Heads. Byrne lived in a big house on Brown Street on Providence's East Side; it's where he began writing "Psycho Killer," the Heads' signature song for quite some time.

Housatonic, MA   *136 miles SW of Boston*
Alice's Church   *4 Van Deusenville Road*
Alice Brock, who operated the restaurant immortalized in Arlo Guthrie's classic anti-war anthem, lived in the bell tower of this converted church during the 1960s. It was here that Guthrie wrote the 18-minute song and 20 others. In early 1992, Guthrie ensured this landmark's preservation by making it the headquarters for his record company and for the Guthrie Center, a nonprofit organization. Unfortunately, Alice's back-alley diner in nearby Stockbridge no longer stands, but the staff at the church sells T-shirts that map out Guthrie's "Garbage Trail."

NEW YORK CITY

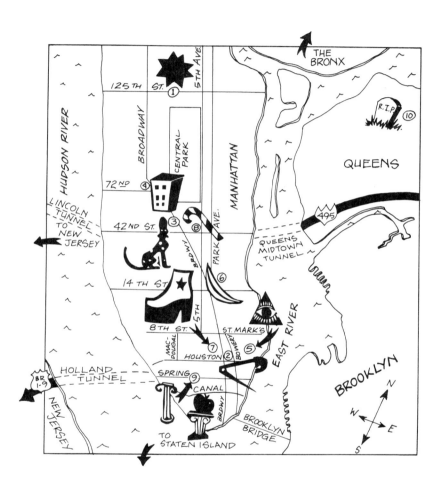

New York City has been a mecca for popular music since the days of Tin Pan Alley and a rock and roll center since the music's inception in the 1950s. The city has spawned many legends of rock and roll (and killed off a few as well, like Sid Vicious), and its rap and underground rock scenes continue to thrive.

The city's rock history began in the early '50s, when its role had more to do with disseminating the music than with creating it. Disc jockeys such as Alan Freed, Jocko Henderson, Dr. Jive, and Mr. Blues created huge audiences for rock and roll by broadcasting rhythm and blues in all its emerging forms. These disc jockeys also promoted concerts around town. Freed's shows at the Paramount in Brooklyn featured the prime attractions of the day—including Buddy Holly, Jerry Lee Lewis, and Fats Domino—and attracted teenagers from all over. The Apollo Theater in Harlem catered to predominantly black audiences and was the other venue of choice for the latest musical stars.

Before long, New Yorkers were attempting their own versions of the new style. Some of the era's best songwriters grew up here, most notably Otis Blackwell ("All Shook Up," "Don't Be Cruel") and the so-called Brill Building songsmiths (including Gerry Goffin and Carole King, Neil Sedaka, Doc Pomus, and Mort Shuman), most of whom didn't actually work in the Brill Building. Jerry Leiber and Mike Stoller ("Hound Dog," "There Goes My Baby") moved here from Los Angeles in 1957 and continued their string of hits. Also emerging in these early years were vocal harmony groups such as Frankie Lymon and the Teenagers (formed in 1954), Little Anthony and the Imperials (1957), Dion and the Belmonts (1958), the Drifters with Ben E. King (1959), teen idols like Bobby Darin,

Cafe Wha? and the Players' Theatre, 1966. (Photo by Fred W. McDarrah.)

and girl-groups like the Chantels (1956), the Ronettes (1959), and the Crystals (1961).

For about five years from the late '50s to the early '60s, five blocks in midtown Manhattan seemed to contain the entire pop industry: a startling number of music publishing companies (in 1650 Broadway and 1619 Broadway), musical instrument stores; rehearsal and recording studios, and the best record stores. (You knew you had a hit record if Colony, then at 52nd and Broadway, played your song out front.)

In the early '60s, New York City's Greenwich Village fostered a folk music revival, inspired by earlier rural performers like Leadbelly and Woody Guthrie. Figures like Bob Dylan and Peter, Paul and Mary got their start at Gerde's Folk City, the Gaslight, Cafe Wha? and other subterranean coffeehouses. After failing as a pop duo in the mid-'50s, Simon and Garfunkel got a second chance in this setting in 1965. The Fugs, who mixed folk, scatology, and politics started out at the Bridge and Players theaters.

A harder form of rock and roll took over the city in the late '60s—with visiting bands generating the excitement. Indigenous groups like the Rascals and the Lovin' Spoonful were by and large overshadowed by the superstars playing Bill Graham's Fillmore East, the Academy of Music (now the Palladium), and Madison Square Garden. The Who, the Jimi Hendrix Experience, the Rolling Stones, and the Allman Brothers Band all put on legendary shows here.

The one homegrown group to achieve a measure of immortality was the Velvet Underground, whose commercial success was all but nil when the band was intact but whose influence remains apparent. That band, with Brooklyn native Lou Reed as its leader, marked the beginning of a distinctive New York City style that extends through today's East Village "noise" bands. These groups thrive on primitive instrumentation, cacophonous effects like feedback and out-of-tune vocals, and grim, streetwise lyrics. The Velvets broke up in 1970, but the New York Dolls formed in 1971 and continued the tradition. They dressed in women's clothing, wore outrageous makeup and created a raw, barely controlled form of rock and roll that inspired future punk bands.

The major styles in New York City's music by the mid-'70s were the twin devils of punk and disco. Punk grew out of the scene surrounding a Lower East Side club named CBGB, which featured raw, "concept" bands like the Ramones, Talking Heads, and Blondie. The aggressive aspects of this scene—as well as its torn fashions—were picked up and pushed to extremes by the more nihilistic punk groups in England. Meanwhile back in Manhattan, Studio 54, the Paradise Garage, the Roxy, and other clubs nurtured disco. Producers Nile Rodgers and Bernard Edwards, both from the Bronx, created key hits of the disco era.

Rap music soon followed, set in motion by DJs in the Bronx who began experimenting with disco songs ("Good Times," for one) at dance clubs and block parties. In the late '70s, figures like Kool Herc, Grandmaster Flash, and Afrika Bambaataa invented and refined the turntable arts of scratching, cutting, and backspinning. By 1980, the focus had turned away from DJs and toward MCs, who were creating an aggressive approach while talking on the mike, or "rapping." In the years since, rap music has been adopted and adapted all over the country, often dominating the charts and the airwaves.

New York's other rock and roll contribution in the last decade came from dissonant Lower East Side bands like Sonic Youth, Swans, Live Skull, and Helmet, who have been inspired by the work of Glenn Branca and his guitar armies. Although many of these bands have either broken up or evolved into more commercial outfits, the No-Wave, white-noise sound lives on.

MANHATTAN

❶ The Apollo   *253 West 125th St.*

It was an uptown variety house—one of many—when Frank Schiffman and Leo Brecher took over in 1935. Since then it's become a world-famous institution, known for its entertainingly brutal Amateur Night competitions and as an important venue for the country's greatest black performers. For decades, it was a key stop on the "chitlin circuit," the network of black theaters that also included the Royal in Baltimore and the Regal in Chicago.

The winners of Amateur Night make an impressive list—the Ronettes, the Isley Brothers, Dionne Warwick, the Jackson Five, and Luther Vandross, among them. And the headliners were always top-notch, including James Brown, the Motown stars, Aretha Franklin, and Sam Cooke (who wrote "I'm Alright" with Little Anthony here).

The Apollo also booked the occasional white act. One of the first, Buddy Holly and the Crickets, appeared there in 1957. That they were white was apparently a surprise to the Apollo's promoters.

One of rock and roll's greatest albums was recorded here: *The James Brown Show at the Apollo.* In the fall of 1962, Brown and his manager went against the advice and wishes of Syd Nathan, the head of Brown's label, King Records, and hired their own engineer to record the final performance of Brown's six-day stint at the theater. They were convinced that Brown's galvanizing live show could translate onto record and they were right. Listeners forced many black radio stations around the country to play it in its entirety and the album spent sixty-six weeks on the pop charts. It marked a turning point in Brown's career.

In the early '70s, Nile Rodgers and Bernard Edwards, the masterminds behind Chic and the producers of disco classics like "Le Freak," "Good Times," and "Upside Down," were both in the house band.

In the mid-'80s, the Apollo went through an expensive series of renovations. Its newly installed entertainment complex, which includes a re-

The Apollo, 1992.

cording studio and television production center, was to make the Apollo the center of revitalization on 125th Street. Instead, the theater has lost $2 million a year since 1988—despite the fact that big rap shows are produced there along with the TV series "It's Showtime at the Apollo." Efforts are now being made to create a nonprofit corporation to keep the theater open.

Bobby's Happyhouse Record Store   *2347 8th Ave.; 301 West 125th St. until 1989*
In this case, the real institution is the man who owns the shop. Bobby Robinson opened his record store in 1946 and soon began booking concerts and starting record labels. His Red Robin label is one of the first black-owned record companies in the country. All along, he's been adept at spotting talent: he produced records for the Orioles and the Ravens, worked with Lee Dorsey and Gladys Knight and the Pips before they were stars, and, with the help of his nephew Spoonie Gee, discovered Grandmaster Flash and the Furious Five. His store has been a popular neighborhood hangout; current stars like producer Teddy Riley used to stop by when they were kids.

The Bottom Line   *Mercer and 4th St.*
Since this Greenwich Village club opened in February 1974 with a show by Dr. John (which ended with a jam session with Johnny Winter, Stevie Wonder, and Dr. John), it has become a key showcase for rising stars.

The Bottom Line, 1992.

Bruce Springsteen's performances here in 1975, for instance, landed him on the covers of *Time* and *Newsweek*. The Bottom Line has also served as an intimate venue for figures like Lou Reed, Marianne Faithfull, and Elvis Costello. And Blue Oyster Cult has played here under their old name, Soft White Underbelly, long after they were famous. Co-owners Allan Pepper and Stanley Snadowsky met as kids in Flatbush and started booking jazz concerts in the mid-'60s. Their current booking policy encompasses every form of pop music except hardcore and rap.

The Brill Building   *1619 Broadway*

Since the late '50s, "the Brill Building sound" has come to stand for the clever, usually uptempo songs that were developed, factory-style, in this building's publishing offices and in those of Aldon Music's offices at 1650 Broadway. These songs include "Calendar Girl," "Teenager In Love," "Save the Last Dance for Me," and "Up on the Roof." Large record labels like Columbia, RCA, and ABC needed a huge supply of potential hit songs for their stable of performers, and songwriters worked all day to answer the demand. Often paired up, they worked in closet-sized cubicles containing just a piano and chair, and came up with smart, relevant songs like "Will You Love Me Tomorrow?" Aldon's stable of songwriters reigned supreme, featuring such teams as Gerry Goffin and Carole King, Barry Mann and Cynthia Weil, Howard Greenfield and Neil Sedaka. When they weren't in their cubicles, many of these songwriter-types could often be found hanging out across the street at the Hotel Forrest.

Doc Pomus and Mort Shuman in
their Brill Building cubicle, circa 1960.
(Courtesy of Sharyn Felder.)

Cafe Bizarre   *106 West 3rd St.*

This tiny Greenwich Village club/tourist trap provided the Velvet Underground with their first "residency" in New York; and it was here that Andy Warhol discovered them and turned them into his very own rock group. In 1965, from August to December, the quartet of Lou Reed, Sterling Morrison, John Cale, and Maureen Tucker played here six nights

The Velvet Underground's "Bizarre"
beginning, 1959.
(Photo by Fred W. McDarrah.)

a week, four times a night—forty minutes on, twenty minutes off. At the end of the year, they instigated their own dismissal because they didn't want to work on New Year's Eve. As Morrison once recalled, "Around December 30th, the lady who owned the cafe came up and said that if we played 'Black Angel's Death Song' one more time we were fired. So we led off the next set with it. A really good version too." Fortunately, Warhol had seen them perform and was impressed. As he wrote in *Popism*, "people would leave looking dazed and damaged." He asked them to join him for a week at the Cinematheque—they would play and he would show movies on them. After that event, Warhol asked for more. According to Reed, "He said, 'Why don't you come to the Factory [231 E. 47th St.], you could be with us. We could go to art festivals and instead of me just showing my movies, I'll show *you*!' " They accepted. The resultant sensory overload was eventually christened "The Exploding Plastic Inevitable."

Cafe Wha? *117 MacDougal*

This basement club was across the street from the Gaslight but much less prestigious. In 1966, however, an unknown guitar player named Jimi Hendrix took advantage of the underutilized space, and used it to try out his compositions and experiment with his band, Jimmy James and the Blue Flames. Soon enough, he attracted fellow musicians. One, an Englishman and former Animal named Chas Chandler, was stunned by Hendrix's performance and promptly whisked him off to London. There Chandler helped put together the Jimi Hendrix Experience. (The media frenzy that followed brought Hendrix back to the United States in 1967.) Next door to the Cafe Wha? was the Players Theatre, which often featured the Fugs.

Carnegie Hall   *154 West 57th St.*

Rock and roll stars have been booked at this prestigious venue since 1955, when Bill Haley and the Comets did a show. The Beatles played their first New York concert here, as did the Rolling Stones. Other stars include Stevie Wonder, Bob Dylan (who flew his parents in for the occasion), the Mothers of Invention, and Ray Charles, who declared in his autobiography, "After Carnegie Hall, I've been more or less nonchalant about all the others."

❷ CBGB   *315 Bowery*

The full name of ex-Marine sergeant Hilly Kristal's rock and roll mecca is CBGB-OMFUG, which stands for "Country, Bluegrass, Blues, and Other Music For Uplifting Gormandizers." But before he could finish putting up the club's awning, Tom Verlaine and Richard Lloyd of Television came by to ask if they could play there. Lloyd remembers saying, "We play blues, bluegrass, anything you want, we'll play it." Kristal penciled them in for the next Sunday, and thus began many years of rock and roll.

This seedy downtown bar became the training ground for seminal punk and new wave bands like the Ramones, Blondie, Television, and Talking

The Ramones at CBGB, 1977. (Photo by Lisa Kristal.)

Heads. Starting in 1973 and continuing today, Kristal's adventurous booking policy gave countless bands an opportunity to test their original material on unusually receptive audiences. Recent success stories include Living Colour, 24-7 Spyz, and They Might Be Giants. CBGB has also served as the first Manhattan venue for an army of raucous bands from outside of New York, including the Police, the Replacements, the Damned, and the Cramps.

Patti Smith's group was the first big attraction, playing for seven straight weeks, four nights a week, in early 1975. Guitarist Lenny Kaye once recalled, "It gave us a chance to continuously work out an act. . . . A lot of songs started off as jams and soon we found that things would organically come together. . . . We became a real band after that." The Talking Heads made their stage debut in June 1975 as a trio, opening up for the Ramones. David Byrne shared a loft with Chris Frantz and Tina Weymouth a few blocks away on Chrystie Street and they just happened to stop by the club while investigating the neighborhood. Other landmark moments at CBGB include rock critic Lester Bangs's wake in 1982 and Linda Ronstadt's speedy departure after a mere ten minutes of the Ramones.

Central Park

In the '60s, this was the site of legendary shows by rising groups like Led Zeppelin, the Young Rascals, and Jefferson Airplane. Since 1980, superstars like Paul Simon, Simon and Garfunkel, James Taylor, Elton John, and Diana Ross have given free concerts at the park's Great Lawn.

❸ The Cheetah   *Broadway and 53rd St.*

Located in the old Arcadia Ballroom, this hip late-'60s disco featured many of the top live acts of the day, from Jefferson Airplane to the Doors. (It was here that Jim Morrison introduced his tightrope act—teetering along the edge of the stage until falling into the audience.) In 1968, powerful '80s Motown exec Suzanne DePasse was the Cheetah's booking agent; Berry Gordy met her here and hired her as road manager and adviser for the Jackson 5. Kool and the Gang, who hail from New Jersey, were first spotted here by producer Gene Redd.

The Chelsea Hotel   *222 West 23rd St.*

The site of several sad endings, this hotel has been a meeting place for both artists and junkies. Bob Dylan stayed up all night here writing "Sad Eyed Lady of the Lowlands." Sid Vicious's girlfriend, Nancy Spungen, and Lou Reed's mentor, the poet Delmore Schwartz, both died here. Keith Richards once observed that "you had to be a certified drug dealer to get a job as a bellboy."

The Continental Baths   *230 West 74th St.*

Bette Midler got a crucial break in her career—and an important training ground—when she was booked here as a solo act in the early '70s. With Barry Manilow as her piano accompanist and musical director, she developed her campy routines and her broad musical repertoire. Frankie Knuckles, the godfather of House Music, also had an important apprenticeship here as a DJ. He was out of a job when the establishment closed in 1976, and soon left for Chicago.

❹ The Dakota   *1 West 72nd St.*

This gothic apartment building has been home to Leonard Bernstein, Roberta Flack, and of course John Lennon. In 1973, Lennon and Yoko Ono bought a sixth-floor apartment here, and later acquired several other units for administrative offices and storage space. Lennon was shot in front of the gates on December 8, 1980, and massive vigils in front of the building lasted for days afterward. A memorial to Lennon, a 2.5-acre area called Strawberry Fields, was created right across from the Dakota in Central Park.

The Delmonico Hotel   *Park Avenue and 59th St.*

Bob Dylan turned the Beatles on to marijuana here on August 28, 1964. (Paul McCartney reportedly declared he was thinking for the first time; he ordered their road manager to follow him around and take note of his brilliant thoughts.)

The Ed Sullivan Theater   *1697 Broadway*

Some of rock and roll's most famous performances were taped here, for *The Ed Sullivan Show* gave millions of teenagers their first real look at such megastars as Elvis Presley, the Beatles, James Brown, and the Doors.

For the Beatles' February 1964 performance, the show received 50,000 applications for the 700 seats in the theater. An audience of 70 million tuned in, and on that one night, America's crime rate was lower than at any time during the previous half-century. In all five boroughs, not a single hubcap was reported stolen.

The Electric Circus   *23 St. Marks Place*

This wild '60s nightspot was created by a young William Morris agent named Jerry Brandt. He transformed a Polish social hall into an overwhelming environment of loud music, light, and strangely costumed revelers. Many top rock groups performed here but their shows were a sideshow event; the club was the star. It lasted from 1967 to 1970. Today the building serves as a social club for recovering alcohol and drug addicts.

Electric Lady Sound Studios   *52 West 8th St.*

Jimi Hendrix's manager had this studio built because Hendrix was spending so much time (read money) at the Record Plant and other studios.

❺ The Fillmore East   *105 2nd Ave.*

In the late '60s, Bill Graham turned a dilapidated old vaudeville theater into the city's most popular rock palace. The San Francisco-based promoter featured the same formula that had worked so well at the Fillmore West: presenting upcoming bands, both local and not, as openers for the biggies. He even went out of his way to match up a group like the Allman

Bill Graham and his Fillmore East, 1968. (Photo by Fred W. McDarrah.)

Brothers Band with their hero, B.B. King. The Allmans were certainly one of Graham's favorites. Whenever the band wanted to play beyond the usual closing time, Graham would announce that he was locking the doors to the auditorium, and that anyone who had to leave should do so. The band would then play on into the night, often until morning. Their classic *Live at the Fillmore East* was recorded here in March 1971.

By the time it closed in June 1971—a few days before Graham's West Coast outpost shut *its* doors—this theater had hosted concerts by all the superstars of the day: Led Zeppelin, the Jeff Beck Group, Creedence Clearwater Revival, Sly and the Family Stone, the Grateful Dead, the Band, Jimi Hendrix (with the Band of Gypsies), and the Who. In May 1969, in fact, the Who's Pete Townshend spent a night in jail for assaulting a man here. Townshend didn't realize that the guy jumping onto the stage during a Who set was actually a plainclothes policeman trying to warn the audience that a fire had broken out. Today the theater is completely boarded up.

The Garrick Theater   *152 Bleecker*

The Mothers of Invention played nearly every night here in 1967. Their posters advertised the show as "hateful, repugnant and a waste of $3." Below the Garrick was the Cafe au Go Go, another '60s hot spot.

The Gaslight   *116 MacDougal*

This club is famous for what happened in it as well as for what happened above it, in a room that Bob Dylan often stayed in. As Wavy Gravy, the Woodstock Festival's MC, recalled, "All the artists used to come up to that little room, smoke some grass, hang out, and sing songs. There was a lot more going on up in that little room sometimes than there was in the Gaslight downstairs. 'A Hard Rain's Gonna Fall' was written up there on my typewriter." By the end of the '60s, the Gaslight featured a new wave of songwriters, folk-rockers like James Taylor. In 1972, John Hammond chose the club to showcase—read audition—Bruce Springsteen.

Gerde's Folk City   *from 1952 to 1956, 11 West 3rd St.; from 1956 to 1969, 11 West 4th St., from 1969 to 1986, 130 West 3rd St.*

In 1952, a Calabrian immigrant named Mike Porco bought a restaurant named Gerde's. By the time he sold the operation in 1979, Folk City had become a cultural touchstone. In the early '60s, the weekly hootenannies were a great source of talent. Performers such as Bob Dylan, Judy Collins, John Phillips, Richie Havens, Peter Wolf, and Peter, Paul and Mary would sing and play for free to showcase themselves or to hone a new song. Important talent scouts and managers such as Albert Grossman, John Hammond, and Jac Holzman looked for new performers here.

Along with the Gaslight down the street, Folk City gave Bob Dylan his start in New York City. Porco helped him get into the union, signing as his guardian because Dylan was only 20. On April 11, 1961, Porco gave Dylan his first paying gig here, opening up for John Lee Hooker. From all reports, it was an electrifying performance, but it wasn't until later that year that Dylan would hit the big time. On September 25, Dylan opened up for the Greenbriar Boys and completely overshadowed them; two days later, he was signed to CBS Records by John Hammond and the day after that, *The New York Times* published an unqualified rave review that established his career. (Despite his star status, Dylan continued to introduce new songs like "Blowin' in the Wind" at Folk City.)

By 1971, Porco found it necessary to book rock bands. Perhaps the most memorable concert of that decade occurred in October of 1975, when the Rolling Thunder Tour was launched. It was Porco's birthday and Dylan gave him an all-star celebration that featured Patti Smith and Bette Midler. The show marked Allen Ginsberg's first performance here and Phil Och's last show ever. (Six months later, he hung himself in his sister's home in Queens.)

In the late '80s, new owners of the club instituted a Wednesday night series of up-and-coming bands: $3 for three bands. Sonic Youth played here then, as did the Smithereens.

King Curtis Home   *150 West 96th St.*

The great R&B saxophonist and bandleader "King" Curtis Ousley lived in this apartment building from the late-'60s until his death in August 1971. He was stabbed nearby, in front of a building he owned at 50 West 86th St.

The Knitting Factory   *47 East Houston*

Opened in 1987 by Bob Appel and Michael Dorf, the space had been "a dirty old Avon Products office." Today the club is at the center of an eclectic postpunk music scene, booking adventurous bands in every genre from funk to jazz to hardcore and hip hop. Appel and Dorf have released a batch of "Live at the Knitting Factory" records, and have syndicated a radio show heard on 200 college stations.

Madison Square Garden   *4 Pennsylvania Plaza*

The venue of choice for supergroups and megabenefits, the Garden has also hosted reunions (both Simon and Garfunkel and Peter, Paul and Mary in 1972), comebacks (including Stevie Wonder's triumphant 1974 appearance seven months after a near-fatal car accident) and a wedding ceremony. On June 5, 1974, Sly Stone married Kathy Silva on stage in the middle of one of his concerts. Silva filed for divorce within six months.

Madonna's First Apartment   *232 East 4th St.*

When she wasn't here plotting her career as a media phenomenon, Madonna Louise Ciccone, age nineteen, worked at Dunkin' Donuts, Burger King, and a Greek restaurant called Amy's.

Manny's   *156 West 48th St.*

Opened in 1933, this is New York City's top musical instruments store. Its walls are lined with photographs of the rock stars who have been

Sid Vicious performs at Max's Kansas City, late 1978, while Nancy Spungeon keeps an eye on him. (Photo by Stephanie Chernikowski.)

customers. In the late '60s, Jimi Hendrix had an open account here and would stop by once a week to try out all the new instruments, distortion devices and accessories; he would buy one or two guitars a week. The store is also a Ramones landmark. In the early '70s, Johnny and Dee Dee Ramone worked at a Times Square construction site and on their lunch hours, they would visit a go-go bar and then move on to Manny's to inspect the merchandise. As Dee Dee recalled, "One payday, we both went over, bought guitars and decided to start a band."

❻ Max's Kansas City   *213 Park Ave. South*
In the late '60s and early '70s, this was the most exclusive nightclub in town, a key hangout for the Warhol crowd and the rest of the glitterati. The Velvet Underground played here frequently; in fact, Lou Reed's last performance with the band was held here on August 23, 1970. (This show was released in 1974 as *Live at Max's Kansas City*.) And the club had its other highlights: a double bill of Bob Marley and Bruce Springsteen; the New York Dolls' series of shows—they were almost a house band; a post–Sex Pistols Sid Vicious performance; and the NYC debuts of the B-52s and the Feelies. This is also the place where Clive Davis saw Aerosmith perform for the first time. In related rock and roll trivia, Debbie Harry was a waitress here before she helped form Blondie, and Iggy Pop met David Bowie here in the early '70s. Max's closed on December 31, 1981 and has since been transformed into a Korean deli.

❼ The Mercer Arts Center   *Mercer and 3rd St.*

> The forerunner of CBGB as a downtown music mecca, the Center consisted of ten rooms at the back end of the Broadway Central Hotel, including an experimental video room (the first incarnation of The Kitchen), a cabaret room, a theatrical room, rehearsal space, a bar and the Oscar Wilde Room (a hangout for the New York Dolls). The Center opened in 1971 and soon became common ground for artists, filmmakers, and musicians, including bands like Suicide and Teenage Lust. But when the front of the hotel collapsed in 1973, the building was condemned.

Metropolitan Opera House   *Lincoln Center at Broadway and 64th St.*

> In 1970, the Who performed *Tommy*, their ninety-minute rock opera, here. Tickets sold out in an hour and the Who's two performances each received ten-minute standing ovations. True to form, leader Pete Townshend bashed his guitar at the end of the first show and threw it into the audience. The second night, he threw his microphone into the audience. The Metropolitan's director Rudolph Bing commented that he'd seen nothing like *Tommy* since the days of grand opera before the war. In 1974, Labelle became the first black band to perform here.

Mira Sound Studios   *145 West 47th St.*

> Ronette Veronica Bennett met future husband and recluse Phil Spector here in early 1963. The studio was located in the back of the disreputable Hotel America but Spector loved the big sounds he could create here.

The Mercer Arts Center, 1972.
(Photo by Fred W. McDarrah.)

The Mudd Club   77 *White St.*

The invention of Steve Mass, a former paramedic from Macon, GA, the Mudd Club was an important site in the New York City underground from 1978 to 1981. It featured elaborate theme parties, and brought in everyone from the B-52's to the Ventures. Some say it was the first rock club to have a restrictive door policy. When a new wave dance club called Danceteria opened, it stole much of the Mudd Club's clientele. Said Mass in 1983, "I lost interest in the club after it became this circus of celebrities kind of scene."

The Night Owl Cafe   118 *West 3rd St.*

The Lovin' Spoonful started their career from this club in 1965. Owned by Joe Marra, it also hosted early shows by the Magicians, the Blues Magoos, and Tim Buckley.

Ondine's   308 *East 59th St.*

In November 1966, this little disco/dive was the site of the Door's first concerts in New York City. According to Warhol, Jim Morrison stood "at the bar drinking screwdrivers all night long, taking downs with them, and he'd get really far gone" The club had opened in early 1965, quickly becoming a hangout for the Warhol gang. Jimi Hendrix—then known as Jimmy James—once sat in with a band called the Druids.

❽ Peppermint Lounge   128 *West 45th St., in the Knickerbocker Hotel*

This club, originally a rather unglamourous Times Square hangout, became the city's hottest spot in 1961 after the house band, Joey Dee and the Starlighters, released "The Peppermint Twist." The song became a number-one hit and suddenly the Lounge was packed nightly with a curious mix of celebrities, teenagers, and diplomats. The Ronettes regularly performed a song-and-dance "Twist" routine here before they were discovered by Phil Spector.

The Pep reopened in the new wave era on Fifth Avenue at 15th Street. It presented bands like R.E.M., Iggy Pop, Sonic Youth, and the Cramps (who recorded the live *Smell of Female* EP here).

P.J. Clarke's   913 *3rd Ave.*

On the day in June 1958 that Buddy Holly met Maria Elena Santiago, receptionist at a music publishing firm, he took her here for dinner. He also proposed to her here and, after some thought, she accepted.

Rusty Beanie's Cycle Shop   *Columbus Avenue and 82nd St.*

The New York Dolls had their first rehearsals here. As one Doll remembered, "He [Mr. Beanie] had amps and drums in there, and we only had three guitars between us."

St. Nicholas Arena   69 *West 66th St.*

This smoke-filled boxing auditorium was the site of the first live revue promoted by Alan Freed, then a WINS DJ in New York City. Selling out a week in advance, two shows were held in January 1955, featuring sixteen acts including Clyde McPhatter and the Drifters, Fats Domino, Ruth Brown, and the Moonglows. Co-promoter Morris Levy was shocked that half of the audience was white, reportedly saying, "Oh my God, this is crazy." The overwhelming audience response prompted a move to less seedy surroundings—the Brooklyn Paramount.

Steve Paul's The Scene   *301 West 46th St.*
At one point in the late '60s, this was the city's most popular rock club. It was also, according to Steve Paul at the time, "part of the continuing search to express myself." Paul was an eager, young entrepreneur who had started out as the Peppermint Lounge's press agent and who knew how to attract massive amounts of media attention. He also had the good judgment to present top bands like the Doors, the Rascals, and the Velvet Underground and to try out lesser known players like Johnny Winter and NRBQ. For a few months in 1968, Jimi Hendrix was a nearly constant presence here. When he wasn't playing at jam sessions with the likes of Jeff Beck, Eric Clapton, and Jim Morrison, he was nearby, recording *Electric Ladyland* at the Record Plant. The club closed in 1969 after several influential years. Today Steve Paul manages Buster Poindexter.

The Strand   *838 Broadway*
Tom Verlaine and Patti Smith both worked at this huge used-book emporium.

Spirit performing at Steve Paul's The Scene. (Courtesy of Sony Music.)

Unitel Video   *515 West 57th St.*
On August 1, 1981, MTV broadcast its first show from this location.
Today 1515 Broadway houses MTV headquarters, as well as VH-1, *Bill-board*, and *Musician* magazine.

Village People Landmark   *500 West 14th St.*
When record producer Jacques Morali visited the Anvil, a West Village
disco, he was impressed by the outfits on the dancers. As he told *Rolling
Stone* in 1978, "Felipe [Rose] was there in a full Indian costume. He was
dancing near a guy who was dressed like a cowboy. Another one wore a
construction hat." Morali realized that the world needed a gay music
group and went about gathering material and men for the group. Morali
made sure to include Felipe Rose.

⑨ White Columns   *325 Spring St.*
At the semilegendary *Noisefest*, held here in June 1981, Sonic Youth
played its first show. The band at the time included guitarists Lee Ra-
naldo and Thurston Moore (who organized the event), bassist Kim Gordon, drummer Richard Edson (who became an actor), with Anne De
Marinis playing keyboards. (The latter two soon departed, and drum
duties passed to Bob Bert, then to Steve Shelley.) Don King, the band not
the guy, also made their debut at the event. Kim Gordon recalled, "The
festival's name was a joke, inspired by the owner of Hurrah who had said
he was gonna close the club because all the bands just sounded like a
bunch of noise. Nobody even knew what a noise band was." In May 1983,
the five-day "Speed Trials" took place here, featuring Sonic Youth, the
Fall, Swans, Live Skull, and the Beastie Boys. The event was preserved
for posterity by Homestead Records.

The White Rock Baptist Church   *152 West 127th St.*
Bronx-born Valerie Simpson was seventeen when she met Nickolas Ashford here in 1964. Simpson was in the choir and was studying music at
the Chatham Square School. Ashford had left his home in Willow Run,
Michigan, to become a jazz dancer in New York City. They began writing
songs together—their first batch sold for $75—and have since produced
a long string of hits including "Ain't No Mountain High Enough,"
"You're All I Need to Get By," and "I'm Every Woman."

👫 Schools

P.S. 75   *735 West End Ave.*
Gene Simmons taught at this elementary school while starting Kiss.

P.S. 109   *215 East 99th St.*
The Bobbettes' 1957 hit song, "Mr. Lee," was inspired by an unpopular
teacher here. Before having the young quintet record their tune, however,
Atlantic Records suggested a change in the lyrics; the line "He's the

ugliest teacher I ever did see" became "He's the handsomest sweetie I ever did see."

New York University   *around Washington Square Pk.*

Def Jam Records, one of rap's most influential record labels, was founded by Russell Simmons and Rick Rubin in 1984; it was initially run out of Rubin's room in NYU's Weinstein dormitory (5–11 University Place). The next year, Rubin, then a twenty-year-old NYU film student, happily ditched his plans to go to law school when he got a $600,000 check from CBS for a distribution deal. Since then, Rubin has produced some of rap's essential releases; Simmons has managed the music's major stars, from Public Enemy to De La Soul. The pair no longer work together, though. Rubin is on the West Coast with a label of his own, Def American.

QUEENS

Andrew Jackson High School   *207-01 116th Ave., Cambria Heights*

The classic girl group the Shangri-Las got started when the two sets of sisters—Mary Ann and Marge Ganser, Betty and Mary Weiss—started singing here as students in the early '60s. In 1964, they were discovered by producer George "Shadow" Morton.

Forest Hills Tennis Stadium   *1 Tennis Place, Forest Hills*

The site of concerts by the Beatles, Talking Heads, and the Jimi Hendrix Experience, its most famous show was held in August 1965. A month after Bob Dylan's disastrous electrified appearance at the Newport Folk Festival, he performed here; the first half of the set was acoustic, the second half with a band that included Robbie Robertson and Levon Helm. The die-hard folkies pelted the stage with fruit and insults, eventually storming out of the amphitheater in great numbers, while the young rock and roll fans stormed the stage in excitement.

🔟 Mount St. Mary's Cemetery   *164th St. and Booth Memorial Avenue, Flushing*

Two New York Dolls are buried here: drummer Jerry Nolan, who died in early 1992, as well as Johnny Thunders, who died the year before in New Orleans.

P.S. 164   *77th Avenue and 137th St., Forest Hills*

Paul Simon met Art Garfunkel here when they were both about nine. They appeared together in a production of *Alice in Wonderland*—with Paul as the White Rabbit and Art as the Cheshire Cat—and soon were in a street corner doo-wop group called the Sparks. By their early teens they had become a duo, singing Simon's tunes at school concerts and local dances. They recorded "Hey, Schoolgirl" in 1957, under the ethnically safe pseudonym of "Tom and Jerry," and had a Top 50 hit. They even wrangled a slot on Dick Clark's "American Bandstand" but had the bad luck of following Jerry Lee Lewis, who performed "Great Balls of

The entrance to Mount St. Mary's Cemetery.

Fire." They broke up after their follow-up songs went nowhere, but met
again in 1962 and hitched on to the emerging folk music revival.

THE BRONX

Dion's Neighborhood

Dion and the Belmonts, creators of such classics as "The Wanderer" and
"Runaround Sue," were raised, not surprisingly, near Belmont Avenue
in the Bronx. On the stoops and streetcorners here, the group (and many
others like it) learned to sing the doo-wop songs they had heard on the
radio. Dion landmarks include 749 East 183rd St. (his childhood home),
Ermondo's (a local hangout where he sang as a child) and P.S. 45 (his
junior high school).

The Franklin Armory Men's Shelter   *1122 Franklin Ave.*

This is the site where Laurence Krisna Parker—now known as KRS-
One—met Scott "LaRock" Sterling, a social worker. In 1986, the two
formed Boogie Down Productions, an important rap outfit, and in 1987
they released a classic album called *Criminal Minded*. In August 1987,
Scott LaRock was fatally shot outside the Highbridge Gardens Homes in
the South Bronx while trying to settle an argument.

The Hevalo   *180th St. and Jerome Ave.*

This West Bronx teen nightclub was host to some of the audio innova-
tions that led to rap music. In 1975, a DJ named Kool Herc (born Clive
Campbell) started programming his customary menu of hardcore funk
hits in a different way. Instead of playing entire songs, he would play the
most intense, or stripped down, section of the song—a thirty-second

"break" segment. These breaks would follow in quick, endless succession, keeping the crowd dancing at a furious pace for hours. Before long, the first "break dancers" were born. Other hip-hop landmarks include **Disco Fever**, where DJ Grandmaster Flash is said to have invented backspinning (turning records manually to make the needle repeat brief lengths of groove) **the Bronx River Community Center**, where Afrika Bambaataa DJ'd many parties, and the **Third Avenue Ballroom**, where "Grand Wizard" Theodore introduced scratching.

BROOKLYN

Abraham Lincoln High School   *Ocean Pkwy. and West End Ave.*
The alma mater of Neil Sedaka, the Tokens, and songwriter Bob Feldman. Feldman was inspired to write "My Boyfriend's Back" after he heard an argument in front of the ice cream shop next door; he used one girl's words, almost verbatim, as the song's intro.

The Paramount Theatre   *DeKalb and Flatbush*
The site of Alan Freed's major triumphs. From 1955 to 1958, the famed DJ put on legendary shows featuring all of the top acts, from Chuck Berry

The marquee is gone, but the Brooklyn Paramount still stands, now property of Long Island University.

and Little Richard to Buddy Holly and Jerry Lee Lewis. To accommodate the demand from concertgoers, the theater scheduled four to seven shows each day. After a controversy over Freed's May 1958 concert in Boston, the Paramount chain refused to book his next big revues. Freed moved down the street to the Fabian Fox Theatre with four of his ten-day revues.

Sedaka and Greenfield Apartment Building   *3260 Coney Island Ave.*
The songwriting partnership of Neil Sedaka and Howie Greenfield began here when teenage tenant Greenfield introduced himself to fellow tenant Sedaka in the hope that his poems might work well with Sedaka's music.

St. Ann's   *157 Montague St.*
This active Episcopal church has featured some extraordinary performances: Aaron Neville on his own, Marianne Faithfull, John Cale's and Lou Reed's *Songs for 'Drella*, and the return of Velvet Underground drummer Moe Tucker.

🦢 DETOURS

NEW JERSEY

This state has long been maligned but rock and roll fans know better. It's been the birthplace of innovators, from Ricky Nelson (Teaneck) and Bruce Springsteen (Freehold) to Queen Latifah (East Orange) and Ice-T (Newark), as well as the site of other historic rock events.

Morris Plains, NJ
Greystone Hospital   *West Hanover Avenue*
Woody Guthrie, the great folk balladeer from Okemah, Oklahoma, was confined to this institution for much of the time between 1956 and his death in 1967. In January 1961, Bob Dylan travelled all the way from Minneapolis in order to meet his idol face to face. Guthrie, though suffering from a debilitating nerve disorder named Huntington's chorea, welcomed the kid heartily. The place is now called Greystone Park Psychiatric Hospital.

Summit, NJ
The Velvet Underground's first concert with Mo Tucker was held at Summit High School on November 11, 1965. The band opened for a pop group called the Myddle Class and were paid $75. There were no encores—just howls of derision.

Freehold, NJ
This is Bruce Springsteen's hometown, and it's best reached from New York City by Highway 9 (immortalized in "Born To Run").

87 Randolph Street

> The Boss lived at this address until he was eight or nine. The house is no longer standing.

39½ Institute Street

> The Springsteen family lived here from 1958 to about 1961.

68 South Street

> Still standing, this house is where Springsteen's family lived from the early '60s. It's also where Bruce learned to play guitar. His parents left in the late '60s for California.

Freehold High School   *Broadway and Robertville Rd.*

> Springsteen, class of '67, formed his first band, the Castiles, when he was a sophomore here.

The Woodhaven Swim Club   *East Freehold Rd., Freehold Township*

> Now replaced by a YMCA, this club hosted the first public performances by the Castiles in 1965.

Asbury Park, NJ

> This Jersey shore town was an important starting point for Bruce Springsteen and the E. Street Band as well as Southside Johnny and the Asbury Jukes.

The Stone Pony   *913 Ocean Ave.*

> This club opened in 1974, and had been an active landmark before closing in late 1991. Southside Johnny and the Asbury Jukes were the club's first house band. Springsteen has played here more often than he has any other stage. Other visiting acts include the Troggs and Iggy Pop.

The Student Prince   *911 Kingsley Ave.*

> Now a bar called Dimples, this club was the site where Bruce Springsteen met Clarence Clemons.

The Upstage   *702 Cookman Ave.*

> Today it is a shoe store, but in the late-'60s this club was the site of countless jam sessions between the top area musicians, including Springsteen, future E. Street Band members Garry Tallent, Danny Federici, David Sancious, Vini Lopez, and Miami Steve Van Zandt, as well as members of the Asbury Jukes.

Hoboken, NJ

Maxwell's   *1039 Washington St.*

> This club opened in 1978 and soon established itself as a haven for alternative rock. It may be most famous for being the place where John Sayles directed Bruce Springsteen's "Glory Days" video, but other noteworthies have played here too, including the Sir Douglas Quintet, the Replacements, Hüsker Dü, the Cult, and Fugazi. Co-owner Steve Fallon had a great deal to do with the "Hoboken pop" scene—featuring bands like the Bongos and the dBs—that was heralded in the mid-'80s. He not only runs Hoboken's best club, he also started a fine record shop (see below) and a now-defunct record label, Coyote, that signed up the scene's best bands. More recently he and partner Bob Mould created SOL (Singles Only Label) to promote favorite overlooked bands.

Maxwell's, a Hoboken institution. (Photo by Steve Fallon.)

Pier Platters   *56 Newark St.*
One of the last great bastions of vinyl (especially seven-inch releases), this store was co-founded by Steve Fallon and Tom Pendergrass in 1982. Fallon pulled out and his partner in the Coyote label, Bill Ryan, moved in. Pendergrass went on to start Bar/None, another Hoboken record label and the first home of They Might Be Giants. Pier Platters also has an outlet around the corner that carries used records and CDs.

UPSTATE NEW YORK AND LONG ISLAND

New York state has significant music sites outside the city, from Adelphi University in Garden City, Long Island (where Public Enemy was formed) and Bard College (where Donald Fagen met Walter Becker) to Woodstock, which has had a strong music community since the turn of the century.

Woodstock, NY   *105 miles NW of New York City*
The adopted hometown of many rock stars, Woodstock was the base of operations for Bob Dylan's longtime manager, Albert Grossman. Dylan's famous, almost-fatal motorcycle crash—which kept him in seclusion for over a year—occurred in the area on July 29, 1966. (The exact site is on

Zena Road, one mile south of Route 212.) And *Music From Big Pink* and *The Basement Tapes* were both recorded nearby, in a big pink house at 2188 Stoll Road in West Saugerties. Although Grossman died in 1986, his Bearsville studio complex on Route 212 has continued on.

Bethel, NY

Fifty miles from the town of Woodstock, this is where the Woodstock Festival actually took place, on August 15–17, 1969. A plaque marks the site on Max Yasgur's farm.

PHILADELPHIA

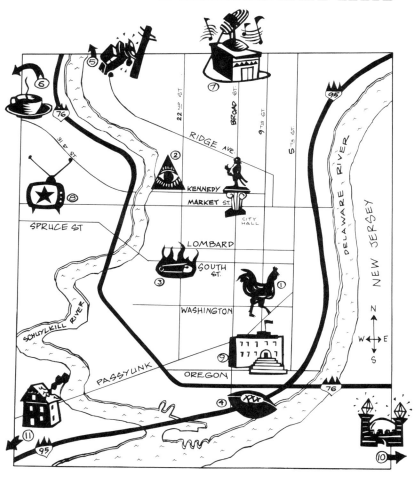

The City of Brotherly Love is best known in the world of pop music for two things: the teen-idol craze of the late '50s and early '60s—almost all of those cute boys came from South Philly—and the sophisticated soul factory operated by Kenny Gamble and Leon Huff in the early-'70s. But many artists from Philadelphia weren't connected to these trends: Solomon Burke, Patti LaBelle, Todd Rundgren, and Fresh Prince, to name a few.

By the mid-'50s, Philadelphia was already an important music market. It was a "break-out city"—music men would test a record here for listener response and promote it elsewhere if it succeeded here. But it was the national broadcast of "American Bandstand" that pushed the city to real prominence. Dick Clark's show became a trendsetter and tastemaker. And because Clark kept an open door to local industry men—who let him in on the financial rewards—the show launched local songs like "At the Hop" and Charlie Gracie's "Butterfly," as well as local "singers" like Fabian and Frankie Avalon. Chubby Checker was also a beneficiary of this accident of geography; his version of Hank Ballard's "The Twist" hit number one. But when the British invaded, local kids lost their appeal and "American Bandstand" moved to the next hip scene: Los Angeles.

The Sound of Philadelphia again became a marketable commodity in the late-'60s. Writer-producers Gamble, Huff, and Thom Bell created a quick succession of smoothly orchestrated pop-soul records. By 1972, their Philadelphia International label had created enormous hits for groups like the O'Jays, Harold Melvin and the Blue Notes (which featured Teddy Pendergrass), and the Trammps.

The American Bandstand *set, 1959. (Courtesy of the Urban Archives, Temple University, Philadelphia, PA.)*

There have been a few break-out artists during the last fifteen years: Major Harris, Jazzy Jeff and the Fresh Prince, and Boyz II Men. Although the local clubs are full of aspiring types, no major rock and roll acts have burst from the scene. The next "sound of Philadelphia" is still waiting to be discovered.

Adelphia Ballroom   *1400 N. 52nd St.*
Daryl Hall met John Oates here in 1967. They were in competing doo-wop groups—the Temptones and the Masters, respectively—in a battle of the bands dance, and shared a freight elevator while trying to escape a gang fight. They both went to Temple University but didn't begin recording together until 1972.

The Bijou   *1409 Lombard St.*
During the '60s, this was a jazz club called the Showboat. It was operated by the Spivak brothers, who joined up with Larry Magid at the end of the decade and opened the Electric Factory. When economics forced that venue to close, Magid and the Spivaks started booking rock shows here. Some of the memorable performances were by Bette Midler (before her first record deal), Joan Armatrading (who made a live recording here), and U2 (their first show in Philly). It was a distinctive club—a three-story building with a gigantic atrium—but apartments took its place in the mid-'80s.

Cameo Headquarters   *309 South Broad*
Cameo/Parkway was one of the city's top independent labels in the late '50s and early '60s. The label's founders, songwriters Bernie Lowe and Kal Mann, signed on local artists such as the Orlons, the Dovells, Dee Dee Sharp, and Chubby Checker and hit big with songs like "The Twist" and "Mashed Potato Time." But Mann and Lowe had lost the pulse of the marketplace by the end of the decade, at one point rejecting the songwriting services of Kenny Gamble. After Cameo folded in 1968, Gamble reportedly took great pleasure in moving his label, Philadelphia International, into this building.

❶ Henry Colt's Poultry Store   *South 9th St. and Washington Ave., The Italian Market*
In 1958, high school student Ernest Evans was just a part-time chicken plucker here. He entertained customers with songs and impersonations, and his boss, Henry Colt, put him in touch with Cameo/Parkway and became one of his managers. In 1959, Evans, now renamed Chubby Checker, was given a song named "The Twist" to record. The rest is history.

Convention Hall   *34th and Civic Center Blvd.*
Rock and roll shows were not commonplace in Philly in the late '50s and early '60s. Each one became an event, and this is where they were held. The Beatles played their first Philadelphia show here, as did the Rolling

The Electric Factory, 1969. (Courtesy of the Urban Archives, Temple University, Philadelphia, PA.)

Stones. One of the more interesting double bills here featured the Supremes and the Kinks.

East Side Club   *1229 Chestnut*

This former Italian social club, located under the Adelphia Hotel, proved to be a key rock and roll club in the early '80s. A fellow named Bobby Start-Up started as a DJ and then became the booking agent, hiring bands like Black Flag, Hüsker Dü, and Minor Threat. The Clash rehearsed here for one of their American tours, playing under a different fake name every night. It's now a dance place called the Cat Club; the hotel is now an apartment building.

❷ The Electric Factory   *22nd St. and Arch*

Philadelphia's "psychedelic ballroom" was created by three brothers in the nightclub and tavern business and their partner, a young music maven named Larry Magid. Though the hall is long-gone, Magid and the Spivaks still work together with Electric Factory Concerts, the city's dominant concert-booking organization.

The hall, a former tire warehouse, was opened to rock fans on February 2, 1968, with the Chambers Brothers as the first headlining act. The huge space featured a fluorescent miniplayground at one end, slanting "body racks" to lie back on when it was time to relax, and shops and amusement stalls dispensing mod clothing and body paint. But the main attraction was the music. All the big names of the day played here, including Van Morrison, the Jimi Hendrix Experience, Derek and the Dominos, and Canned Heat. The Who performed the American debut of *Tommy* here on December 24, 1969.

But city authorities apparently weren't rock and roll fans. In the fall of 1968, then-police commissioner Frank Rizzo had the city file a case against the hall on the grounds that it was a "public nuisance" and a hangout for drug dealers. The next April, seventy-one-year-old Judge Joseph Sloane ordered it closed, writing "This place of amusement is not a place of quiet mirth and enjoyment." Nor was it advertised that way! The Electric Factory stayed open on appeal, and the Judge eventually dissolved his injunction, noting that no trouble had been detected at the Factory for almost two years. Unfortunately, the costs of booking major rock acts had multiplied, and the hall was forced to shut its doors in November 1970. The building was torn down and replaced with condos.

The Hot Club, 1980. (Courtesy of the Urban Archives, Temple University, Philadelphia, PA.)

❸ The Hot Club   *21st St. and South St.*

Owned and operated by David Carroll, this spot developed into the city's best new wave/punk club in the late '70s. Carroll had opened the city's first rock and roll bar, Artemis, and seen the need for a live music venue. The Dead Boys opened the club in 1977 and closed it in 1980. Other acts included Elvis Costello and the Attractions, Iggy Pop, and Talking Heads. The walls were painted fire-engine red, and the club is remembered fondly.

J.C. Dobbs   *304 South St.*

This small club opened in 1975, and has been presenting original local bands and touring alternative groups ever since. It can claim several success stories. First off was a blues guitarist from Delaware who used to do three sets on Saturday night, sleep over on the couch upstairs, and then perform four sets on Sunday afternoon. That was George Thorogood. Next up were the Tom Cats, a rockabilly band that played on Sundays. A British bartender at Dobb's, Tony Bidgood, saw their potential and urged them to go to England to cash in on the rockabilly craze there. Brian Setzer took his advice, reformed the band in his native Long Island, and hired Bidgood as their manager. The Tom Cats made it big as the Stray Cats. Songwriter Robert Hazzard was also "discovered" here, while playing with his locally popular band, the Heroes. Kurt Loder, then of *Rolling Stone*, wrote a feature on the group. Hazzard was soon signed up; his biggest success came when Cyndi Lauper covered his song, "Girls Just Want To Have Fun." And Kenn Kweder, Philadelphia's own rock and roll bard, has been a steady draw here for years.

❹ J.F.K. Stadium   *On Broad St., next to the Spectrum*

As host of Live Aid in July 1985, this football stadium helped let loose years of all-star rock and roll telethons. Organized by Bob Geldof and Bill Graham, the American portion of the concert meant to benefit African famine relief efforts, went off smoothly, in safe twenty-minute sets. Hyped as "the Woodstock for the post–Baby Boomers," Live Aid was completely televised and partially underwritten by Pepsi, Chevrolet, and AT&T. Unlike the chaotic rock festivals of the late '60s and early '70s, this event yielded no births or deaths, although one fan was transported by air from the arena to undergo a long-awaited kidney transplant. The structure was scheduled for demolition in 1992.

❺ Lincoln Drive   *outside of city center, from Main St. to Allen Ln.*

In the spring of 1982, along this twisting stretch of highway near Clifford Park, Teddy Pendergrass crashed his green Rolls-Royce into a pair of trees. He was left paralyzed, and his career has yet to recover from the blow.

❻ The Main Point   *874 Lancaster Ave., Bryn Mawr*

This intimate coffeehouse, tucked away in the suburbs but close to several colleges, was started up in 1964 by four couples who were fans of folk music. But though this partnership eventually dissolved, the Main Point went on to become a legendary club. It served as a home-away-from-Asbury Park for Bruce Springsteen, and featured every prominent "folk-rock" act of the day including Jackson Browne, James Taylor (and all of his siblings), Joni Mitchell, and even the Talking Heads. The Main Point managed to survive into the early '80s, long after the rest of the city's coffeehouses closed.

Mount Lawn Cemetery *84th St. and Hook Rd., Sharon Hill suburb*
Both Bessie Smith, who died in 1937, and Tammi Terrell (born Thomasina Montgomery), who died thirty-three years later, are buried in this graveyard. Smith's grave was unmarked until 1970, when a woman named Juanita Green and one of Smith's biggest fans, Janis Joplin, split the cost of a tombstone.

Pep's *South and Broad*
This club was a popular stopping point for the top R&B artists in the '60s and '70s. The groups on the Philadelphia International label—Harold Melvin and the Blue Notes, the O'Jays—would often try out new material here. The owner of this club also ran Loretta's Hi-Hat Club in nearby New Jersey. Out-of-town acts would play at Pep's on Fridays and Saturdays and then move over to Loretta's on Sunday night.

Schuylkill Expressway
This roadway joined Route 66 in musical legend when it inspired the Soul Survivors' "Expressway to Your Heart," the first national hit for producers Gamble and Huff.

Sciolla's *521 West Pike St.*
A popular supper club during the '60s, Sciolla's featured performers like Frank Sinatra, Bobby Rydell, and Connie Francis. Teddy Pendergrass's mother worked here and he got the opportunity as a kid to learn several instruments, using the club's equipment. Pendergrass's first job with Harold Melvin and the Blue Notes was as their drummer. It was only after the group's lead singer left that he got the vocal spot.

The 2nd Fret *1902 Sansom St.*
Manny Rubin owned this '60s club, said to be the city's best coffeehouse. Present-day luminaries like Joni Mitchell and Carly Simon (then in the Simon Sisters) played here early on. Bob Dylan auditioned but didn't make the cut. When the appetite for folk music dwindled in the mid-'60s, Rubin started booking acts like the Byrds, the Electric Flag, and Moby Grape. In 1967, he opened the first psychedelic club in Philadelphia: the Trauma.

Sigma Sound *212 N. 12th St.*
This facility was the city's top recording studio in the 1970s. Record companies had to compete for time here with Thom Bell and the team

Sigma Sound Studios, 1979. (Courtesy of Joseph Tarsia.)

of Gamble and Huff; at one point, the studio was open and running seven days a week, twenty-four hours a day. Bell produced hits for groups such as the Stylistics ("Betcha By Golly Wow," "Stone In Love With You") and the Spinners ("I'll Be Around," "Mighty Love"). After successes with artists like Jerry Butler and Wilson Pickett, Gamble and Huff created a string of lushly orchestrated hits for their own label, including "Backstabbers," "Bad Luck," "Kiss And Say Goodbye," and "TSOP." This last song was recorded by MFSB, the house band that was actually a mini-orchestra. These players were given freedom to experiment once they learned the basic structure of the songs. As Sigma Sound's owner Joe Tarsia says, "There was no such thing as MIDI recording . . . The energy and excitement came from the interplay of a lot of creative musicians."

Some of the other hits recorded here are "Hello It's Me" by Nazz, *Young Americans* by David Bowie, and "Macho Man" by the Village People.

Solomon's Temple Baptist Church   *1633 North Willington St.*
The great soul singer Solomon Burke was anything but a neglected child. Twelve years before he was even born, his grandmother, Eleanora A. Moore had a dream about him and founded a church on his behalf—Solomon's Temple: The House of God for All People. Burke delivered his first sermon when he was seven. At nine, he was a preacher and choir soloist. At twelve, he had his own gospel radio show and was touring the gospel circuit as "the Wonder Boy Preacher." But it was through a talent show at Philadelphia's **Liberty Baptist Church** (24 North 37th St.) that he was discovered and signed to the Apollo record label.

South Street

Philly's pop group of the '60s, the Orlons, had a hit that sang the praises of this street. It used to be the main drag for entertainment, from strip joints to nightclubs. Now it's a cleaned-up version of the same, with used bookstores, record and fashion shops, a few clubs and lots of food. (The street was mentioned in Fear's "I Don't Care About You," as part of a list of decadent city landmarks.)

Town Hall   *150 North Broad St.*

Todd Rundgren's first recording band, the Nazz, made their debut here in July 1967, opening up for the Doors. The building, a former Masonic Temple, was demolished in 1983.

The Trauma   *2121 Arch St.*

Before the Electric Factory, this second-story ballroom (complete with psychedelic light show) was the top nightspot in the city. It was operated by Manny Rubin, who claims it was the first psychedelic club on the East Coast. Upcoming bands like the Mothers of Invention played here, but it was forced to close down a year after the Electric Factory opened its bigger operation across the street. City Hall's antagonistic attitude toward nightclubs also played a part in its demise. The Trauma then became a club called Memphis. From the mid-'70s to the early '80s, it was a nightspot called Just Jazz, which booked R&B types, too. It's now a disco called Rhythmz.

Treegoob's   *41st and Lancaster Ave.*

In 1954, Herb Slotkin owned this record store and Jerry Ragavoy was a young musician who worked as a clerk. That year, a black doo-wop group called the Castelles recorded a song called "My Girl Awaits Me" on a record-your-voice disc for twenty-five cents and brought it to this store in order to hear how it sounded. Ragavoy liked it and persuaded Slotkin to become the group's manager. Slotkin went further and formed a label, Grand Records, to record the group. The group traveled to New York for a session and the song was a hit, especially among soldiers stationed in Korea. Ragavoy went on to a series of classic New York "Hit Factory" productions in the '60s.

❼ The Uptown   *Broad St. and Dauphin*

In the late '50s and '60s, this theater was used for R&B extravaganzas, ten or twelve 10-day shows that were conveniently scheduled immediately after welfare and government pay checks were due. These shows featured local groups as well as the major artists of the day, such as Ray Charles, Jackie Wilson, and Marvin Gaye. (It was here in fact that Ray Charles found his first Raelettes—they were singing here as the Cookies.) The groups would vie for a good place in the line-up; no one wanted to start the show, everybody wanted to end it. Several albums were recorded here, including Atlantic Records' *Saturday Night at the Uptown.* One act, Patti LaBelle and the Blue Belles, was subsequently signed to Atlantic. Like other theaters on the chitlin circuit, the Uptown did not fare well in the late '70s and '80s, when the area surrounding it, filled with drugs and guns, became known as "The War Zone." As with the Howard in D.C., the many plans for renovations and revitalization have not yet been carried out.

⑧ WFIL-TV   *46th and Market*

In 1952, a show called "Bandstand" began local broadcasts from this television studio. It became the city's top-rated daytime program, and it continued to be taped here even after ABC decided to turn it into a national show—the nationally broadcast "American Bandstand"—in August 1957. Five days a week, host Dick Clark delivered the top stars (who lip-synched) and the latest dance crazes (the Hully Gully, the Fly, the Pony) to the teenage masses. Alongside bona fide big names like Jerry Lee Lewis, Bill Haley, Chuck Berry, and the Everly Brothers, "American Bandstand" introduced unknown Philadelphia singers to the world. It also boosted Philadelphia's writers and producers into the mainstream of the national music industry.

The Uptown Theater today.

John Bartram High School (Courtesy of the Urban Archives, Temple University, Philadelphia, PA.)

 ## Schools

John Bartram High School   *67th St. and Elmwood Ave.*
This is the alma mater of Patti LaBelle (then Patricia Holt) and Earl Monroe. In fact, LaBelle made her first appearance outside of church at a talent show here. A teacher gave her the sheet music to "You'll Never Walk Alone," and she performed it here, later turning it into a hit with her group Patti LaBelle and the Blue Belles. In 1992, she recorded it again, for an AIDS walkathon organization.

High School for the Creative and Performing Arts   *11th and Catherine*
The four members of Boyz II Men were students here when they sought out Michael Bivens (of Bell Biv Devoe) after a talent show. He became their manager and got them signed to Motown. They were nominated for a Best New Artist Grammy in 1991.

⑨ South Philadelphia High School   *Broad and Snyder*
Fabian and James Darren were both spotted by desperate "talent scouts" while they were students here. Their telegenic looks and lip-synching abilities took them far. Chubby Checker is another alumnus.

🔙 Detours

⑩ Cherry Hill, NJ
The Latin Casino/Emerald City
Although it's in another state, this club served as an important venue for the city's music fans. It's only ten minutes away, after all. In the '60s and most of the '70s, it was called the Latin Casino and featured everyone

from Frank Sinatra and Tony Bennett to Al Green and the Four Tops. (Its low point came on September 25, 1975, when the great Jackie Wilson suffered a heart attack while performing here. He went into a coma and never really recovered.)

In 1978, the club underwent an expensive renovation to accommodate the disco boom, becoming Emerald City. It continued to feature live shows, though, including Prince, Talking Heads, David Johansen, and the Psychedelic Furs. The club closed in October 1981, making way for Subaru's national headquarters.

⓫ Chester, PA   *14 miles SW of Philadelphia*
The former home of Bill Haley was demolished after a fire but musical notes (the Comets) and a star (Haley) are still embedded in the sidewalk at the corner of Crosby and Fifth streets.

Wilmington, DE   *29 miles SW of Philadelphia*
In 1966, Bob Marley lived with his mother here and worked at the Chrysler factory in nearby Newark (550 South College Ave). He returned to his native Jamaica when it looked like he might be drafted. This is also the hometown of guitarist Tom Verlaine.

Dover, DE   *75 miles SW of Philadelphia*
In mid-March 1956, Carl Perkins was riding high with his pop, country and R&B hit, "Blue Suede Shoes." It was selling 20,000 copies a day, and Perkins and his band were touring around the country promoting it. On March 22, they were headed for New York City and the Perry Como show when their car crashed into a poultry truck on Route 13 just south of Dover. Carl and his bandmates were badly hurt and, for a variety of reasons, Perkins never regained the momentum of his career.

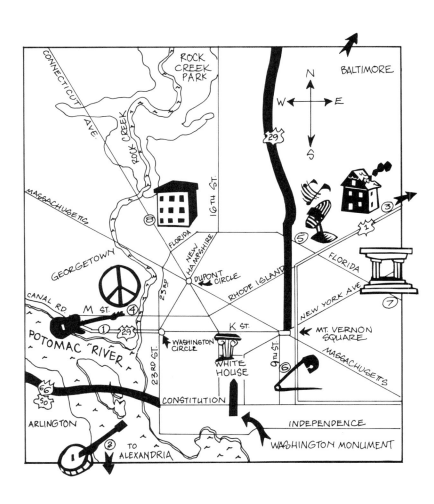

The nation's capital has produced some megastars of American music—Duke Ellington and Marvin Gaye, to name two—but for the most part they have had to leave town to get a record contract and national exposure. For years the city had no recording industry whatsoever, and labels like Atlantic, Chess, and Motown gladly poached D.C.'s local talent.

D.C.'s music makers have always kept up with the nation's most popular styles, though, and the area has several legendary venues. In recent years the city has also generated some styles of its own. Go-Go, an ultra-rhythmic, richly textured brand of dance music, developed in Southeast Washington, one of the city's most deprived areas. And hardcore (or harDCore, as it's spelled here), an offshoot of punk rock, had strong exponents in Georgetown and the city's white suburbs. The "straight edge" ethic—steering clear of alcohol and drugs—first took hold in this scene.

❶ The Bayou   *3135 K St. NW*
The city's top showcase venue, the Bayou is located in a building that's been a nightclub since Prohibition. In 1980, Cellar Door Productions, the largest concert promoter in the area, took it over and has presented shows by stars such as R.E.M, U2, Joe Jackson, Dire Straits, and Guns N' Roses.

❷ The Birchmere   *3901 Mt. Vernon Ave., Alexandria, VA*
For years, Washington has been considered the bluegrass capitol of the country, and this club has been at the center of the scene. Since 1976, it has been the homebase for the Seldom Scene, D.C.'s legendary bluegrass group, who have played there nearly every Thursday. The Birchmere has also booked acts such as the Dixie Dregs, Lyle Lovett, and Marshall Crenshaw.

❸ Bo Diddley's House   *2600 Rhode Island Ave. NE*
In 1957, Marvin Gaye and his struggling doo-wop group, the Marquees, were introduced to rock and roll pioneer Bo Diddley, who was living in town at the time. Diddley took an interest, letting them hold jam sessions in his basement. He even took the Marquees to New York, and produced

The Birchmere, bluegrass haven.

a record date for them. The resulting songs—"Wyatt Earp" and "Hey, Little School Girl"—went nowhere but the group was encouraged to persist.

The Capitol   *1st St., between Constitution Ave. and Independence Ave.*
The rock and roll biz gets a Congressional going-over here about every twenty-five years. In 1959, hearings began investigating payola for radio and television play. Alan Freed was nailed, and clever Dick Clark emerged unscathed. In 1985, naughty rock lyrics were exposed and analyzed by the likes of Tipper Gore, Susan Baker, and Nancy Thurmond.

The Cellar Door   *1201 34th St. NW*
This club was opened in 1961 and remained very popular into the '70s. Neil Young heard local guitar wiz Nils Lofgren here and helped him launch his career. But when its legal capacity was cut in half by the police—from 250 people to 125—the building was sold and torn down.

d.c. space   *443 7th St. NW*
This gallery and performance space was, perhaps unwittingly, one of the birthplaces of harDCore. In December 1980, it hosted one of the crucial events of the time, The Unheard Music Festival. Put together by Mark Halpern of the new wave band the Nurses, the show featured ten bands over two nights. For S.O.A. and Government Issue, it was their first show. For most of the others, it was their first show at a "legitimate" venue after performing at plenty of parties and at the Madam's Organ artists' collective.

The bands played short sets. And, following the lead of the Teen Idles, seven other bands performed the old Monkees song "Stepping Stone," each in their own distinctive style; G.I. did a ten-second version, for example. A live album was planned to commemorate the raucous event but it never materialized. The money raised from the show may well have gone to Mark Halpern's drug habit; he overdosed and died a few months later.

The Teen Idles played two or three more times at d.c. space, but were "banned for life" when the bathroom was destroyed during one of their multibill shows here. Songwriter/bassist Ian MacKaye says his group wasn't involved: "we were not going to do the cliché rock and roll things, like stealing stuff or breaking things. After all, the bathroom is our friend." But it was three or four years before any other rock shows were put on here.

In recent years, the venue featured appearances by Holly Hughes, Henry Rollins, as well as bands like the Holy Rollers, Fugazi, and Tiny Desk Unit (their first and last shows). The space closed at the end of 1991 and may have since found another location.

Dischord House   *3819 Beecher St. NW*
This was the childhood home of Ian MacKaye, a member of three of the city's most important bands: the Teen Idles, Minor Threat, and Fugazi.

Dischord band, Fugazi. (Photo by Pat Graham.)

He co-founded the Dischord label in 1981 to document the fledgling harDCore scene, and ran it from this house. Label headquarters have since moved to a cottage in Arlington, VA.

❹ Emergency *2813 M St. NW*

Now a French restaurant, this small club was an important center for D.C.'s counterculture from the summer of 1969 to January 1, 1972. It was a place—the only place—for local bands with original material to perform, and it also featured rising touring acts like the Bob Seger System, Fairport Convention, and the Kinks.

The club started off as a community project by a handful of Georgetown teenagers, who had gotten financial help from their parents for a nonalcoholic teen hangout. It met with predictably antagonistic community reaction and strict zoning regulations. But while it lasted, Emergency was an exciting place. The entrance was through a narrow, yellow-painted record store; once inside the club, the young patrons sat along a carpeted floor that sloped downward to the stage.

In 1991, Emergency's staff and regulars held a reunion at the Bayou, which attracted people from all over the country. It featured the temporary reformation of local music legends like Sageworth and Drums, Itchy Brother, Rent's Due, and Claude Jones, a band often described as "the Grateful Dead of the East Coast."

FBI Headquarters *Pennsylvania Ave. between 9th and 10th St. NW*

Elvis was given a private tour of the building in 1970 but he didn't get to meet J. Edgar Hoover, as he had wished.

Georgetown University   *37th and O St. NW*

WGTB Radio Station

>   In 1979, after this student-run 50,000-watt station aired an advertisement
>   for Planned Parenthood, Georgetown U.'s then-president Timothy Healy
>   sold it to the University of the District of Columbia for one dollar. The
>   outcry from the student population was enormous, and resulted in the
>   Hall of Nations benefit.

Hall of Nations

>   The benefit for WGTB was held here on February 3, 1979—and it became
>   the concert event of the year. The show featured the Cramps, and it
>   quickly sold out—but that didn't keep hundreds of kids from pouring in
>   through the windows. The creepy looking Cramps put on a galvanizing
>   show—Lux Interior even threw up for the occasion—and the entire
>   crowd showed their appreciation throughout by jumping up and down
>   on the tables in the hall. At one point, all of the tables started collapsing.
>   No one was seriously hurt, but the benefit made no profit at all. Neverthe-
>   less, impressionable teenagers were present and many of them—such as
>   Ian Mackaye and Guy Picciotto—immediately formed bands. With their
>   wild, confrontational show, the Cramps had overturned the staid stereo-
>   types of '70s arena rock. As MacKaye once recalled, "It was the first time
>   I realized that anyone could do it and that it was more fun to go out and
>   play and potentially totally suck than being holed up in your cellar
>   practicing your guitar and being oppressed by your fear of sucking!"

Go-Go Landmarks

>   Although the D.C.-bred go-go style—that thumping, thick mix of funk,
>   jazz, soul, and Latin percussion—has yet to go global, or even national,
>   Southeast D.C. is still ringing with the sound of that music. It's been
>   almost thirty years since the term was applied to the celebrated Thurs-
>   day-night dance parties at the Knights of Columbus Hall (10th and K
>   streets, NW), but the actual style of music began to be developed in the
>   late '70s.
>
>   Great-grandfather Chuck Brown is go-go's acknowledged godfather.
>   After learning guitar during a mid-'60s stint in jail (Lorton Penitentiary),
>   he formed a Top-40 cover band and started playing all-ages shows all over
>   the city. The style evolved as the group started to fill in the dead space
>   between songs; the drummer kept a beat going, and Brown would "talk"
>   to the audience, welcoming back any return visitors to the go-go, which
>   is what the event was called. Over time, the entire band (with up to ten
>   members) joined in. R&B bands around town started adopting the sound
>   of Chuck Brown and the Soul Searchers—which was drawing the city's
>   largest crowds—and a phenomenon was born.
>
>   Most of the first venues were in Southeast D.C., many of them affiliated
>   with the Catholic Church or the Knights of Columbus: the **Shelter Room**,
>   the **Satellite Room**, **Our Lady of Perpetual Help's Panorama Room**, and the
>   **Maverick Room**. There was also **Byrne Manor**, right across the Maryland
>   border. One of the first halls that was privately owned was the **Black Hole**
>   (3401 Georgia Ave.), which is now operating under the name of Capitol

City Pavilion. **Breeze's Metro Club, Cheriys,** and **The U Street Temple** are other go-go spots, past and present. These clubs and halls are often forced to close or change names because of violence that occurs outside the venue. Another scapegoat for urban ills. At its height, however, go-go events were promoted at R.F.K. Stadium and the Washington Coliseum.

Unfortunately, the style has not traveled well; unlike rap, it can't be compressed into four-minute, radio-ready songs. A 1985 movie about the scene, "Good to Go," was laughably bad, which of course didn't help.

Chuck Brown continues to perform here—and up and down the East Coast—with his band the Soul Searchers, as do other scene stalwarts such as Rare Essence, Junkyard, C.J.'s Uptown Crew, and Little Benny and the Masters. At last count, there were at least fifty go-go bands in the area. And one of them performed at Mayor Sharon Pratt Dixon's inaugural ball.

⑤ The Howard   *620 T St. NW*

With its considerable black population (remember the Parliament song "Chocolate City"?), Washington D.C. was a key stop for black performers; and the Howard was the city's link in the nation's chitlin circuit. The first legitimate theater in the America built for blacks, it became a grand social institution, hosting all the big names from Count Basie and Duke Ellington to Bo Diddley and James Brown to Sly and the Family Stone. The Howard also launched many careers. Pearl Bailey started as a member of the chorus in 1934, and amateur night contests brought attention to Bill Kenny of the Ink Spots and Billy Eckstine, among others.

Ahmet Ertegun, an eventual co-founder of Atlantic Records, was lucky

The Pump Blenders at Cheriys, 1984. (Photo by W. G. Allen.)

The Howard Theater today. (Photo by W.G. Allen.)

enough to be in Washington in the '30s and '40s, when his father was
the Turkish ambassador. In a documentary on the theater, Ertegun commented, "The Howard Theater taught me more about black music than
anything else, because that's where I heard all the great musicians."
Among Ertegun's first successes with Atlantic were two Washington-
based acts, the Clovers and Ruth Brown.

The theater's decline started in the mid-'60s, as the Shaw neighborhood
itself declined. The theater couldn't keep up with the rising costs of name
performers, and black and white fans became increasingly hesitant about
turning out for shows. It never recovered from the riots of 1968, finally
closing in 1970. The city purchased the theater in 1986, and in late 1990,
then-mayor Barry announced plans to begin a $5.6 million renovation of
the eighty-year-old theater. Those plans are currently on hold.

Right nearby the Howard was Cecelia's, a restaurant/nightclub/room-
ing house for performers to hang out before or after showtime. In November 1958, Harvey Fuqua was staying in a room here while his group, the
Moonglows, were performing at the theater. He was unhappy with the
group's current line-up and allowed a young local group called the Marquees to audition for him here. He was impressed, especially with a
singer named Marvin Gaye.

Lisner Auditorium   *21st and H St. NW, George Washington University Campus*
This theater has seen many rock and roll shows, from Bill Haley and the
Comets in the '50s to Jane's Addiction in 1990. This was also the favorite

hall of Lowell George, Little Feat's vocalist/guitarist/guiding spirit. Little Feat's live album, *Waiting For Columbus*, was recorded here, and this was the last place George performed, on June 29, 1979. He had a fatal heart attack at his hotel the next morning.

Madam's Organ   *2318 18th St. NW*

This artists' cooperative witnessed early performances by the Bad Brains, the Teen Idles, and other harDCore stars.

Mr. Henry's   *601 Pennsylvania Ave. SE*

Roberta Flack was discovered at this Capitol Hill nightclub by Les McCann in the fall of 1967. (After graduating from Howard University, she had been a public school music teacher in the city.)

❻ The 9:30 Club   *930 F St. NW*

This has been a top alternative club since the late '70s, when it was called the Atlantis. It became the 9:30 Club in 1980 and soon became headquarters for the local hardcore scene. Bands like the Bad Brains and Minor Threat didn't mind that there wasn't a real stage or P.A. system. Since then, touring bands such as Sonic Youth (opening for Egoslavia), the Cramps, Living Colour, the Red Hot Chili Peppers, and Nirvana have stopped by on their way up. The 9:30 has also booked go-go bands regularly. In fact, Spike Lee saw E.U. perform here and featured them—and their song "Da Butt"—in his 1988 movie, *School Daze*.

The club is on the ground floor of a building that has been condemned for fire code violations, but the club itself shows no sign of budging.

The Bad Brains at the 9:30 Club, 1982. (Photo by Leslie Clague.)

Parents' Music Resource Center   *1500 Arlington Blvd., Arlington, VA*
Stop by and visit Tipper Gore and Susan Baker, two of the co-founders of this "music monitoring" organization. Congratulate them on their record labeling system, which only seems to alert kids to the explicit lyrics contained on a record—and probably makes them listen to the words more carefully.

7-11   *Wisconsin and Q St. NW*
Henry Rollins, lead singer for LA's now-defunct Black Flag and now fronting the Rollins Band, grew up in the D.C. area as Henry Garfield. He was in an early harDCore band called S.O.A., and this particular convenience store was a key hangout for him back then. In 1985, he wrote a loving tribute to the 7-11 chain in *Spin* magazine.

❼ The Washington Coliseum   *3rd and M St. NE*
This sports arena was the site of the Beatles' first U.S. concert, on February 11, 1964. The group had appeared on the Ed Sullivan Show two nights before, and 7,000 teenagers packed the venue. The stage was set in the center, surrounded by the audience, and the group's publicist Brian Sommerville had to keep running out onstage to turn them all in a different direction. They played twelve songs.

❽ The Washington Hilton   *1919 Connecticut Ave. NW*
In September 1967, this hotel's ballroom was the unlikely site of a very, er, interesting performance by the Doors. Jim Morrison had spent his high school years in nearby Alexandria, VA, and his parents now lived in Arlington, VA. His mother, Clara, hadn't seen the boy in several years and tried to contact him at the hotel before the show. His entourage kept her away, according to Morrison's wishes, but she did get a chance to hear his version of their Oedipal epic, "The End," complete with the line that got the band thrown out of the Whisky: "Mother? I want to . . . FUCK YOU!" When she went to see him after the show, he had already left for New York.

Washington Monument
During the historic March on Washington on August 28, 1963, musical performances were given on a stage here by, in order, Joan Baez, Odetta, Josh White, Peter, Paul and Mary, and Bob Dylan, who brought up the SNCC Freedom Singers from Albany, Georgia.

Waxie Maxie's   *1836 7th St. NW*
Initially called the Quality Music Shop, this record store was a key part of the Shaw neighborhood from its opening in 1938 until the day it burned down in the 1968 riots. Max Silverman was a jukebook entrepreneur when he opened the shop as an outlet for jukebox records that had been used and discarded. This store became the first in a chain of more than twenty stores in the area; in 1991, it was sold to the Strawberries record chain.

Located right around the corner from the Howard theater, the record shop offered half-price specials for the featured performer's records after the shows. The lines stretched half the block. The store also proved to be a frequent hangout for Ahmet Ertegun. Silverman once guessed that the young Turk spent at least twelve hours a day there, listening to the latest R&B releases. The two men even started a record label, which—without a single release—never quite reached the stature of Atlantic Records, Ertegun's next venture.

Yesterday and Today Record Store   *1327-J Rockville Pike, Rockville, MD*
This mostly vinyl shop opened in the summer of 1977 and continues to stock new and used, mostly independent releases—and just a few CDs. In the late '70s and early '80s, the store owners also ran a record label, Limp Records. It released vinyl by local bands like the Slickee Boys and the Shirkers as well as three compilations—*30 Seconds Over D.C.*, *Best of Limp* and *Connected*—which included early tracks by the Bad Brains and Black Market Baby.

Schools

Ballou High School   *4th and Trenton SE*
Members of Rare Essence and Junkyard, two of the city's top go-go groups, went here.

Cardozo High School   *13th and Clifton NW*
Marvin Gaye formed his first group, the DC Tones, while a student here. He played the piano but didn't sing. Gaye never graduated but he returned in May 1972 for a concert in the school auditorium; it was the city's official Marvin Gaye day. He sang "What's Going On" with the school band, signed autographs, and gave a brief speech.

George Washington High School   *1005 Mt. Vernon Ave., Alexandria, VA*
In 1958, Jim Morrison's father was assigned to the Pentagon. The family moved from Alameda, California, and the young Lizard King attended this school for two and a half years. He graduated in the spring of 1960 but, not surprisingly, he didn't bother to attend the ceremony. He used to regale his teachers with elaborate stories involving gypsies and bandits when he was late, absent, or inattentive. One gullible teacher fell for his story that he had a brain tumor and had to leave class for an operation to remove it.

Howard University   *2400 6th St. NW*
This black institution is the alma mater of, among others, Roberta Flack, Donnie Hathaway, members of the go-go group Trouble Funk, and Crystal Waters, who hit it big in 1991 with "Gypsy Woman." Flack and Hathaway were classmates here in the late '60s and later sang such classic duets as "The Closer I Get To You." Most recently, Michael Ivey recorded *Play With Toys*, Basehead's debut album, while a full-time student here.

Ivey played all the instruments on the hip-hop/rock record, and then assembled a band for playing live.

Wilson High School   *Nebraska and Chesapeake NW*
The Teen Idles formed here in 1979.

↳ DETOUR

Baltimore, MD   *45 miles NE of Washington, D.C.*
The birthplace of doo-wop pioneers the Orioles as well as Jerry Leiber, Frank Zappa, David Byrne, and Joan Jett. The Basement Boys are the latest local hit makers. In 1990, the production team (who actually work out of their basement) scored with Crystal Waters's "Gypsy Woman." **The Royal Theater** (1329 Pennsylvania Ave.) was an important, though intimidating, stop along the chitlin circuit; audience members came prepared with bottles, rotten heads of lettuce, tomatoes, and eggs. It was demolished in 1971.

The South

MEMPHIS

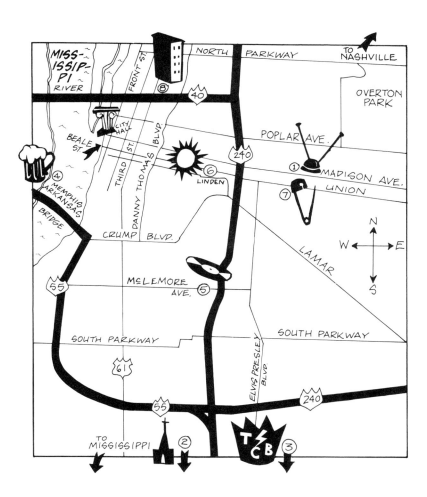

This Tennessee city had its pop music heyday in the '50s and '60s with two pioneering hit factories—Sam Phillips's Sun studio and Jim Stewart and Estelle Axton's Stax outfit—but its intriguing musical tradition extends back to the '20s and continues to this day. Many legends, from Elvis Presley and Jerry Lee Lewis to Al Green and Alex Chilton, have made Memphis their home, and history has been made here many times over. WDIA-AM, the first radio station in the country to have

61

all-black programming, was born in Memphis; it featured B.B. King and Rufus ("Funky Chicken") Thomas spinning records and performing daily.

By the time Sun Records put Memphis on the pop-music map in 1954, the area had a thriving live music scene. Clubs along Beale Street (a stronghold of the blues), in West Memphis, Arkansas, and in East Memphis were packed with listeners paying to hear live rhythm and blues, raw country music, and their emerging hybrids.

But while the city continues to have top-notch recording studios, the live music scene hasn't kept pace. Into the '60s, session musicians from Sun and Stax and Hi Studios performed regularly at clubs in the area, but that tradition had fallen apart by the '80s. Today the city is pushing for a return to musical prominence, with a major overhaul for Beale Street and W.C. Handy Park. Most of the clubs and bands there cater too strenuously to tourists, but places like the Rum Boogie Cafe do have good nights. And the unpretentious Green's Lounge, outside of the city center, does even better.

But good clubs or no, visitors will continue to come to Memphis, virtually descending on the place when the anniversary of Elvis's death rolls around.

❶ Antenna Club   *1588 Madison Ave.*

Memphis's premier new music club—at times its only one—since March 1981. Mark McGehee, who runs the Antenna with his brother Steve, says they opened the club out of "a passion for decent music in a town full of crappy music." The men evidently have an ear for the raw and adventurous. The club has booked early shows by the Replacements, the Red Hot

Antenna Club, with metaphysical graffiti, 1990. (Photo by Jim Cole.)

Chili Peppers, Concrete Blonde, and R.E.M. (tickets were $2 and they still couldn't fill the place) as well as local legends like Panther Burns and Cordell Jackson.

Arcade Restaurant   *540 South Main St.*

Memphis's oldest restaurant, the Arcade was featured in Jim Jarmusch's *Mystery Train*—and still serves good breakfasts. The real structural star of the film, the Arcade Hotel down the street, was closed in 1983. It may still be for sale.

Ardent Studio   *2000 Madison Ave., since 1971; 1457 National, 1966–1971*

This studio opened up in 1966 and was soon handling lots of projects, including the overflow work that the city's already famous studios couldn't handle. The breakthrough LP from Stax writer/musician/producer Isaac Hayes, *Hot Buttered Soul*, was recorded here because there was no open time on East McLemore. But what seems to have brought bands like the Replacements and R.E.M. to the studio in the '80s was the fact that Big Star, the legendary Memphis pop group, recorded here in the early '70s. In fact, the Replacements recorded "Alex Chilton," their ode to the former Box Top and Big Star member, in these studios. (Big Star changed its name from Ice Water after seeing the big store across the street from the National Avenue studio: the Big Star Foodmarket.)

Baptist Memorial Hospital   *899 Madison Ave.*

Lisa Marie Presley was born here in February 1966. Her daddy was pronounced dead here eleven and a half years later, though he actually died in his bathroom.

Burnettes' First Home   *583 Pontotoc*

Rockabilly pioneers Dorsey and Johnny Burnette spent their first years in a house at this address. Their house has since been torn down.

❷ Church of the Full Gospel Tabernacle   *787 Hale Rd.*

The Reverend Al Green, who recorded his first hits in this town, has been the pastor of this church since 1985. When he presides over Sunday services, he sometimes sings these hits along with the gospel numbers—much to the pleasure of out-of-town fans.

The Eagle's Nest   *Clearpool and Lamar*

Jim Stewart, the co-founder of Stax Records, was a country fiddler in the house band for this now-defunct club in the mid-'50s, when an unknown Elvis Presley played during the intermissions. Stewart now says Presley's meteoric rise got him interested in producing some records.

Flamingo Room   *140½ Hernando Rd.*

In the '50s, black kids hung out at this club owned by Clifford Miller. A five-man singing group called the Del Rios (which included William Bell) were regular performers here. And at fourteen Booker T. Jones was snuck

Wayne Jackson and Duck Dunn in Hernando's Hideaway band. (Courtesy of the Center for Southern Folklore © 1992.)

in to play bass or baritone sax with Willie Mitchell's band. Mitchell's drummer was the late, great Al Jackson, Jr., and the pair became half of Booker T. and the MGs.

❸ Graceland

See The Homes of Elvis on pages 71–73.

Hernando's Hideaway   *3210 Hernando Rd.*

This club opened in 1957 and quickly gained a reputation as a wild place to spend an evening—its nickname used to be "the pressure cooker." It's long been a notorious Jerry Lee Lewis hangout; a lot of his parties have been held here. The current owner has even built a special room for Lewis so that he won't be bothered by the other patrons.

Holiday Inn   *1441 East Brooks Rd., off Route 55*

This is where the Sex Pistols stayed during their 1978 visit to Memphis's Taliesyn Ballroom.

Hotel Chisca   *Main St. and Linden*

Now the Church of God in Christ World Headquarters, this building used to house the WHBQ radio station studios. Dewey Phillips, a notorious but well-loved Memphis DJ, broadcast his "Red Hot and Blue" show from the mezzanine and was the first DJ to play "That's Alright (Mama)." When a dozen positive listener calls came through, Phillips hauled Elvis in for his first-ever interview. (The legend goes that he didn't tell Elvis the microphone was on because the future King seemed so nervous.) The building's basement has its own legend: Elvis played a handful of parties here before he made his first recording.

Jerry Lee Lewis's Downfall *4908 East Shore Dr., near Coro Lake*
The home of Lewis's cousin, J.W. Brown, this was also the blessed abode of Brown's daughter, Myra Gale. Jerry Lee met Myra as soon as he arrived in Memphis in November 1956. She was twelve, he was already married, but their love seemed to conquer all. On December 11, 1957, they married. It shocked Myra's parents first, then the entire British population during his 1958 tour of England. The loving couple lived at 4752 Dianne St., and then 5042 East Shore Drive. They divorced in 1970.

The Lorraine Motel *406 Mulberry St.*
Before Martin Luther King, Jr. was assassinated in 1968, this was a popular place for out-of-town musicians to stay. (The Stax studios were only a half-mile away.) Several songs, including "Knock On Wood," are said to have been written here. It was closed as a lodging house in 1988 and opened up in 1991 as the National Civil Rights Museum. The interior has been gutted and rebuilt to make room for exhibitions, but the exterior remains as it was.

Mitchell's Hotel *207 Beale St.*
Like the Dew Drop Inn in New Orleans, this establishment provided fine shelter and a top-notch club for touring musicians from the '40s to the '60s. Run by Andrew "Sunbeam" Mitchell, who operated many night-clubs before he died in 1989, the hotel and Club Handy upstairs hosted the likes of Johnny Ace, Bobby "Blue" Bland, and Little Richard. The house band included heavyweights like George Coleman, Phineas Newborn and Charles Lloyd. (Mitchell's wife Ernestine is famous for her bowls of chili.) Sunbeam's last venture was a converted bowling alley he named the **Club Paradise** (645 E. Georgia Ave.). It's still running and the stars still love it. In fact, Carla Thomas recently claimed it was her favorite club.

Overton Park Shell *1928 Poplar Ave.*
It wasn't the site of his first concert, or even of his first outdoor concert. But when Elvis Presley performed here in August 1954, it may well have been the first time he shook and made the girls—including Sun Records's Marion Keisker—go crazy. Since then, Overton Park has been the site of frequent spring and summer concerts. One recent show of note was given by Memphis's latest potential male superstar, guitarist Eric Gales.

The Palace Theater *318 Beale St.*

Stax artist Rufus Thomas started hosting amateur night here right out of high school. Men such as B.B. King, Johnny Ace, and Bobby "Blue" Bland got important exposure here. The theater was torn down in the '60s.

④ The Plantation Inn *3600 East Broadway, 3 miles from the bridge in West Memphis, Arkansas*

This legendary club (now Pancho's Mexican Restaurant) was opened in the 1940s by a Cesar Romero-type named Morris Berger and his wife Clemmye. These charismatic hosts knew how to throw a good party—the club's slogan, "Having Fun With Morris," was, from all accounts, an understatement. In the late '50s, the local R&B bands booked here were the best, led by Phineas Newborn, Sr., Ben Branch, and Willie Mitchell. Other regular attractions included William Bell and the Del Rios, talented precursors of groups like the Temptations; and a waiter known as Charlie Turner, Wild Charlie, and Tennessee Turner who would deliver over-the-top renditions of songs like "Jim Dandy to the Rescue." Climbing the walls with microphone in hand, this showman made Little Richard look tame.

One group in the audience that was listening to the house bands partic-

A vintage advertisement for the Plantation Inn.

ularly carefully was made up of underage white boys such as Packy Axton (whose mother and uncle later founded Stax), Duck Dunn, Steve Cropper, Don Nix, and Jim Dickinson. They would sneak in as much as they could and sit near the stage. "When the heat was on [from the authorities]," Dickinson recalls, "the bouncer, Raymond Vega, would let us sit in the parking lot while they ran the music through a speaker."

Memphis clubs closed at 1 A.M. but the Arkansas clubs kept going for many hours after that. Nearby in West Memphis were **Danny's Club** and the **Cotton Club**, which gave Jerry Lee Lewis his first local performing job—with Clyde Leoppard and the Snearly Ranch Boys. Sadly, none of these nightspots survived the '60s.

Poplar Tunes   *308 Poplar Ave.*

This famous Memphis record store was opened in July 1946 by two childhood friends, Joe Cuoghi and Johnny Navarese. Cuoghi, who also started up the Hi record label, died in 1970 but Navarese continues to run the shop—8:30 A.M. to 9 P.M., same hours as always. Elvis lived in the neighborhood back in the early '50s and, Navarese remembers, he used to come by nearly every day. When he got his first hit, he bought copies for the local kids. One night, Elvis stopped by to show off his brand new white Lincoln Continental. After spending a few minutes inside the store listening to music, he went outside to discover that some fervid female fans had covered his entire car with rouge and lipstick. Recalls Navarese: "Joe told him to drive it home, to never wash it and to never take it out in the rain. I just couldn't believe there was that much lipstick in the world." Other luminaries have stopped by the store, as well: Brenda Lee, Johnny Cash, Roy Orbison, and Sam Phillips, to name a few.

Royal Recording Studios   *1320 South Lauderdale*

This was the Royal Theater before Joe Cuoghi and his partners in the Hi record label turned it into a studio. The first hit generated here was "Smokie, Part II," but the label's greatest successes came when band-leader/trumpeter Willie Mitchell came into the business. His own instrumentals, especially "Soul Serenade," did well; even better were his classic productions with Al Green, including "Tired Of Being Alone," "Let's Stay Together," and "I'm Still In Love With You." Mitchell and the studio are still going strong; one recent project was the M Team, a rap group featuring his two grandsons.

❺ Satellite Record Shop   *926 East McLemore*

Run by Estelle Axton as an adjunct to the Stax record label, this store served as more than a revenue generator, though that function was very important early on. Axton and her brother Jim Stewart both learned about the changing tastes of the young customers, and they often tested the latest Stax songs on the kids, making changes or canning certain songs according to criticism and comments. The operation also gave some Stax

Rufus Thomas at the Satellite Record Shop. (Photo by Don Nix.)

artists and producers an initial foot in the door as well as a steady job. Steve Cropper and Homer Banks both worked as counter help.

❺ Stax Studios   *926 East McLemore*

Founded by Jim Stewart and his sister Estelle Axton, the *Stax* label turned out some of the best Southern soul hits of the 1960s, most notably Otis Redding's entire catalogue of classics. In 1959, the pair had turned the Capitol Theater, an abandoned moviehouse, into company headquarters. The stage became the control booth; the seats were torn out to make room for two recording spaces; and the old candy and popcorn stand turned into a record store where demos could be consumer-tested (*see* **Satellite Record Shop**).

The label drew on a racially mixed group of performers, producers, and writers, and developed legends like Redding, Sam & Dave, Booker T & the MGs (the first house band), and Isaac Hayes. The string of hits began with Carla Thomas's "Gee Whiz" in November 1960 and ran until Johnnie Taylor's "I Ain't Particular" in April 1968.

The building was bought by the Church of God in Christ and torn down—famous marquee and all—in 1991.

❻ Sun Studios   *706 Union Ave.*

In January 1950, a radio station engineer named Sam Phillips opened a studio to record local blues and country artists. He ended up capturing some of the earliest—and best—moments of rock and roll.

The first few years of the business were financially bleak but artistically impressive. Phillips recorded blues and R&B artists such as Bobby Bland, James Cotton, Howlin' Wolf, B.B. King, Ike Turner, and Jackie Brenston. One Brenston/Turner collaboration—"Rocket 88," from 1951—is considered by Phillips to be the first rock and roll record ever made.

In 1952, Phillips started his Sun record label, and within two years, he had found the performer to shoot him past solvency. Elvis Presley was an insecure teenager when he walked in, but Phillips evidently saw something more and hooked him up with two session musicians, Bill Black and Scotty Moore. They went to work at finding a suitable style for the uncrowned King, and while fooling around, came up with the magical sound of "That's All Right (Mama)." After a string of Presley hits, Phillips sold Elvis's contract to RCA Records for $40,000, a grand sum at the time.

Hoping to follow in Presley's footsteps, hundreds of young rock and rollers trooped off to Sun Records for an audition. Among the winners were Carl Perkins, Jerry Lee Lewis, Johnny Cash, Billy Riley, and Roy Orbison (who recorded his big hits later in Nashville).

Phillips opened a new studio at 639 Madison in 1960, leaving the historic, slightly grimy and very cramped Union Avenue facility behind.

Stax headquarters—out front are the MGs and friend. (Courtesy of the Center for Southern Folklore/Deanie Parker Collection © 1992)

Sun Studio: where it all began?

Today, happily, recording sessions have resumed, and tours are given daily.

❼ Taliesyn Ballroom   *1447 Union Ave.*
This venue, now replaced by a Taco Bell, was the site of the Sex Pistols second performance in the United States. (The Pistols almost didn't make it—their plane from Atlanta was struck by lightning.) Jim Dickinson, a legendary Memphis musician and producer, was in the audience: "It changed my life. It was a part of rock and roll I thought was gone forever. Rock and roll was really supposed to be something that your mother didn't like."

👫 Schools

Booker T. Washington High School   *715 South Lauderdale*
Alma mater of Johnny Ace and Stax stalwarts like Rufus Thomas, Booker T. Jones (his father taught science and math here), David Porter, Roosevelt Jamison, and Homer Banks.

Hamilton High   *1478 Wilson*
Carla Thomas was a senior here when she made her first record, " 'Cause I Love You," a duet with her father, Rufus.

L. C. Humes High   *659 North Manassas Ave.*

Elvis Presley's alma mater. He majored in shop, didn't make the football team and won a talent contest in his senior year.

Immaculate Conception High School   *Central Ave. and Belvedere Blvd.*

Priscilla Beaulieu attended this all-girls Catholic school from spring 1963 to June 1964. Elvis kept her out late at night—sometimes until 5 A.M.—but she managed to stagger off to classes almost every day so that her parents back in Germany wouldn't force her to return. When she graduated, Elvis gave her a beautiful red Corvair.

Manassas High   *781 Firestone Ave.*

Isaac Hayes's alma mater.

Messick High School   *703 South Greer*

The alma mater of Steve Cropper, Duck Dunn, Packy Axton, Terry Johnson, Charlie Freeman, and Don Nix, who formed a white R&B group called the Royal Spades while there. That group evolved into the Mar-Keys, which had a hit, "Last Night," on Stax Records. According to Peter Guralnick's *Sweet Soul Music,* Cropper decided to become a rock and roll guitarist in his sophomore year when he saw an upperclassman perform at the school's Friday morning chapel program.

🏠 The Many Memphis Homes of Elvis

572 Poplar Ave.

Now a vacant lot, this address served as the Presley family's first home in Memphis. Vernon, Gladys, Elvis, and Grandma Minnie occupied one room—sharing one double bed—while other welfare recipients resided in the other five rooms of the wooden-frame, double shotgun house. According to a contemporary, Elvis's father often slept off his hangovers outside on the porch. In those days, beer joints lined Poplar, which apparently pleased Vernon just fine. The family lived here from mid-September 1947 until mid-January 1948.

⑧ 85 Winchester/Apt. #328

The Presleys lived in this apartment in the Lauderdale Courts, a well-kept city housing project, from January 1948 to early 1953. It was while living here that Elvis got his first guitar lessons from Jesse Lee Denson, a young neighbor down the block. He often practiced singing and playing his guitar on the stairway to the basement because there was a nice echo there. This building still stands, but the neighborhood has deteriorated.

698 Saffarans

After being evicted from Lauderdale Courts, the Presley family lived in a now-demolished house at this address for four months in early 1953. Located right behind Humes High, it was the home of Bill Phelps, a paint contractor who employed Vernon once in a while.

462 Alabama St.

The Presleys lived here for a year and a half, beginning in the spring of 1953. In May or June 1954, Sam Phillips's assistant Marion Keisker gave Elvis a call here and had him come down to sing a song called "Without You." The house was right across the street from the home of musicians Bill and Johnny Black. Also living nearby were the young Burnette brothers, who apparently played in some casual jam sessions with Elvis back then.

2414 Lamar

After the success of Elvis's recordings with Sun, the Presley family moved to this modest, four-room brick house. They moved in at the end of 1954, and moved out in the middle of 1955. The house is still there, but it's run-down and may be demolished sometime soon.

1414 Getwell

The Presleys stayed a little longer at this address, renting it from mid-1955 to May 1956. (Elvis was touring around the country most of the time.) The house has been replaced by a Chief Auto Parts store.

1034 Audubon

This was the first house that the King actually bought, but the family lived here for less than a year. Elvis had a brick wall built around the house and then had tall metal spikes added, but that apparently didn't stop his avid fans from invading. A move to more secluded parts was necessary.

Young Elvis and his friend, Betty McMahon, across from the Lauderdale Courts. (Courtesy of J.L. Denson.)

③ Graceland *3717 Elvis Presley Blvd.*

Elvis bought this modern-day shrine on thirteen-and-a-half acres for $100,000 in 1957. Elvis soon added a kidney-shaped pool, big white pillars out front and his own inimitable decorating style. Some of the highlights: a gold-plated grand piano in the music room, the pool table room covered with pleated fabric, and the shag carpeting on the walls and ceilings of the Jungle Room. Elvis also surrounded himself with an entourage, the so-called "Memphis Mafia," who wore gold medallions and T-shirts with the message, "TCB" topped with a lightning bolt—short for "Taking Care of Business in a Flash." Gladys Presley died at Graceland in 1958, and her son died here nineteen years later, after many parties and more pills than one man can count. They are buried in the Meditation Garden, alongside Grandma Minnie, Vernon, and Jesse Garon (Elvis's stillborn twin).

In 1982, on the anniversary of Elvis's death, Graceland was officially opened to the public. Although it draws about 650,000 people annually, Elvis's Aunt Delta still lives here.

Forest Hill Cemetery *1661 Elvis Presley Blvd.*

Elvis was buried next to his mother here in August 1977. But after attempts were made to steal the King's body, Vernon asked that both Elvis and Gladys be brought back to Graceland. The task was accomplished in October 1977.

↳ DETOURS

Nashville, TN   *210 miles NE of Memphis*

This Tennessee city isn't known for its rock and roll scene—it's the capital of Country. Few rock stars hail from here, even if you count Jason and the Scorchers, who didn't succeed nationally. But the city's studios have captured some of the best early rock and pop hits, including Gene Vincent's "Be Bop A Lula" and Roy Orbison's "Only the Lonely." And the 50,000-watt radio station, WLAC, was a crucial transmitter of R&B in the '50s. Kids from all over the country, and from Canada to Jamaica, listened closely to disc jockeys Glen Nobles, Hoss Allen, and John "R" Richardson when they took over the country station at night.

Bradley's Barn *Bender's Ferry Rd., Mt. Juliet*

Owen Bradley recorded everyone from Brenda Lee to Moby Grape at his legendary studio headquarters.

RCA Recording Studios *1525 McGavock St.*

All of the Everly Brothers' early hits, including "Bye Bye Love" and "Wake Up, Little Susie," were recorded here. And when RCA bought Elvis's recording contract, the King came here to record such songs as "Heartbreak Hotel" and "I Want You, I Need You, I Love You." Chet Atkins often supervised sessions here.

Bradley's Barn near Nashville, Tennessee. (Photo by Stephanie Chernikowski.)

Florence, AL   *165 miles SE of Memphis*

Florence and its surrounding towns—Sheffield and Muscle Shoals—have played major roles in the history of rock and roll and soul. Sam Phillips was born and raised here. It's also the site of legendary recording studios. Rick Hall's Fame Studios (603 East Avalon Ave. in Muscle Shoals) produced such classics as "I Never Loved a Man (The Way I Love You)," "Land of 1,000 Dances," and "One Bad Apple." Muscle Shoals Sound (3614 Jackson Highway in Sheffield) was the site of the "Wild Horses" and "Brown Sugar" sessions, among many others.

THE MISSISSIPPI DELTA

This rural area—which, loosely speaking, extends from Vicksburg to Memphis—was the breeding ground for the blues in the first half of this century. It's covered with the landmarks of bluesmen like Robert Johnson, Charlie Patton, Muddy Waters, and Howlin' Wolf, as well as blueswoman Memphis Minnie. Most of these players eventually followed the Mississippi River north—to Memphis and Chicago—to gain a wider audience. From the '30s to the '50s, Clarksdale was the center of most of the Delta blues activity. Today it's home to the **Delta Blues Museum** (114 Delta Ave.), the impressive **Stackhouse/Delta Record Mart** (232 Sunflower Ave.), and several beloved juke joints, like **Margaret's Blue Diamond Lounge** (4th and West Tallahatchie) and **Smitty's Red Top Lounge** (377 Yazoo Ave.). Other sites of note:

Dockery Farms   *Highway 8, between Cleveland and Ruleville*

This huge plantation may have been the birthplace of the Delta blues. Guitarist Charlie Patton—considered to be the music's founder by several blues historians—learned to play here from a man named Henry

Sloan, who never recorded. Patton continued the teaching tradition—his students include Son House and Howlin' Wolf.

Highway 61

This road, visited and revisited by Bob Dylan and countless others, extends from New Orleans to Memphis and beyond. The Mississippi stretch alone accounts for more than its share of legends. The most famous of course is that of "the crossroads," the place at which Robert Johnson sold his soul to the Devil in exchange for guitar-playing genius. This hallowed ground is said to be near the center of Clarksdale, where Highway 61 intersects Highway 49.

Ike Turner Residence   *304 Washington, Clarksdale*

The notorious bandleader/songwriter/husband Izear Luster Turner was born in this city on November 15, 1931. The son of a Baptist minister, he began playing piano behind the likes of Sonny Boy Williamson and Robert Nighthawk at the age of eleven. He formed his first band in high school, recording "Rocket '88" at Sun Studio in 1951, and then worked as a talent scout and producer. In 1956, Turner and his band moved to St. Louis, where he soon met Annie Mae Bullock.

The Riverside Hotel   *615 Sunflower Ave., Clarksdale*

Before being turned into a hotel, this building served as the G.T. Thomas Afro-American Hospital; in September 1937, Bessie Smith died here after

ZZ Top and waxman Muddy Waters in the Delta Blues Museum in Clarksdale, Mississippi.

a car accident. Since 1944, it's been a comfortable, temporary home for luminaries like Sonny Boy Williamson, Ike Turner, and the Staple Singers.

Stovall's Plantation   *Oakridge Rd., 9 miles from downtown Clarksdale*
McKinley Morganfield, aka Muddy Waters, lived on a small patch of this enormous piece of land from age three to age twenty-six. He learned to play the harmonica and bottleneck guitar here, and his house was used as a juke joint on weekends. At twenty-six, he was discovered—and recorded—by Alan Lomax and John Work, folk song collectors from the Library of Congress. Within a few months, he left Stovall's for the lights of Chicago.

Three Forks   *5 miles south of Itta Bena*
More than fifty years after his death, there is still controversy over where and how the great blues guitarist Robert Johnson died in August 1938. The current consensus—by no means unanimous—holds that he was poisoned with strychnine-laced whiskey at a juke joint in Three Forks. His killer was supposedly an angry, jealous husband. Johnson was twenty-six years old; his grave is in the Zion Church graveyard, off Highway 7 in Morgan City.

Tupelo, MS   *100 miles SE of Memphis*

This town may one day be called Elvisville—if Memphis doesn't get to the name first. Streets, parks, and a highway have been renamed after Tupelo's famous native son—so it's just a matter of time. The main attraction is undoubtedly the "authentic recreation" of Elvis's birth-shack, complete with painted and papered walls, lush landscaping, and an $800,000 memorial chapel. It's located at 306 Elvis Presley Drive (formerly Old Saltillo Road). The family didn't stay here for long, however; before moving on to Memphis in 1947, they also lived on Berry Street, Reese Street, Adams Street, and several others. Even the town's **McDonald's** outlet (327 South Gloster St.) is Elvis-oriented. It displays photos, documents, and panels of narration about the departed King. And the etched-glass portraits are something to see.

ATLANTA/ATHENS

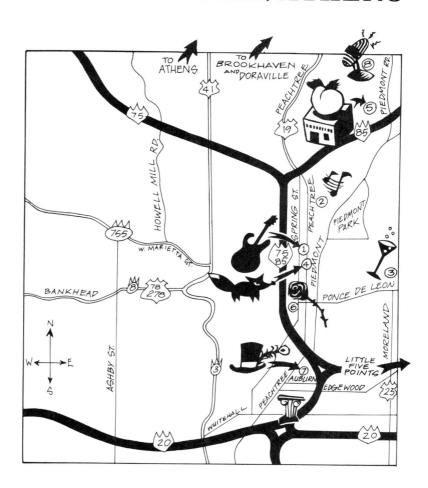

Georgia has produced some of the greatest figures in American pop history, including a remarkable number of raucous R&B pioneers like Little Richard, James Brown, Ray Charles, and Chuck Willis. Otis Redding and the Allman Brothers Band burst out of Macon at opposite ends of the '60s. And the explosion of inventive bands out of Athens that started at the end of the '70s made it clear that the South had risen again. Here are three crucial cities in American pop music history:

ATLANTA

Atlanta was a booming black entertainment center after World War II—
it was full of nightclubs and top-notch talent. Billy Wright, James Brown
and Little Richard were just the *local* scenemakers. But the city took
its time in developing its own music industry—recording studios and
independent labels have been scarce until recent years. The most important local music biz figure has been Bill Lowery, who started out as a
disc jockey and moved, with spectacular success, into music publishing
and recording studios. He has helped launch pop songwriters like Joe
South and Buddy Buie, and his studios have recorded everyone from Lynyrd Skynyrd to the Black Crowes.

Although Atlanta has produced few white rock and roll stars, the city
has plenty of local legends to keep the scene moving along. One of the
most enduring is Bruce Hampton, who began his band in the mid-'60s
and released his latest album in 1992. In the '70s, the reigning bands were
the Swimming Pool Qs, the Fans, and the Brains. But when the Athens,
GA, music scene took the spotlight at the end of the decade, few Atlanta
bands could escape from the shadow. Two exceptions were the Georgia
Satellites and the Indigo Girls. Then the Black Crowes burst onto the
national scene, having been transformed from a mild-mannered R.E.M.-
influenced rock and roll band to wild rock stars. Other emerging bands
are Drivin' 'N' Cryin', Follow For Now, and Uncle Green. In addition,
native (and very young) talents like Another Bad Creation and Kris Kross
have been discovered (some would say manufactured) in this city.

The R&B scene may now be headed for better things: Top producers
L.A. Reid and Babyface have moved here, as has Bobby Brown. They join
royalty like Curtis Mayfield, Isaac Hayes, and Larry Blackmon of Cameo.

❶ Agora Ballroom   *665 Peachtree*
> In the mid-'70s, a promoter named Alex Cooley turned this old hotel
> space into the Electric Ballroom, a full-time showcase. He booked mostly
> rock and roll, including Bruce Springsteen and the Tubes (who created
> something of an uproar in town). It later became another link in the
> Agora chain, featuring acts like Pylon, the Gang of Four, Talking Heads,
> and R.E.M. It has since made way for a parking lot.

Atlanta Motor Speedway   *1500 Highway 41, Hampton*
> Formerly called the International Raceway, this was the site of the first
> "Atlanta Pop Festival." On July 4 and 5, 1969, 140,000 fans came out to
> see performances by Janis Joplin, Johnny Winter, Led Zeppelin, the Staple
> Singers, and Creedence Clearwater Revival. Tommy James and the Shon-
> dells also showed up. This was the first pop music venture of Alex Cooley,
> now the city's most prominent promoter, who organized that historic
> festival with sixteen other partners. (The Second Atlanta Pop Festival,
> 90 miles south in Byron, didn't go nearly as well. It attracted 400,000

people, who left the area damaged and dirty. The end of the era of rock festivals was near.)

Auburn Avenue

In the '50s and early '60s, this street was the musical center of black Atlanta. Clubs like the Royal Peacock, the Poinciana, the Congo, the Auburn Avenue Casino, and the Zanzibar were packed with black patrons, as well as a few whites. With the exception of the Royal Peacock, these clubs closed in the late '60s and early '70s; others opened up in the outer stretches of the city, where the black population was moving. The Martin Luther King, Jr. Center for Nonviolent Social Change is also along this street . . . U2 has been known to stop by.

Bailey's 81 Theater   *81 Decatur St.*

In the '50s, this movie theater used to put on live shows before the films. Little Richard performed here early in his career. And Lee Angel, Little Richard's sometime-girlfriend, was a stripper here.

❷ The Catacombs   *1172 Peachtree St. NE*

This legendary late '60s nightspot was in the basement of an old mansion. It was perhaps the first club in the city to allow local bands to play original music. One memorable performance by the legendary Hampton Grease Band was capped off when Bruce Hampton swung from a water pipe, ripping it from the ceiling and letting loose a flood of water.

❸ The Clermont Lounge   *789 Ponce de Leon Ave.*

On Thursday nights, this sleazy strip bar turns into a great rock and roll club, featuring local bands like the Jody Grind and Big Sky.

❹ Fox Theater   *660 Peachtree St.*

This lavishly conceived national landmark opened in 1929, and many rock and roll stars have graced its stage, from Elvis Presley in 1955 to Prince and Iron Maiden in the '80s. Most thrilling of all, Lynyrd Skynyrd's famous live version of "Free Bird" was recorded here.

❺ The Great Southeast Music Hall   *2581 Piedmont Rd. NE*

This was the site of the Sex Pistols first stop on their one and only American tour. When determining the itinerary, Pistols' svengali Malcolm McLaren supposedly decided to forego punk rock strongholds like New York and Los Angeles, and go straight into the heartland. In reality, the band couldn't get their papers in order fast enough for the New York City show. This Atlanta site was particularly well chosen—it was located in a shopping mall—now known as the Lindbergh Plaza Shopping Center—on the former site of a Winn Dixie grocery store.

Their performance on January 5, 1978 caused quite a stir in the community, musical and otherwise. Opinions vary on whether the band stank or triumphed. Johnny Rotten had his own view, asking the audience, "Aren't we the worst thing you've ever seen?", then adding, "You can

The grand interior of the Fox Theatre.

all stop staring at us now.'' Other Pistol points of interest:

Squire Inn   *2115 Piedmont*

This motel, now the La Quinta Inn, is where the Pistols stayed.

Victoria Station   *631 Lindbergh Way NE*

Before the show, the group ate prime rib at this now-demolished restaurant.

Municipal Auditorium   *30 Courtland St. SE*

In the '50s and '60s, this was the principal venue for big touring shows. Everybody from Buddy Holly to Bob Dylan to the Allman Brothers Band played here.

Piedmont Park

In the late 1960s, this was the site of some very influential free concerts. The Hampton Grease Band started playing there out of frustration; there were few venues for local bands that didn't want to play cover tunes. They found a bandshell here that had a working outlet and they just plugged in. Audiences began to gather, and they put on several shows here before it became necessary to get a permit from the city. One of the biggest shows, featuring the Allman Brothers Band, Chicago, Delaney and Bonnie, and the Grateful Dead, was put on by Alex Cooley. As Cooley says now, "We made money on the Atlanta Pop Festival—and that was very uncool at the time—so we spent it on a free concert."

⑥ Rose's Cantina *688 Spring St.*

This was the first Atlanta club to feature new wave and punk bands. The Swimming Pool Q's and the Nasty Bucks played here all the time, and the Police and Squeeze both played here on their first tours. The club lasted through the '70s and then turned into the legendary 688 Club.

⑦ The Royal Peacock *186½ Auburn Ave.*

This club was known as the Top Hat Club until the '40s, but it gained stature as the Peacock. Other clubs and theaters had several acts per night, but this swanky joint usually presented just one special show, by performers like Sammy Davis, Jr., Jackie Wilson, and Sam Cooke.

The Royal Peacock has also been the site of some historic events, though it doesn't seem to have been, as legend has it, the place where Jimi Hendrix met Little Richard for the first time. It was here that Ray Charles first showed off his new band to Atlantic's Ahmet Ertegun and Jerry Wexler. The pair heard them do "I Got A Woman," and were impressed enough to record them the next day. (*See* **WGST**.)

The club was co-owned by Carrie Cunningham, who had other prize pieces of real estate along the block, too—the Royal Hotel and the Savoy Hotel. After several changes of ownership, the club now serves up salsa music.

The Royal Peacock today.

Kevn Kinney of Drivin' N' Cryin' at the 688 Club, 1987. Iggy Pop's set list is visible at back. (Photo by Ruth Leitman.)

6 688 Club   *688 Spring St.*

This sorely missed venue of the '80s hosted many landmark events. Iggy Pop played here for a week (and even left the set list painted on the stage), Hüsker Dü and the Minutemen did great all-ages shows here, and the Replacements managed several sober sets here. Let's Active and Drivin' 'N' Cryin' chose the 688 for their professional debuts.

Southern Tracks   *Brookhaven*

Bill Lowery, a former "radio personality" at radio station WGST, started in the music publishing business in 1951 and soon proved that a significant, successful music company could stay put in Atlanta. He opened his first studio in the '50s but this facility, initially called Master Sound, was far more successful.

Housed in the auditorium of the Brookhaven Elementary School, the stage was the control room and the seats were removed for a recording area. "Down in the Boondocks" and hits by the Classics 4 were recorded here. When it was torn down by the city in 1984, Lowery says, "most of the artists didn't want to go to Studio One downtown because they thought it was too fancy." Now the Brookhaven Marta [mass transit] station stands on its site.

Stone Mountain Studios   *2895 Buford Hwy. NE*

In February 1978, the B-52's recorded their first songs—"Rock Lobster" and "52 Girls"—here. Danny Beard financed the session and put out the single on his just-then-created label, DB Records. (Beard's company has gone on to release records by Georgia bands such as Pylon, Love Tractor, the Coolies, and the Jody Grind.)

Studio One *3864 Oakcliff Industrial Ct., Doraville*

This was another Bill Lowery studio, which was run in partnership with songwriter Buddy Buie. Lynyrd Skynyrd's first album was one of the first recordings here. The Atlantic Rhythm Section recorded all of their hits here.

Wax 'N' Facts *432 Moreland Ave.*

This excellent vinyl emporium in the bohemian/skinhead neighborhood of Little Five Points is owned by Danny Beard, the man behind DB Records, and his partner Harry DeMille. It celebrated its fifteenth anniversary in 1991.

❽ WGST Radio Station *550 Pharr Rd. NE*

In the early '50s, record companies often used the facilities of this state-owned station to record local artists. In fact, Little Richard's first recording session was held here in October 1951. His friend and mentor Billy Wright had helped set it up with RCA and with WGST's white R&B DJ Zenas Sears. This day's work produced a local hit, "Every Hour." Little Richard was eighteen. In 1954, another milestone was recorded here when Ray Charles cut his first records with his own group: "I Got A Woman," "Blackjack," "Come Back Baby," and "Greenbacks." Recording here had its disadvantages: The band had to stop playing every time the broadcasters did the news.

The White Dot *239 Ponce de Leon Ave.*

This now-defunct club was a starting point for a lot of local bands, including Follow For Now, Mr. Crowe's Garden (later the Black Crowes), Michelle Malone, the Indigo Girls, and Mary My Hope.

WRAS Studios *University Center*

On a promotional visit to this Georgia State University radio station, Bob Geldof read a wire report that told of a California schoolgirl shooting kids on a playground. He went back to his hotel room and wrote "I Don't Like Mondays"—the Boomtown Rats' biggest hit.

Schools

Emory University

Peter Buck went here for a year and helped promote the first Atlanta show by the B-52's here—in the Coke Room. The Indigo Girls also attended the school.

ATHENS

Sixty-six miles east of Atlanta, this college town gave rise to a rock and roll renaissance in the late '70s. The B-52's got the record spinning, and were quickly followed by equally inventive pop bands such as Pylon, the

Side Effects, the Method Actors, R.E.M., and Love Tractor. The next
generation included Flat Duo Jets and the Chickasaw Mudd Puppies, and
these days, the scene is more professional but still appealing with groups
like Widespread Panic, Roosevelt, and Daisy.

By almost all accounts, the local music offerings were fairly dismal
in the '60s and '70s. Perhaps this is why students generated their own
entertainment, their own wild parties, and then their own eccentric rock
and roll bands. But whether it was something in the water or something
in the beer, the bands formed went on to great critical acclaim and, in
some cases, commercial success.

Allen's   *1294 Prince Ave.*
Before they became famous B-52's, Kate Pierson, Ricky Wilson, and Keith
Strickland frequented this dark, dusty bar in Athens's Normaltown section. The 1989 B-52's song, "Deadbeat Thing," celebrates those days—
twenty-five-cent beers and all.

Barber Street   *north of Prince Ave.*
In the late '70s and early '80s, members of Pylon, R.E.M., the Side Effects,
Love Tractor, and the Method Actors lived along a two-block stretch of
this street. It soon became known as the Street of Stars—a patch of
cement here still bears that legend along with the names of the bands.
The two principal sites:
169 Barber Street
This rambling, majestic house, the site of countless parties, was once
home to Michael Stipe and scenemakers like Linda Hopper, Leslie Mi-
chel, and Mark Phredd Rizzo. Dancing and tickling games were all part
of the fun. R.E.M. practiced in a room here for a time.

*R.E.M. in front of 285 Barber Street, Mike Mills' and Bill Berry's early 1980s
home. (Photo by Sandra-Lee Phipps.)*

Dreams So Real in front of the fourth 40 Watt club, 1986. (Photo by Terry Allen.)

Pylon Park

Six doors down from 169 Barber, this house gave shelter to members of Pylon, Love Tractor, and the Side Effects. Michael Lachowski, the founder and bassist of Pylon, turned his answering machine into a party hotline; it provided the relevant information for parties planned around town.

The El Dorado *199 West Washington*

In the mid-'70s, this vegetarian restaurant employed Fred Schneider as a waiter. He sometimes served food in bikini. The B-52's practiced their songs behind the El Dorado, in the blood-letting room of an old funeral home.

The 40 Watt Club

So far there have been six different versions of this world-famous club:

171 College Ave.

The first space with the 40 Watt moniker was inaugurated with a raucous Halloween party in 1979. The space had been abandoned for nine years, but two young men named Curtis Crowe and Bill Tabor saw the possibilities beneath the dirt and dead pigeons. They cleaned it up and threw several legendary wild parties. The Halloween party saw the debut performance for Pylon, for which Crowe played drums.

101 College Ave.

In the spring of 1980, Curtis Crowe's friend Paul Scales, who managed the Sub and Steak Sandwich shop at this address, took over an upstairs space that had been used as a lounge bar. It inherited the name and the spirit of the 40 Watt across the street and opened on May 20 with a show by the Side Effects. Love Tractor played the next night. "There was a lot of experimentation with concept, but simultaneously it was like a sybarites' ball," Love Tractor's Mark Cline once recalled. It lasted here until 1982, shortly after Crowe turned the club over to Scales.

256 West Clayton

Scales moved the club over here because the increasing crowds were making the shaky floorboards at College Avenue more precarious than ever. A fellow named Doug Hoechst took it over when Scales ran into financial trouble.

364 East Broad St.

In 1984, the 40 Watt Uptown was given an air of legitimacy, undesired by the scene pioneers certainly, when Hoechst moved it into this building; it came complete with brass railings and a liquor license. National acts played here but local legends like Love Tractor were reticent about entering. It closed in March 1987, but two of its top employees quickly took over the mantle:

256 West Clayton

Jared Bailey and Barrie Buck, the wife of R.E.M. guitarist Peter Buck, opened their version of the 40 Watt in June 1987. Here and in its present location (285 West Washington), the Buck-Bailey 40 Watt has featured alternative touring acts such as Fugazi and the Violent Femmes as well as local bands. They've also hosted poetry readings, experimental film screenings, and a lot of benefits. And Athens's biggest selling group, R.E.M., has been known to play here unannounced.

Hunan   *2139 West Broad St.*

The B-52's were formed in October 1976 after the five members spent a night drinking flaming volcanoes at this Chinese restaurant. It is now located at 1075 Baxter.

Ort's Oldies   *on Jackson, between Clayton and Washington*

Ort, a legendary Athens eccentric whose full name is William Orten Carleton, started the first used-records store in town in the early '70s. He employed Fred Schneider and turned him into a record nut.

The Potter's House   *285 West Washington until 1988; now 434 and 450 Prince Ave.*

This thrift store, packed with clothes as well as with random collectibles, was frequented by the cream of Athens's rock and roll royalty, starting with the B-52's, when they were daring and on a tight budget. The Rag Room featured particularly cheap and strange clothing items. The latest incarnation of the 40 Watt is now in its former location.

R.E.M. Church   *394 Oconee St.*

A lone steeple today marks the spot of the first performance by R.E.M.

This converted Episcopal church was a key Athens party location even before Peter Buck began living here in the summer of 1979. He and a friend named Kathleen O'Brien took over the lease in the fall, renting the spare rooms out to three others, including Michael Stipe. Stipe and Buck gradually, haltingly, worked up some songs with the young Macon-bred rhythm section of Bill Berry and Mike Mills. It was O'Brien who forced their hands. She asked them to perform for her big birthday party on April 5, 1980. They obliged. This show led to gigs at the Koffee Klub and Tyrone's, and to gold records, world tours, and Grammies.

Tyrone's   *110 Foundry St.*
Perhaps the most beloved club of all, Tyrone's hosted the nightclub debuts of R.E.M. (opening for the Brains) and Love Tractor (opening for R.E.M.) before burning down in January 1982. For most of the '70s it had booked blues acts, but in the spring of 1979, the booking agent hired an art band called the Tone-Tones. From there on in, the local alternative bands dominated the place (although bands like the Gang of Four and the Stranglers also played here). From late 1980 to early 1981, R.E.M. played here nearly every weekend.

Wuxtry   *College and Clayton*
Kate Pierson worked as a clerk at this record store before joining the B-52's. Furthermore, Peter Buck, a Wuxtry clerk, and Michael Stipe met each other here in 1978. They shared an admiration for Patti Smith and the Velvet Underground as well as the latent desire to form a band, and became housemates and songwriting partners in the fall of 1979. (Buck still gets an employee discount here.)

Pylon performing at Tyrone's, 1980. (Photo by Terry Allen.)

 **Schools**

Athens High School   *500 College Ave.*
> Future B-52 Ricky Wilson met fellow future B-52 Keith Strickland here. Ricky's sister Cindy, another B-52, also went here.

University of Georgia
Department of Art
> A sizable number of Athens's famed musicians were enrolled here, including Michael Stipe and two members of Pylon, Curtis Crowe and Michael Lachowski. Few ended up graduating. (Fred Schneider, for his part, dropped out of the Forestry School.)

Memorial Hall
> The B-52's played here in November 1978.

Reed Hall
> In the late '70s, this was the only coed dormitory on campus. As such, it was the home of women like Sandra-Lee Phipps, Carol Levy, Linda Hopper, and Kathleen O'Brien, important catalysts in the Athens music scene. They formed an antisorority sorority here called D Phi U. Bill Berry lived here in his freshman year.

⤷ DETOURS

Macon   *85 miles SE of Atlanta*
> After World War II, this city was full of clubs and auditoriums, a good environment for locals like Little Richard and Otis Redding, both of whom began performing around town in their early teens. James Brown made Macon his base after getting out of the juvenile prison in Toccoa.
>
> But the city's first important label, Capricorn, didn't materialize until the late '60s, when Phil Walden, Redding's manager, was forced to do something else after Redding died. Capricorn thrived in the '70s with acts like the Allman Brothers Band and the Outlaws, but collapsed during the 1979 record–industry recession. Two members of R.E.M. are also from Macon: drummer Bill Berry and bassist Mike Mills met in high school.

Allman Brothers Band First Macon Home   *309 College St.*
> The boys in the band played raucous games when they got home from rehearsals at 4 A.M.; instead of complaining, the other tenants simply moved out. The bank later moved to "the Big House" at 2321 Vineville.

Capricorn Studios   *535 Cotton Ave.*
> The Allman Brothers recorded their first albums here.

The Douglass Theatre   *355 Broadway*
> This now-abandoned venue was the site of breakthrough performances by Little Richard, Otis Redding, Lena Horne, and James Brown.

Duane Allman Crash Site   *Hillcrest Ave. and Bartlett Square*
> Allman was killed in a motorcycle accident here on October 29, 1971. He was almost twenty-five. A few blocks away, at Napier Avenue and

Rock and roll diner, the H&H Restaurant. (Photo by Feathers/ Feathers & Jed.)

Inverness Street, the band's bassist Berry Oakley died in a car crash a year later.

H & H Restaurant *807 Forsyth*

The Allman Brothers Band stopped by this soul food cafe regularly while recording their first album; proprietor Mama Louise extended weekly credit to the group. Not to be missed: the mural of Duane Allman and Berry Oakley as angels with guitars.

Miss Ann's Tick Tock Club *408 Broadway*

When he was thirteen, Little Richard was kicked out of his family's house—he's claimed it was punishment for his homosexuality—and moved in with a white couple, who ran this club. Before long, he began performing here, and then branched out with shows at the Douglass Theater and, occasionally, the City Auditorium.

Rose Hill Cemetery *Riverside Dr., east of Interstate 75*

When the Allman Brothers Band first moved to Macon, they used to relax and write songs here. The most famous, "In Memory of Elizabeth Reed," was inspired by a 19th-century gravestone here. 150 yards away are the graves of Duane Allman and Berry Oakley.

The Tindall Heights Housing Projects *985 Plant, Bellevue*

Otis Redding's first Macon home, Tindall Heights was in a neighborhood nicknamed Hellview.

The Two-Spot Bar *5th St. and Broadway*

James Brown got his start here as a teenager with the Famous Flames.

The graves of Duane Allman and Berry Oakley at the Rose Hill Cemetery. (Photo by Feathers/Feathers & Jed.)

WIBB Radio   *830 Mulberry St.*
This black radio station, now at 369 2nd Street, was where James Brown made his first recording, a demo of "Please Please Please." (Brown had to stand on a Coca-Cola® crate to reach the microphone.)

 Schools

Ballard-Hudson High School   *1070 Anthony Road*
Otis Redding and Little Richard both went to school here. When Redding quit in the tenth grade to help support his family, he joined up with Little Richard's old band, the Upsetters.

NORTH CAROLINA: WINSTON-SALEM AND CHAPEL HILL—RALEIGH—DURHAM

In the last fifteen years, these Southern towns have witnessed a pop explosion, not unlike what's been going on in Athens, GA. Like the Athens scene, bands usually formed in college and started performing at campus parties. The first wave included groups like the Sneakers, which featured Mitch Easter and Chris Stamey; and Arrogance, with Don Dixon. More recently, bands such as Superchunk and Johnny Quest have broken out. Area bands are well supported by the college radio stations, the college press, and the many record labels that have sprouted up.

Reynolds High School   *301 North Hawthorne*
Perhaps the premier alternative rock high school. Alumni include three former members of the dB's (Chris Stamey, Gene Holder, and Peter Holsapple), and Mitch Easter of Let's Active. In 1985, many musical alumni

returned for a benefit at the school. Remarked Holder, "It was really weird. Everybody's parents were there."

Cat's Cradle   *206 West Franklin St., Chapel Hill*

Run by a popular figure named Frank Heath, this ten-year-old club has been an ideal training ground for local bands like the Connells, Superchunk, Snatches of Pink, and Dillon Fence.

Drive-In Studios   *Outskirts of Winston-Salem*

Parked in the two-car garage of Mitch Easter's parents, this facility has been used by post-punk stars, R.E.M. (*Chronic Town* EP), Pylon (*Chomp* LP), the Individuals (*Fields* LP), the Bongos, and Chris Stamey. Mitch's mother has been particularly appreciated—she often serves coffee and donuts to the bands.

Lloyd Street Studios   *116C West Main St., Carrboro*

Formerly a jail, this "rehearsal/recording house" gave the Connells their start.

Among the noteworthy area record stores: **School Kids Records** (144 E. Franklin St., Chapel Hill) and **Poindexter** (756 9th St., Durham).

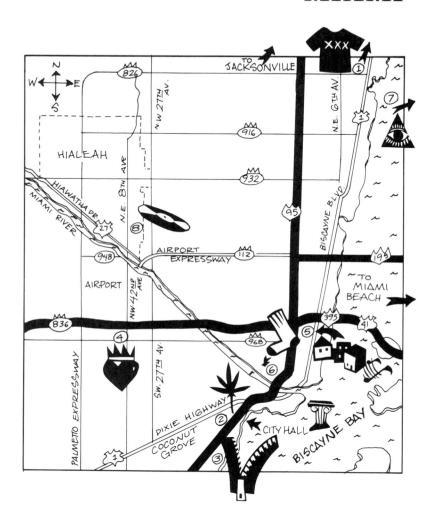

F lorida's northern cities may have produced more rock and roll stars than Miami—Tom Petty hails from Gainesville, for instance, and Lynyrd Skynyrd and the Allman Brothers Band both formed in Jacksonville—but Miami has long been a strong music town. In the '50s and '60s, the area near downtown called Overtown Square was an exciting place for black entertainment. Major stars, including locals Sam & Dave, performed here into the early morning hours. In the mid-'60s, Collins

Avenue was the main drag for the go-go discotheque craze; almost all of the hotel lounges here hired bands and dancers.

In the '70s and '80s, Miami gave pop an infusion of Latin rhythms—courtesy of, among others, Gloria Estefan and her Miami Sound Machine—and top-of-the-line dance hits. What's more, the city has lately seen a resuscitation of its dormant rock and roll scene.

The Miami area has also proven to be the perfect setting for scandal: consider Jim Morrison's infamous 1969 concert (*see* **Dinner Key Auditorium**) and 2 Live Crew's raunchy, arresting 1990 performance (*see* **Club Futura**).

Cedars of Lebanon Medical Center *1400 NW 12th Ave.*
On May 11, 1981, Bob Marley died here of cancer—seven months after he was first diagnosed with the disease.

Churchill's *5501 NE 2nd Ave.*
Run by British expatriate Dave Daniels, Churchill's is a British pub tucked away in Little Haiti. For several years, it was the center of the local alternative rock scene. Daniels has brought in all sorts of touring acts—from the Silos to Joe "King" Carrasco—and has booked local bands like the Goods and the Mavericks (who played their first show here). Another regular was Charlie Pickett, a Miami legend who's given up music for law.

❶ Club Futura *Hollywood Blvd. and Dixie Highway, Hollywood*
This adults-only nightspot was made famous on June 10, 1990, when three members of the rap group 2 Live Crew were arrested following a performance here. Band leader Luther Campbell and two others in the

Churchill's in Little Haiti.

2 Live Crew at Club Futura, the night of the big bust. (Photo by Mike Stocker. Courtesy of the Miami Herald.)

group were charged with violating local obscenity laws. Two detectives had attended and tape-recorded the Club Futura show, and the case went to trial the following October. After two weeks of testimony—much of it based on the nearly unintelligible recording—the jury deliberated for about two hours and acquitted 2 Live Crew. For a time, Club Futura sold T-shirts with the legend "Broward County: Censorship Capitol of the World," but owner Kenneth Geringer closed the club at the end of 1990.

❷ Coconut Grove

In the 1960s, this nearby "village" was home to an active folk music scene. It was also the best place to buy marijuana. Now it's an enclave for the upwardly mobile.

Criteria Recording Studio   *1755 NE 149th St.*

Over 150 gold and platinum records have been created here. Although it's been active since the 1950s, the studio's business began in earnest only when Atlantic producer Jerry Wexler moved to the area in the late 1960s. He lured Tom Dowd, engineer extraordinaire, and a group called the Dixie Flyers to be the studio band, and together they created hits for the likes of Aretha Franklin and Wilson Pickett. The Bee Gees made the transformation from British Invasion has-beens to disco superstars with resident producers Albhy Galuten and Arif Mardin.

The most famous song recorded here is probably "Layla" by Derek and the Dominos, which featured a guest spot by Duane Allman and, of course, the impassioned pleading of Eric Clapton. Allman apparently added the legendary five-note intro as an afterthought one night, while he and Clapton were listening to the playback of the recorded song.

❸ The Dinner Key Auditorium   *3360 Pan American Dr.*

The sordid details of March 1, 1969, are still in dispute, but this auditorium, now called the Coconut Grove Convention Center, is the site of the Doors' first and last Florida concert, for which Jim Morrison was charged with one felony (lewd and lascivious behavior) and three misdemeanors (indecent exposure, open profanity, and drunkenness). The band started their show late and then played an hour-long set of slurred words and confused musical signals. Jim Morrison was apparently influenced equally by an all-day drinking binge and a recent performance he'd seen of the confrontational theater piece, *Paradise Now*. Between song fragments, he delivered a confused harangue to his audience of 17,000. He invited the audience to join him on stage, and berated them when they didn't. We may never know whether Morrison actually "did lewdly and lasciviously expose his penis . . . and simulate the acts of masturbation upon himself and oral copulation upon another," as he was charged. But either way, Morrison was entangled in Miami's court system for the rest of his short, sweet life.

Gulfstream Park   *901 South Federal Highway, Hallandale*

This famous racetrack was the site of the Miami Pop Festival in December 1968. The show lasted for three days and featured the pop music gamut, including Chuck Berry, the Grateful Dead, Steppenwolf, and Marvin Gaye. The acid trips were plentiful.

The Hotel Deauville   *6701 Collins Ave., Miami Beach*

On February 16, 1964, the Beatles made their second live appearance on the Ed Sullivan Show from this hotel's Mau Mau Club. The Fab Four stayed at the hotel for several days, made virtual prisoners by their desperate, screaming fans waiting outside. (They did manage to escape to a drive-in, though, as well as a meeting with Cassius Clay.)

❹ The King o' Hearts   *6000 NW 7th Ave.*

The great R&B duo Sam and Dave was formed at this Miami club in 1961. Samuel Moore had a solo act here, and he would occasionally bring up another performer, David Prater, for a song or two. Eventually, they began to sing together. "We looked pretty funny," Moore once recalled. "Up to that point, a pair of singers had never been done . . . not like *we* did it. We were considered quite radical for that time."

Club owner Johnny Lomelo hooked them up with their first label, Roulette, but it wasn't until they worked with the Memphis-based producers at Stax Records in the mid-'60s that their careers took off.

Liberty Park

A black community since the '30s, it is also the homebase for Luther Campbell, founder of Luke Records and leader of the lewd rap group, 2 Live Crew. His label is located here at 8400 N.E. 2nd Avenue.

Open Books and Records   *44 NW 167th St., North Miami*

Now in its fourth location, this store was opened in 1979 as an outlet for independent labels, imports and music magazines. Founded by Leslie Wimmer and Ted Gottfried, the store also spawned a label. Open Records's first releases were by Charlie Pickett, including a live recording at the Button, a now-defunct Ft. Lauderdale rock club. A compilation called *The Land That Time Forgot* followed in 1982. Wimmer owns and runs the place now; Gottfried moved to New York City in 1984 and opened a music book and magazine store called See Hear.

⑤ Overtown Square

Now sadly run-down, this North Miami area was an exciting center for black entertainment from the '20s to the '60s. From 6th to 20th streets along NW 2nd Avenue, clubs, theaters, and hotels were packed with black entertainers and music lovers. A few of the hotspots:

Harlem Square Club   *10th St. and NW 2nd Ave.*

This big hall held 2,000 people and booked the most popular acts. One of the most famous shows here—certainly the best documented—was Sam Cooke's performance on January 12, 1963. A fine recording of the night was released twenty-two years later. Advance tickets were $2.

The Knightbeat   *in the basement of the Sir John Hotel, 6th St. and NW 2nd Ave.*

Run by legendary local impresario Clyde Killens, this venue featured performers like Count Basie, the Drifters, Jackie Wilson, and Solomon Burke.

The Mary Elizabeth Hotel   *642 NW 2nd Ave.*

This seventy-room hotel opened in 1905 and was considered the best in Overtown, especially after a renovation in 1947. Its Zebra Room was one of the busiest lounges in the area, open twenty-four hours a day. When black entertainers finished their sets in the white Miami Beach clubs, they came back here and started jam sessions. These often lasted until one or two the next afternoon. White celebrities like Walter Winchell would often stop by.

⑥ The Place   *1410 NW 7th Ave.*

This teen club—no alcohol was served—and its "show dances" were a galvanizing force for the city's garage-rock bands. Along with other teen venues like the World and the Hibiscus Auditorium in Miami Beach, it lost its luster once a spot called Thee Image came onto the scene.

The Zebra Room of Overtown's Mary Elizabeth Hotel. (Courtesy of the Black Archives, History and Research Foundation.)

7 Thee Image   *18330 Collins Ave., Miami Beach*

Touted as Miami's Fillmore, this ballroom was the city's top rock and roll venue in the late '60s. The Collier brothers—Kenneth and James— brought in big touring acts like the Grateful Dead, Country Joe and the Fish, Led Zeppelin, and the Mothers of Invention, and he hired upcoming local bands like 7 Of Us (which evolved into NRBQ), the Bangs, and Blues Image as openers. Blues Image got their recording contract after Jimmy Page saw them perform here and declared them "the most dynamic sound in the country." Community pressure shut the place down in April 1969, one month after the disastrous Doors show at Dinner Key Auditorium, which the Colliers had promoted. (The brothers subsequently left the world of concert promotion and entered the murkier depths of politics. Jim Collier is locally notorious for his charges of a nationwide vote-fraud conspiracy; he's sued everyone from ABC-TV to the U.S. Department of Justice.)

❽ TK Studios   *485 SE 10th Court, Hialeah*

Henry Stone has been crucial to the Miami music industry since arriving in town in 1946. A soul and R&B devotee, he started out as a distributor. "My real love was producing records," Stone says, "but to survive I had to sell records. In the early years, I always had a studio in the back." He recorded Ray Charles, James Brown, and Sam and Dave before they were famous, but it was at this Hialeah studio that Stone had his greatest string of hits. This lucky streak started shortly after Rick Finch, one of the studio's engineers, and Harry Wayne Casey, one of Stone's warehouse helpers, started working together in the studio. They had recorded an instrumental track when a young truck driver named George McRae dropped off his wife, singer Gwen McRae, at the studio. Stone says he suggested that George go upstairs and try the vocal. The song turned out to be "Rock Your Baby." Finch and Casey went on to create disco anthems like "Get Down Tonight" and "That's The Way (I Like It)" for their group, K.C. and the Sunshine Band. Also from T.K.: "Ring My Bell" by Anita Ward, "Get Off" by Foxy, and "Dance With Me" by Peter Brown.

Tobacco Road   *626 South Miami Ave.*

The city's oldest bar has become one of the city's best clubs over the last few years. The extremely popular house band is called Iko-Iko, and the owners book the best blues players currently touring.

👫 Schools

Miami Beach High   *2231 Prairie Ave., Miami Beach*

Luther Campbell graduated in 1978 and went on to promote rap concerts at Miami High School, skating rinks, and armories. He's now considered

Blues haven, Tobacco Road.

The Einstein a Go-Go in Jacksonville.

the godfather of the local Miami rap scene, and is involved in local politics.

Southwest Senior High School   *8855 SW 50th Terrace*
The alma mater of several local-legend garage bands of the '60s: the Montells, Evil, and the Shaggs (a group unrelated to the fabulous Wiggin sisters from New Hampshire). Their stories can be found in Jeffrey Lemlich's 1992 book, *Savage Lost,* a chronicle of south Florida rock in the '60s.

🦶 DETOUR

Jacksonville, FL   *348 miles NW of Miami*
In the late '60s and '70s, this north Florida city rivaled Macon as the center of "Southern rock." It may have lost when the Allman Brothers left and adopted the Georgia city as their homebase, but stalwarts like Lynyrd Skynyrd, Molly Hatchet, and .38 Special kept the tradition alive. This city has other virtues, too: Gary "U.S." Bonds was born here—as Gary Anderson—in 1939, and Elvis inspired his first riot here on May 13, 1955.

Einstein a-Go-Go   *324 North 1st St., Jacksonville Beach*
The Faircloth family have run this alternative-music landmark since 1985, booking bands like Jane's Addiction, Nirvana, Chickasaw Mudd

Puppies, Love Tractor, the Reivers, and the Beggar Weeds. One reason for its popularity with touring bands: Father Faircloth makes dinner for them; his specialty is fried chicken. Located in what's known as "the blighted area," the Einstein building has long been slated for redevelopment. Visit while you still can.

Robert E. Lee High School   *1200 South McDuff Ave.*

The first version of Lynyrd Skynyrd—then called My Backyard—formed while attending this place of learning. The band was eventually named after Leonard Skinner, an unpopular gym teacher here who was hard on kids with long hair.

Jacksonville Memory Gardens   *111 Blanding Blvd., Ocean Park suburb*

Three members of Lynyrd Skynyrd—Ronnie Van Zant, Steve Gaines, and his sister Cassie—were killed in a plane crash near Gillsburg, Mississippi, on October 20, 1977. This is where they're buried.

NEW ORLEANS

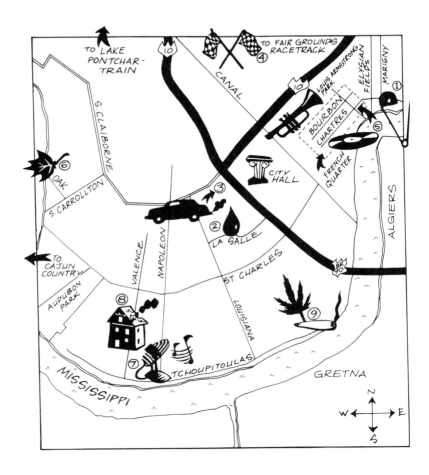

The city is known as the birthplace of jazz and the home of Dixieland but it also produced some of the best early rock and roll hits— "Tutti Frutti" among them—and still has an active pop music scene. It's the hometown of giants like Fats Domino, Randy Newman, and Dr. John, and in the '50s it developed into a much envied recording center. In fact, more than sixty Crescent City productions made it into *Billboard's* Hot 100 charts in 1962 and 1963 alone.

The local industry centered around a handful of legendary figures, some of whom worked at everything from performing on records to owning recording studios and labels. People like Cosimo Matassa, "the master of one track," and Allen Toussaint have maintained their base in the city for over thirty years, and have no plans to leave. The city also has a rich live performance tradition—perhaps the richest of any city when you consider Congo Square, the only spot on the continent during the eighteenth century that allowed blacks to gather, play drums, and dance.

The city seems to have made a specialty of producing piano-playing geniuses—think of Professor Longhair, James Booker, Art Neville—and quirky vocalists like Frankie Ford, Lee Dorsey, and Clarence "Frogman" Henry. But it's also produced some great bands—from the session players at Matassa's studios to the Meters to the Dirty Dozen Brass Band. Curiously, the number of rock and roll bands coming out of New Orleans has been low, despite the fact that one of the best rock and roll anthems, the Showmen's "It Will Stand," was recorded here. Today the Neville Brothers remain New Orleans's first family and help bring recording artists like Daniel Lanois, Robbie Robertson, and Linda Ronstadt to the city.

❶ The Beat Exchange *2300 Chartres*
> This club was New Orleans's premier rock and roll club/multimedia space from 1979 to 1982. It looked like a New York City nightclub—dark with lots of art and video monitors. Bands from all over the country—such as the Bush Tetras, Black Flag, James White and the Blacks, the Residents and the Skunks—stopped by. The Exchange also presented an early show of the Dirty Dozen Brass Band. R.E.M. was seen here by the president of the I.R.S. label in March 1982 and, despite what the band thought was a terrible show, they were soon signed to the label.
>
> The house mascot, a French poodle named Sir Nicholas de Alpaca, is also remembered fondly. During a show by a particularly bad punk group, the dog jumped on the stage and threw up. Members of the audience applauded his honesty. Barbara Hoover, the owner of the club and the poodle, has gone on to work on many film and music projects, including Daniel Lanois's Kingsway Music USA. Many of the artists she featured at the club—including Skip Bolen, Mike Staats, Carlo Ditta, and Bunny Matthews—have gone on to successful careers.

The Caldonia Inn *St. Phillip St. and St. Claude Ave.*
> Roy Byrd got his nickname of "Professor Longhair," as well as his first big break, here. Dave Bartholomew's band was booked, but when the pianist took a break, Byrd stepped in. The band was fired and Byrd was hired. His ethnic/ragtime/boogie-woogie style helped define New Orleans music, influencing Allen Toussaint, Dr. John, Fats Domino, and plenty of others. His 1959 "Go to the Mardi Gras" became the unofficial theme song of the carnival.

Calliope Housing Project   *3440 Earhart Blvd.*

The Nevilles grew up in this piece of city housing. (Saxophonist Red Tyler lived in the apartment below them.) As Charles Neville recalls, "It was a nice place back then, a real close-knit community. People had homes they could be proud of." It was situated near a gathering spot of the Mardi Gras Indians, the black fraternal organizations that parade through the back streets of the city on Mardi Gras. The influence certainly comes through in the Neville Brothers' music.

Charity Hospital   *1532 Tulane Ave.*

New Orleans legend James Booker was born here in December 1939 and died here forty-four years later. Ernie K-Doe was born here in 1936 as Ernest Kador.

❷ The Dew Drop Inn   *2840 LaSalle St.*

Owner Frank Painia started his entrepreneurial career with a two-chair barbershop in the '30s. He gradually acquired a bar, hotel, and restaurant, and by 1945, he had New Orleans's swankiest club. For the next twenty years, it was the most popular nightspot around for black entertainers. National stars like James Brown, Ray Charles, Little Richard, Sam Cooke, and Otis Redding performed here, but the local R&B performers were often attraction enough. Painia became the city's premier black business-

The Dew Drop Inn in its heyday. (Photo by Ralston Crawford. Courtesy of the William Ransom Hogan Jazz Archive, Tulane University Library.)

man and a strong advocate for integration, running the place until he died in 1972.

With weekly amateur contests and almost nightly jam sessions that would last until dawn and beyond, the Dew Drop provided a training ground for young musicians like Tommy Ridgeley and Allen Toussaint, who began sneaking in in his early teens. Painia also ran a successful booking agency, and the club became a central meeting place for musicians. When the bands came in from out of town, the musicians were dropped off here. Painia's hospitality—as well as the good food he served—were appreciated by touring musicians. And for a time, James Booker and Earl King both lived here.

The Dew Drop floor shows were legendary. Starting with a comedian or emcee—usually an exotic gay singer called Patsy Valdalia—the show would proceed with shake dancers, female impersonators, and comedy skits. The house band was led by luminaries like Dave Bartholomew and Edgar Blanchard and featured future stars like Allen Toussaint, Art and Charles Neville, Earl King, Bobby Marchan, Guitar Slim. The Dew Drop still stands today.

Doc Wonder's Curio Shop   *Dryades St., between Josephine and St. Andrew*
The sign in the window read HOUSE OF HOPE—DR. MIGHTY THE VOODOO MAN, but this establishment was a fascinating mixture of voodoo shop (candles, mojos, incense, wonder water, and ointments could be purchased), record store and rehearsal hall. Run by Victor "Doc" Augustine, it provided local musicians with a place to hang out and jam with each other. In 1949, Augustine discovered Earl King singing gospel songs on a corner and told him to stop by his shop. There King met Huey "Piano" Smith and began learning the guitar. He also rehearsed here with his trio. Johnny Vincent, the head of Ace Records, heard Smith and King rehearsing here, and recorded them both on his label.

❸ Ernie the Whip's   *Martin Luther King, Jr. and Clara*
Lee Dorsey was discovered at this auto body repair shop in 1959. He went on to sing such classics as "Ya Ya," "Ride Your Pony," and "Workin' in a Coal Mine." Until he died, in 1986, Dorsey had his own body repair shop in the Seventh Ward. As he once said, "I love to sing, but if they don't give me the money I want, I'll just go back to fender and body work. I love that just as much."

❹ Fair Grounds Racetrack   *1751 Gentilly Blvd.*
The site of the legendary Jazz and Heritage Festival, which got its start in 1969, and takes place here each Spring. It has featured every major name in contemporary New Orleans music, from Professor Longhair to Allen Toussaint to the Zion Harmonizers. Its eleven stages present all sorts of styles, including gospel, zydeco, and bluegrass, over the festival's ten days.

Doug Kershaw at the New Orleans Jazz and Heritage Festival. (Photo by Michael P. Smith.)

🏠 Fats Domino Homes

2407 Jourdain Ave.
Antoine "Fats" Domino was raised at this address in the lower Ninth Ward. He left school at fourteen to work in a factory by day and at clubs by night. In late 1949, when he was twenty-one, he was discovered by Dave Bartholomew and Lew Chudd (*see* **The Hideaway**).

Marais St. and Caffin Ave., NW Corner
With such huge hits as "Blueberry Hill," "I'm Walkin'," and "My Blue Heaven," Fats Domino is probably the most financially successful performer to emerge from New Orleans, but he still lives near the house in which he grew up. Look for the big house with surveillance cameras.

The Glass House   *2519 South Saratoga St.*
The Dirty Dozen Brass Band got their start here and the Rebirth Brass Band were regulars until the club closed in 1991.

The Hideaway   *2900 Desire St., Ninth Ward*
Twenty-one-year-old Fats Domino was playing piano here one day in late 1949. As the legend goes, he was spotted here by Dave Bartholomew and Lew Chudd. They immediately set up a recording session (at Cosimo Matassa's studio, of course) and came up with "The Fat Man," an even-

tual million-seller. Over the next twenty years, Domino and Bartholo-mew came up with a huge string of hits.

The Ivanhoe   *601 Bourbon St.*
In the late '60s, before they had recorded a note, the legendary instrumen-tal group called the Meters had a long residency at this French Quarter nightclub; it was a key site in the development of the great Meters' sound. As bassist George Porter once explained, "We played as free as we wanted. No one was restricted . . . Everybody just felt good and comfort-able. Really, playing that gig at the Ivanhoe was the thing that got us tight, 'cause we were playing six nights a week." It was also here that they were first seen by Allen Toussaint, who remembers it as "the most exciting thing I'd heard in years." Before long, the group was recording classic instrumentals under their own name and as the house band for the Sea Saint recording studio.

J&M Music Shop/Cosimo's Studios
North Rampart and Dumaine
Cosimo Matassa was born and raised in the city's French Quarter. In 1945, he and a friend opened the J&M Music Shop, which dealt in every-thing from pinball machines and jukeboxes to records and phonographs. Initially, the studio was almost incidental, tucked away in the back. Little did he know that his studio (wherever it was located) would become the only place in town to record for the next two decades. Matassa has been present at many historic and semihistoric occasions:

In 1947, bandleader Dave Bartholomew began broadcasting a regular Sunday night show for Dr. Daddy-O on WMRY from this shop. That same year, Roy Brown recorded "Good Rockin' Tonight" here. In Novem-ber 1953, Professor Longhair recorded "Tipitina" for Atlantic records here. Participants remember the recording sessions at these studios as fun, spontaneous, and quick. "There was certainly no pretension," Ma-tassa says today.
523 Governor Nicholls St.
In 1956, Matassa moved the operation to this location, formerly a cold storage warehouse. But within a few months, he moved next door to larger quarters.

❺   525 Governor Nicholls St.
This was Matassa's first sizable studio—it even had parking in the back. Record companies held several auditions here, in which all the aspiring amateurs of New Orleans would line up outside the door. Huey Smith's first chance to record came after a giant Savoy record audition here. And after playing piano for some Minit Records auditions here, Allen Toussaint was offered a contract. It was the site of great sessions by Big Joe Turner, Little Richard, and many others. One of the most disputed sessions was "Tutti Frutti." Did Little Richard write the words, as he claims, or did Dorothy La Bostrie, as she claims? Matassa can't say for sure; he thinks she may have cleaned up his bawdy club tune—he's sure she did have *something* to do with it.

748 Camp St.

Initially called Cosimo's, as the two previous ones were, this studio was renamed "Jazz City" after a business failure. Aaron Neville's "Tell It Like It Is" was recorded here in 1967, and the studio closed shortly after. But Matassa continued to work in the local music industry, helping to open Sea-Saint, the next great New Orleans studio.

Jimmy's *8200 Willow St.*

This nightclub was opened in April 1978 by Jimmy Anselmo, the son of a locally famous nightclub and restaurant owner who went by his boxing name, Jimmy King. Anselmo's first act was Lil Queenie and the Percolators; next was the Neville Brothers. Since then, he's kept up this fine tradition with acts like the Radiators, the Fabulous Thunderbirds, Dr. John, Joe "King" Carrasco, and Irma Thomas. One particular highlight in Jimmy's history was the 1980 benefit for WWOZ, the city's inventive community station. It featured Professor Longhair, the Neville Brothers, and James Booker, who played here most Wednesdays during the early '80s. Neighborhood boy Harry Connick, Jr. used to come by when he was a young teenager.

Kingsway Music USA *544 Esplanade*

In 1989, producer Daniel Lanois came down to New Orleans to record the Neville Brothers' album, *Yellow Moon*. He decided to stay and had this recording studio compound (with living quarters) designed from an

Daniel Lanois and cohorts at Kingsway Music USA, 1992. (Photo by Stephanie Chernikowski.)

old mansion. He's worked on several albums here, including the acclaimed debut from guitarist Chris Whitley.

⑥ The Maple Leaf   *8316 Oak St.*

This longstanding club has booked its share of local legends. In the early '80s, pianist James Booker and his band played here on Monday nights. His last public performance was held here on October 31, 1983; he died before the next show. Cyril Neville and his group, Endangered Species, immediately took over the Monday slot with a type of music they dubbed "Booker-woogie," inspired by and dedicated to James Booker. More recently, the Rebirth Brass Band has had a regular gig here.

Municipal Auditorium   *1201 St. Peter*

In the '50s and '60s, this was the main venue for the big touring shows. In 1957, for instance, it hosted "the Biggest Show of Stars" revue, featuring Chuck Berry, the Drifters, Frankie Lymon and the Teenagers, and Clyde McPhatter. (Buddy Holly, the Everly Brothers, Paul Anka, and Jimmy Bowen didn't appear on this date because of the city's segregation laws; black and white acts weren't allowed on the same stage.)

The New Orleans Jail   *730 South White St.*

Jerry Jeff Walker wrote "Mr. Bojangles" here in 1967. He was spending the night for disorderly conduct.

Papa Joe's   *423 Bourbon St.*

There have been a few special clubs on New Orleans's most famous street; in the mid-'60s, this was one of them. The house band included little-known musicians like Freddy Fender, Mac Rebennack, Joe Barry, Skip Easterling, and Ronnie Barron.

The Pepper Pot   *4th St., Gretna*

This was a key Professor Longhair hangout back in the '40s. It's where he wrote his anthem, "Mardi Gras in New Orleans," and also the place he was seen and approached by Atlantic Records honcho Ahmet Ertegun. (He eventually signed with Atlantic but at the time he was contracted to Mercury.)

The Pimlico Club   *2727 South Broad St.*

Irma Thomas was a waitress at this cocktail lounge in 1959 when she sat in with Tommy Ridgley's band. The club owner fired her for neglecting her customers, but Ridgley hired her for his band and hooked her up with Ron Records. Within a week she recorded her first hit, "Don't Mess With My Man."

Sea-Saint Recording Studios   *3809 Clematis Ave.*

This facility is owned jointly by Allen Toussaint and his partner, Marshall Sehorn, who both say it probably would not have been built if financial problems hadn't closed Cosimo Matassa's last studio. Since it opened in 1972, Sea Saint has produced such classic albums as Dr. John's *In the Right Place* and Labelle's *Nightbirds*, which includes the New Orleans setting of "Lady Marmalade." For many years, the unbeatable funk band the Meters was the house band. More recently, the studio has been the site of sessions by Paul Simon, the Neville Brothers, and Allen Toussaint himself.

St. Peter Guest House *1005 St. Peter*

In April 1991, former New York Doll Johnny Thunders died in this French Quarter hotel. As one friend said sadly, "He didn't even get to unpack."

Tiajuana Club *1201 South Saratoga*

This club vied with the Dew Drop Inn for customers and performers. In the '50s, though, both were packed with patrons. Ernie K-Doe emceed the shows, which also featured shake dancers and female impersonators. When Earl King's group won the talent show at the Dew Drop too many times, he went over here, where he met his biggest inspiration, Guitar Slim. Like the Dew Drop, the Tiajuana was frequented by talent seekers like Art Rupe and Dave Bartholomew of Specialty Records and Johnny Vincent of Ace Records.

7 Tipitina's *501 Napoleon Ave.*

In 1977, a group of dedicated Professor Longhair fans took over the 501 Club, at one point a Klan hangout, and named it after one of Longhair's most famous tunes. The revered pianist played here all the time, but the Neville Brothers are the reigning players these days. It's the first place they played as a group. As Aaron Neville once said, "It's our stage. We're the Uptown kings there."

Allen Toussaint's Childhood Home *3041 College Court*

It was here, in his parents' front room, that songwriter-pianist-producer and all-around legend Allen Toussaint developed his first Crescent City hits. Friends like Ernie K-Doe, Aaron Neville, Benny Spellman, and Irma Thomas would drop by and Toussaint would write songs for them, one by one. The others would sing backup or play in the band. "When I woke up in the morning," he recalls today, "some of the artists would be sitting on the porch waiting . . . We had fun all day long."

8 Valence St.

This street in the Uptown area of the city has been dubbed "singers' row" because figures like George Landry, head of the Wild Tchoupitoulas, and his nephews Art, Charles, and Aaron Neville, have all lived here. Benny's, the nightclub, is also located on this street. Indeed, Aaron Neville reportedly moved out of the neighborhood because the music from Benny's was keeping him awake.

The Warehouse. (Courtesy of Clayton Faught.)

⑨ The Warehouse   *1820 Tchoupitoulas*

This huge, old coffee warehouse was used from 1969 through 1982 for rock and roll concerts. It became a favorite for both touring musicians and New Orleanians who had an understandable adversity to frequenting touristy Bourbon Street.

The first shows here featured a triple bill of the Flock, the Grateful Dead, and Fleetwood Mac on a Friday and Saturday. On Sunday, a benefit was thrown for the Dead, who had gotten busted smoking pot in the French Quarter. From there, the Warehouse booked all sorts of performers from Bob Dylan to David Bowie. The Doors' last concert was given here on December 12, 1970, and it was a disaster. Jim Morrison lost all concentration and energy in the middle of the set, and did the sensible thing: He picked up his mike stand and bashed it into the stage until he'd made a big hole. Then he sat down and stared, and that was the show. Don Fox, who ran the Warehouse, says he refrained from fixing the hole for quite a while—out of a sense of history.

👫 Schools

Booker T. Washington High School   *1201 South Roman*

Earl King, Joe Jones, and Allen Toussaint all attended this school. Sam Cooke once played a concert in the school's auditorium, where he met one of his biggest fans, teenager Aaron Neville.

Jesuit High School   *4133 Bank St.*
Dr. John attended this school when he was still called Malcolm Rebennack. He formed a band for the talent show and never looked back. He
dropped out in his junior year.

Joseph Clark High School   *1301 North Derbigny St.*
Shirley Goodman and Leonard Lee were students here when they recorded "I'm Gone" in 1952. They soon left to tour the country and
performed together until 1962, singing such hits as "Let The Good Times
Roll."

✦ DETOURS

Cajun Country   *130 miles from New Orleans*
Cajun Country, aka Acadiana, which includes towns like Lafayette,
Breaux Bridge, and Opeloussas, is the home of zydeco and Cajun music,
the accordion-driven dance musics of the Louisiana bayous. The many
dance halls have produced such legends as Clifton Chenier, Doug Kershaw, Buckwheat Zydeco, and Beausoleil.
   The area is also the home of "swamp-pop," melancholy-tinged R&B
tunes like Phil Phillips's "Sea of Love," Dale and Grace's "I'm Leaving
It Up To You," and Freddy Fender's "Wasted Days, Wasted Nights" (1960
version). Some bayou landmarks:

Richard's Club   *on Highway 190, Lawtell*
A popular zydeco spot since the '60s, it featured early shows by luminaries like Clifton Chenier. Rounder Records has released a number of records that were recorded here.

Jay Miller's Studio   *314 North Parkerson, Crowley*
It's been called "the home of the swamp-pop sound." Producer Jay Miller
has had top-notch house bands—one featured Warren Storm on drums—
and has generated many local hits as well as a few national ones. La
Louisianne in Lafayette is another durable studio.

Kaplan
The birthplace of Huey Meaux, the self-proclaimed "Crazy Cajun," who
maintained a barbershop in Winnie, Texas while getting all sorts of
classic pop songs recorded and played.

   The top clubs today include **Fred's Lounge** (420 6th St., Mamou), the
Triangle Club (Highway 93, Scott) and **El Sid O's** (1523 Martin Luther King
Dr., Lafayette).

Ferriday, LA   *180 miles NW of New Orleans*
This town, which is right on the Mississippi border, is the hometown of
several pop culture luminaries: cousins Jerry Lee Lewis, Mickey Gilley
and Jimmy Lee Swaggart. They hung out together at spots like the Assem-
bly of God church (100 Cypress Ave.), Lake Concordia (at the eastern
edge of town), the Arcade Theatre (Louisiana Ave.) and a now-defunct

Club owner Sid Williams and Buckwheat Zydeco in front of El Sid O's.

nightclub called Haney's Big House (Highway 65). Haney's booked the best of the black players then touring the South—everyone from Sunnyland Slim to Muddy Waters to up-and-coming types like Ray Charles and Bobby "Blue" Bland. It was off-limits to white customers, but Jerry Lee and Jimmy Lee often managed to sneak in and soak up the music and the atmosphere.

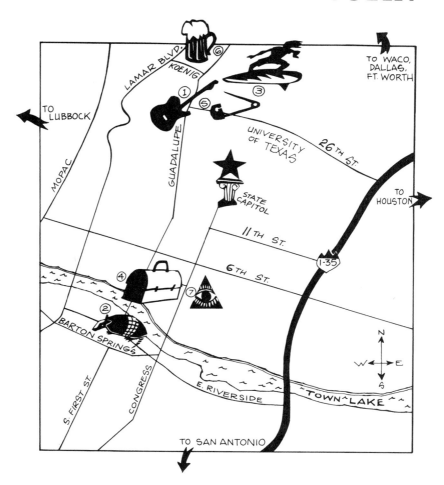

E ven considering its size and diversity of cultures, Texas has produced more than its share of distinctive music makers. For rock
and roll alone, the list starts off with Buddy Holly (from Lubbock)
and Roy Orbison (from Wink) and includes the likes of Janis Joplin, Steve
Miller, Sly Stone, Doug Sahm, and, of course, the Butthole Surfers.

Many Texas cities can claim important nightclubs and musical scenes.
One of the most significant clubs was certainly Don Robey's Bronze

Peacock in Houston. Along with Robey's labels Duke and Peacock, the Bronze Peacock helped launch influential Southern artists like Bobby "Blue" Bland, Junior Parker, Clarence "Gatemouth" Brown, and the late, great Johnny Ace.

But, since the late '60s, no city has had a live music scene to compare with Austin's. Not much of a recording mecca—only a few studios are state-of-the-art—its many halls, clubs, and barrooms have nurtured some of the best talent in Texas and in the country. The first of these talents was of course Janis Joplin, who attended the huge University of Texas here and much preferred the humble surroundings of a refurbished gas station named Threadgill's. Blues, folk, and country dominated the local scene then, but the 13th Floor Elevators, one of the town's first rock and roll bands, has also had a lasting influence. Formed in 1965 and featuring the quirky brilliance of Roky Erickson, it was one of the first psychedelic bands, performing in San Francisco so often they were sometimes assumed to be a Bay Area group.

But the similarity between the two cities goes deeper than that. Austin had its own significant underground community, full of musicians, artists, and hippies searching for entertainment outside of the mainstream. Like the Family Dog collective in San Francisco, a group of Austin-based music lovers got together and put on their own concerts, eventually opening their own venue, the Vulcan Gas Company. When that shut down three years later, some were inspired to try again—thus the Armadillo World Headquarters was born. The Armadillo continued in the Vulcan's experimental vein and sustained an eclectic booking policy—everything from blues and jazz to funk and punk was welcome.

Apart from these two major venues were lots of smaller clubs, many of them dusty dives that lasted only a few years but which were well-loved nonetheless. In addition, one of the country's top blues clubs, Antone's, opened in the '70s, and several punk clubs made their marks in the early '80s. And groups as varied as the Reivers, the ARC Angels, the Butthole Surfers, and Poi Dog Pondering have been nurtured in the last decade. (These last two bands were on the soundtrack of another of Austin's recent cultural exports, the independent cinematic hit, *Slacker*, which captured the "new" subculture of deadbeat youth.) With a supportive, occasionally smothering, music press and plenty of college kids to lure in, Austin's clubs have maintained their vitality through the years. The annual South by Southwest Conference gives the scene an extra added boost.

Alamo Hotel   *400 West 6th St.*
> Before its demolition in 1985, Texas singer/songwriters like Joe Ely, Butch Hancock, Jimmy Dale Gilmore, and Lucinda Williams often played in the lounge here. Lester Bangs called the Alamo Austin's Chelsea Hotel

because LBJ's brother Sam Houston Johnson drank himself to death in
one of the rooms here.

① Antone's   *from 1975 to 1978, 141 East 6th St.; from 1978 to 1982 Anderson Lane;*
from 1982 to present, 2915 Guadalupe

Clifford Antone opened his first club on July 15, 1975—"the minute we
got liquor by the drink"—on a street that he says reminded him of a
ghost town. Today Sixth Street is booming, resembling tourist-soaked
Bourbon Street. Although Antone was forced out of the area by high
rents, he's maintained the reputation of his top-notch blues club and has
gone on to start his own record label and record store. The club's first
headliner was Clifton Chenier—"he got us started right"—and Antone
went on to book every great blues artist around. The club gained the
most attention, however, in the '80s, when the white blues performers
that he'd been booking for years became superstars; The Fabulous Thunderbirds featuring Jimmy Vaughan and the Cobras featuring Vaughan's
little brother, Stevie Ray, had been Antone's house bands.

② Armadillo World Headquarters   *525 Barton Springs Rd.*

This fabled counterculture concert hall opened in August 1970 to fill the
gap left by the closing of the Vulcan Gas Company. Located in an old
national guard armory, it ended up doing much more. Its demise, at the
end of 1980, is still lamented.

The hall's name was inspired by the work of artist Jim Franklin; he
had first featured the armored animal in a 1968 concert poster, and it

*Jerry Jeff Walker at the Armadillo World Headquarters. (Photo by Burton
Wilson)*

had quickly become the mascot of the whimsical Austin underground. Franklin was also one of the founders of the 'Dillo; along with site-finder Eddie Wilson, then the manager of Shiva's Head Band; Mike Tolleson, an entertainment lawyer; and Bobby Hederman, who had been involved with the Vulcan. The hall didn't start off with much financial backing—and it never made huge profits—but its dedicated, imaginative staff helped establish the Armadillo—and Austin itself—as an important music center.

The huge cavernous hall became a home for every type of music, from country, jazz, and rock to punk and funk. It thrived on the diversity of Austin's cultures and spurred the cross-fertilization that had always gone on within the music created there. The 'Dillo also played a part in launching careers. For former Nashville tunesmith Willie Nelson, it was his second career. It was here that Nelson first won over a rock and roll crowd with his brand of outlaw country music. Cosmic cowboy rock also gained a foothold when artists like Jerry Jeff Walker and Michael Murphey became regulars here.

The Armadillo's huge barren room was considerably enlivened by gigantic surrealist murals—the most famous showed Freddie King with an Armadillo bursting out of his chest. The kitchen also added a human touch, serving fresh baked bread, cookies, and the famous Armadillo nachos. The Armadillo Beer Garden, an institution in itself, was opened in 1972. It served cold pitchers of draft beer and featured bands like Greezy Wheels, the Flatlanders, and Omar and the Howlers.

❸ The Beach   *2911 San Jacinto*

Owned by Chris Mossler, who was killed in a car accident in 1990, this unpretentious little club made its mark in the mid-'80s by launching a host of original local bands: True Believers, Dharma Bums, Glass Eye, the Reivers, the Texas Instruments, and Doctor's Mob. Mossler didn't seem real picky at first. As John Croslin, formerly of the Reivers, recalls: "We gave him a cheap demo we had made at our practice warehouse and he said okay, you can play on this and this and this date." The club didn't have many amenities—it had no PA system to speak of—and the decorative surfboard sometimes fell down on band members when they jumped around on stage, but the club drew a devoted following. Unfortunately, it closed shortly after Texas raised its drinking age to twenty-one in September 1986. The site is now occupied by the Crown and Anchor Pub.

Black Cat Lounge   *309 East 6th St.*

Owned by Paul and Robert Sessums, this club had been aptly described as "a real dive, with real music, on the most bogus street in Austin." It books the best of the upcoming bands, and is often packed to the rafters.

Cannibal Club   *306 East 6th St.*

Run by Brad First, a key figure behind the Austin club scene, this club has been important for local groups. Once a week, First booked three brand new bands; Bouffant Jellyfish, Retarted Elf, and many others started out this way. The Reivers had their last performance there in late 1991. In December 1991, First changed the name of the club: now the Jelly Club hosts music upstairs and the Jar Bar downstairs has pool tables and other games. Drinks and beer are served in big mason jars.

Club Foot   *110 East 4th St.*

A much loved venue set up in an old warehouse, Club Foot opened in 1981. Antone's and the Armadillo had just closed—the former only temporarily—so it was able to book the best small- to medium-size road shows of the day. It also featured the stars of the vibrant local scene, most notably Joe "King" Carrasco and the Crowns.

In May 1983, the club's owner fired the club's staff and changed the club's name to Nightlife. He closed it at the end of the year, reportedly because the surrounding urban renewal raised property values beyond what he thought he could afford.

The Continental Club   *1315 South Congress*

Built in the '40s, this building has housed a succession of establishments named the Continental Club. Initially it was a swanky watering hole. In the '60s, it was a topless bar. From '83 to '87, new music fixture Mark Pratz ran it and gave a huge number of local bands their first gig. In October '85, *Live at the Continental Club* was recorded live on two-track, bringing together dissimilar local favorites like Joe "King" Carrasco, the Leroi Brothers, the Squeezetones, the Kill, Bubble Puppy, and the Cobras. In recent years, the legendary barrelhouse pianist Roosevelt Thomas Williams—better known as Grey Ghost—has often played here. It still has a great jukebox, featuring the Meters, Jackie Wilson, and ? and the Mysterians.

The Doris Miller Auditorium   *Rosewood Ave. and Chestnut Ave.*

This East Austin gymnasium has been used for concerts since the '50s. Johnny Holmes of the Victory Grill presented performers here that were too popular for his compact club: Count Basie, James Brown, and Aretha Franklin, for instance. In the late '60s, a hippie coalition calling themselves the Electric Grandmother chose this spot for their first concert promotion. After a few successes here, they looked around for a larger location, eventually settling upon the Vulcan Gas Company.

Duke's Royal Coach Inn   *316 Congress Ave.*

On the site of the Vulcan Gas Company, this club was a Mexican beer bar when it started booking rock and roll bands in the early '80s. The final performances of local bands like Terminal Mind were commemorated with graffiti tombstones on the wall in the back.

The Eleventh Door   *Red River and 11th St.*

This was the first place Janis Joplin sang professionally; she was booked here just before leaving for San Francisco. Unlike the jam sessions at

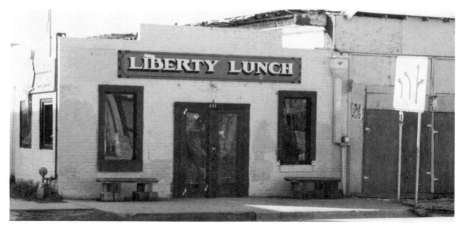

Liberty Lunch, 1992.

Threadgill's, a performance here entailed a microphone and a PA, a paying audience, and actual payment. It is now called Symphony Square.

The Hole in the Wall   *2538 Guadalupe*
At one point this small dark hole in the wall was Doug Sahm's favorite hangout. It was also an important place for Timbuk 3. Ed Guinn, formerly of the Conqueroo, saw the group here and recorded them in his own studio. That demo was sent to the IRS label, which eventually signed the band. Omar and the Howlers also played early shows here.

The Jade Room   *16th and San Jacinto*
This club brought together the Austin teen scene and the hip college crowd with shows by two local rock and roll groups: Roky and the Spades, and the Wigs. Sixteen-year-old Roky Erickson was the big attraction, singing like anybody from Buddy Holly to Little Richard—and screaming like nobody else. His next band, the legendary 13th Floor Elevators, gave their first live performance here. The club's owners were upset that the band didn't dress alike—all other local rock and roll bands did in those days—so the band had to lure their friends to the shows to prove they were a good draw. It's now a parking lot.

KLRU   *26th and Guadalupe*
This Austin PBS station has hosted the long-running television series, "Austin City Limits." It's been crucial for the national exposure it's given local artists, from the "outlaw" country singers to the eccentric rockers Timbuk 3.

❹ Liberty Lunch   *405 West 2nd St.*
Before becoming one of Austin's most popular clubs, this site was, among other things, a wagon yard, America's first mechanical tortilla factory

and the city's first Cajun restaurant. In May 1976, Liberty Lunch's live music policy was instituted, featuring Beto y Los Fairlaines on Thursdays and The Lotions, the city's first reggae band, every Tuesday. But something was keeping it from the profit margin: It had no roof. As co-manager Mark Pratz once recalled, "Rainouts murdered us." So in the winter of 1988, the staff built a roof that could be rolled back when the weather was hospitable. Highlights of the last decade include a tribute/benefit to Roky Erickson in February 1990, and performances by k.d. lang and the Neville Brothers.

The One Knight   *8th and Red River*
This early '70s dive was admired for its great roster of regular blues bands, its coffin-shaped door, and its nonexistent entrance fee. The only time the three owners charged a cover was for a Willie Nelson benefit, and they lost money. The bands included players like Jimmy and Stevie Ray Vaughan, Paul Ray, and Otis Lewis. As Paul Ray recalls, "There were about five bands from different configurations of twelve people."

❺ Raul's   *2610 Guadalupe*
This punk rock landmark near the UT campus started as a bar featuring "Mexican music, a little reggae, a little bit of everything," according to manager Joseph Gonzalez, Jr. It became a rock and roll venue in early 1978, shortly after the legendary Sex Pistols concert in San Antonio. A fellow named David Abbott, who had been hanging around, told Gonzalez and his cousin, Raul, that he could bring in some local bands that would pack the place. Fortunately he was right; the Violators and the Skunks drew a crowd, and punk rock now had a home.

For several months, Raul's booked these two bands and others that had recently formed. The club did well but it wasn't until a huge police raid in September of that year that business started booming. The Austin

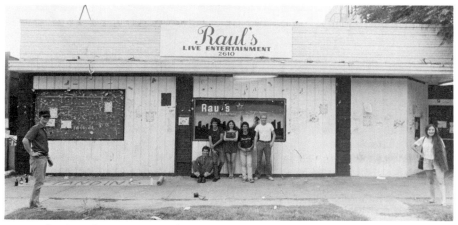

The Standing Waves in front of Raul's, 1979. (Photo by David Fox.)

The refurbished Threadgill's, 1989. (Photo by Burton Wilson.)

band the Huns had put up inflammatory posters, and half of the local police force turned out in riot gear to enforce the peace. They arrested members of the band and the audience—and suddenly the club was in the headlines, even making *Rolling Stone*. Out-of-town acts—from the Plugz, the Nuns, and the Dils on the West Coast to Elvis Costello and Patti Smith—started calling up for gigs. (All of the charges were eventually dismissed except for a contempt of court citation for Huns leader, Phil Tolstead.)

Soon after releasing a *Live at Raul's* album, featuring the Skunks, the Next, Standing Waves, Terminal Mind, and the Explosives, Raul and Joseph Gonzalez sold the club to a fellow named Steve Hayden, who instituted an all-hardcore policy that didn't go down very well with many of the regulars. Another live album, this one starring the Big Boys and the Dicks, was recorded here before the club closed in March 1981. A packed Raul's reunion at Liberty Lunch in 1988 proved its memory lives on.

Soap Creek Saloon   *707 Bee Cave's Rd. from 1973 to 1979, 11306 North Lamar Blvd., then 1201 Congress Ave.*

This significant Austin venue had three locations before closing in the mid-'80s. It featured performers like Delbert McClinton, Doug Sahm, Willie Nelson, and Joe Ely. (When Nelson gave a big kiss to black country artist Charlie Pride on stage here, it caused a minor uproar.) The Saloon started out ten miles outside of town, then took over the old Skyline Club, which was the last place Hank Williams played.

❻ Threadgill's   *6416 North Lamar Blvd.*

After purchasing Austin's first beer license on the day that Prohibition ended in 1933, Kenneth Threadgill turned an abandoned gas station on the outskirts of town into a bar. He ended up with a cultural institution and a campus favorite until its closing in 1973.

Threadgill's fame derives from its Wednesday night acoustic jam sessions, which were attended by a special bunch in the early '60s, including Powell St. John, Tary Owens, and Janis Joplin. The musicians would gather around a big table, passing the microphone and performing anything from blues to hillbilly music to ethnic folk songs. Threadgill, a great Jimmy Rodgers-style yodeler, would sometimes join in too. Participants were paid $2 a night and all the beer they could drink, and they were happy for the forum. In time, the jam sessions grew so popular that they had to be moved to the Split Rail Inn. Threadgill's bolstered the local music scene immeasurably, giving rise to folk coffeehouses and clubs like the Jade Room, the Eleventh Door, the IL, and the Saxon Pub.

Since 1981 the building has been owned by Eddie Wilson, one of the original masterminds behind the Armadillo World Headquarters, who has turned it into a restaurant and reinstituted the Wednesday-night jam sessions.

The Victory Grill   *1104 East 11th St.*

From the '20s to the '60s, East 11th Street was the center of entertainment in East Austin, the city's black neighborhood. Eight or nine clubs on the street would be busy every night of the week. The Victory Grill is the most enduring; it opened in 1945 and still struggles along. Through the years, it has nurtured the local blues scene, and has brought in nationally known acts as well: Freddie King and Gatemouth Brown, for instance. In the '40s, Bobby "Blue" Bland entered and won the club's talent contest so often that owner Johnny Holmes had to ask him to let others have a chance.

❼ The Vulcan Gas Company   *315 South Congress Ave.*

Frustrated by the lack of spaces for original musical entertainment, a coalition of musicians and their friends took over this rather barren hall

The Johnny Winter trio at the Vulcan Gas Company, 1968. (Photo by Burton Wilson.)

in 1967. For three years, it was the city's counterculture center, giving local bands like the Conqueroo, the 13th Floor Elevators and Shiva's Head Band a place to perform and experiment in a suitably psychedelic environment. (The Vulcan's vibrant light shows rivaled those in San Francisco halls, with up to twelve overhead projectors of photo slides, motion pictures, and free form water/oil reflections.) Electric blues legends like Lightnin' Hopkins, Muddy Waters, Mance Lipscomb, Big Joe Williams, and Freddie King were also regularly booked. The biggest star to emerge from the Vulcan was probably Johnny Winter from Beaumont, who was signed to a record deal after a *Rolling Stone* profile in 1969. He made his first live record here, as did the Velvet Underground.

Not surprisingly, city officials and newspaper editorialists were not overjoyed with the chaotic scene being created before their eyes. The hall had no liquor license but there were generous amounts of marijuana and hallucinogenic drugs being passed around. The Vulcan eventually closed in 1970, mainly because the owners couldn't survive without liquor revenues.

Waterloo Records   *600-A North Lamar*
This is Austin's top record store. Its annex is filled with vinyl, and it has employed a lot of local celebrities—like Alejandro Escovedo, formerly of the Nuns and the True Believers.

🏠 Hangouts and Homes

For years, Austin musicians have appreciated the city's affordable housing. Here are some of the places they lived in the '60s:

The Ghetto   *2812½ Nuecas*
This was the nickname for a run-down building in which many of the prehippie hippies lived in the early '60s; it sparked the start of the Austin bohemian scene. Twenty people lived in eight one- or two-room apartments (rent was $40 a month) and every day thirty or forty others—including Janis Joplin—came by daily to hang out. Joplin rehearsed with the Waller Creek Boys here, and these sessions would always evolve into a party. The original tenants—folks like Powell St. John and Tary Owens—left after getting paranoid about all of the police and university surveillance, but others promptly moved in: the founders of the Vulcan Gas Company and members of the blues-rock band the Conqueroo.

33rd Street
Janis Joplin, Johnny Winter, Denny Freeman, Doug Sahm, and Paul Ray all crashed in pads along this street. As Ray once commented: "That was the real Austin, you know—Greezy Wheels on the front porch on 33rd Street, dogs laying in front of the band. They oughta take that whole block and encapsulate it."

1404 West Avenue
The Conqueroo were living at the Ghetto when they met novelist Bill Brammer, who set them up in his apartment, the top floor of this Victo-

rian mansion. Before long, many of their hippie friends and acquaintances stopped by at night to sleep on their floors. As scene historian Jan Reid wrote, "The object of the game in the daytime was to take as many drugs as physiology and peer pressure would allow." Also of note, Ken Kesey and his Merry Pranksters stayed here for a week during one of their trips across the country. Today the mansion has been restored to its pre-'60s luster and is rented out for receptions.

Schools

Travis High School   *1211 East Oltorf*
Roger Kynard "Roky" Erickson was kicked out during his senior year because his hair went past his ears.

The University of Texas
This huge university has attracted many musicians to Austin—including Janis Joplin, Tary Owens, John Croslin of the Reivers—but few have graduated. Sterling Morrison, the bassist of the Velvet Underground, left the band in 1971 to teach English here.

↖ DETOURS

San Antonio, TX   *79 miles SW of Austin*
Randy's Rodeo   *1534 Bandera Rd.*
The site—in January 1978—of the Sex Pistols' infamous San Antonio show. Over 2,000 Texans, many from Austin, paid the $3 cover charge to be insulted and entertained in this big ballroom that was once a bowling alley. The audience pelted the group with beer cans as they came onstage, and Sid Vicious answered: "You cowboys are all a bunch of fucking faggots!" By the end of the night, Johnny Rotten had been hit in the face with a pie, and the stage had been covered with cans. It was a cathartic show for all. Last time we checked, the venue had been turned into a Cardi's.

Sam Houston High School   *4635 East Houston*
Doug Sahm (Class of '60) had his first local hit, "Why, Why, Why," while a student here.

Wayfarer Motel   *601 East Elmira*
In late 1964, the legendary crazy Cajun Huey P. Meaux set out to compete with the British Invasion by locking himself into a room here with a cheap record player, a case of Thunderbird wine, and a load of Beatles records. As he once told it, "When I rented three rooms, I told the [desk clerk] I'm going to be in the middle room drunk on my ass. I don't want these people on each side of me awake. I knew I had to get into a subconscious state of mind so I could get deep inside that music to see what the pattern was. So then I figured out it was the beat on the beat. It was something I had been playing with my dad in cajun music for

The 13th Floor Elevators, circa 1966. (Courtesy of Evelyn Erickson.)

years." He called Doug Sahm over, explained the secret pattern and Sahm came up with "She's About a Mover," the first hit for the Sir Douglas Quintet.

Houston, TX   *186 miles SW of Austin*

This oil city can boast of hometown musicians ranging from Lightnin' Hopkins and Johnny Guitar Watson to Lyle Lovett, the Geto Boys and King's X. Kenny Rogers is another native son. In the late '60s, his brother, Lelan, ran a psychedelic-oriented label called International Artists Records, which released vinyl by the 13th Floor Elevators, the Moving Sidewalks (which featured ZZ Top guitarist Billy Gibbons and had a hit with "99th Floor"), and Red Krayola.

The Bronze Peacock   *2809 Erastus*

Don Robey owned this legendary club as well as the Duke, Peacock, and Backbeat record labels. He used the club as a source of new talent and a place to develop it. Robey's roster included Clarence "Gatemouth" Brown, Big Mama Thornton, Johnny Ace, Bobby Bland, Junior Parker, and some of the biggest gospel stars of the day.

Houston City Auditorium   *Texas Ave. and Louisiana St.*

In December 1954, R&B singer Johnny Ace was in the midst of a promotional tour for "Pledging My Love" when he shot himself in the mouth while playing Russian roulette backstage. He died the next day. The building has since been replaced by a park.

Rusk, TX   *220 miles NE of Austin*
Rusk Hospital for the Criminally Insane   *Highway 69*

The 13th Floor Elevators were a true psychedelic band. Introduced to LSD by their songwriter/jug player Tommy Hall, singer Roky Erickson and other members of the band reportedly took the drug daily. It did more for their lyrics than for their judgment. In 1968, Erickson was arrested for possessing a small amount of pot; he pled not guilty by reason of insanity in order to avoid a serious prison term. He ended up spending three years here and was given Thorazine and other mood-stabilizing drugs. The experience supposedly inspired his song "I Walked With A Zombie." Sadly, Erickson today is said to be reclusive, unstable, and often incoherent.

Lubbock, TX   *390 miles NW of Austin*

This is the hometown of Texas's first rock and roll star, Buddy Holly. (The best time to visit may be during Budfest, the birthday celebration that takes place during the first week of September.) Lubbock is also the home of a legendary group called the Flatlanders, made up of Joe Ely, Jimmy Dale Gilmore, and Butch Hancock. They started their careers here in the mid-'60s as the T. Nickel House Band, and later moved to Austin.

Buddy Holly's First Home   *1911 6th St.*

This is where the Holley family lived when their fourth child, Charles Hardin Holley, was born on September 7, 1936. (Buddy dropped the "e" in Holley for simplicity's sake once he went professional.) An empty lot stands where the three-room wood structure used to be.

Buddy Holly's Late-'50s Home   *1305 37th St.*

While Buddy was growing up, the Holleys moved to a different rented house almost every year. But this is where they lived in 1957 and 1958. It was here that Holly married Maria Elena Santiago. Peggy Sue, the wife of Holly's drummer Jerry Allison, was matron of honor.

Hutchinson Junior High   *3102 Canton*

Buddy met his first partner in music, Bob Montgomery, while a student here. They played guitar together at school functions, calling themselves "The Buddy and Bob Show."

Lubbock High   *2004 19th St.*

Holly wasn't a great student, but he did end up graduating.

Fair Park Coliseum   *Avenue A and 10th St.*

In the mid-'50s, Buddy Holly and the Crickets played on the bottom of bills headed by Elvis Presley and Bill Haley and the Comets.

Lubbock Cemetery   *eastern end of 34th St.*

Buddy Holly's original gravestone was stolen but has been replaced with a duplicate, which shows a guitar leaning against a Doric column.

Buddy Holly Statue   *8th St. and Avenue Q*

This 8½ foot bronze likeness of Buddy and his guitar stands at the entrance to Lubbock's Civic Center. It is surrounded by a walk of fame honoring other local musicians like the Crickets, Waylon Jennings, Mac Davis, and Roy Orbison.

Lubbock High School, 1992. (Photo by William Griggs.)

Clovis, NM   *90 miles NW of Lubbock*

This Southwestern town is famous for its role in the too-short saga of Buddy Holly's career. A local bandleader named Norman Petty ran a studio at 1313 West 7th Street, and one of his customers was the Lubbock-based Crickets. In 1956, they came by to record some demos; in 1957 and 1958, Buddy Holly and his crew recorded such classics as "That'll Be The Day," "Maybe Baby," "Think It Over" and "Not Fade Away." Other hits captured in Petty's Clovis hotspot include: Buddy Knox's "Party Doll," Jimmy Bowen's "I'm Sticking With You," and Jerry Gilmer and the Fireballs' "Sugar Shack." Petty acquired a new studio at 206 Main Street in 1968, but the original has been partially restored and is occasionally open for tours.

Tulsa, OK   *450 miles NE of Austin*

This city can claim its own music landmark in **Cain's Ballroom** (423 North Main St.), built in the '20s and still standing. It was homebase for Bob Wills and the Texas Playboys, who broadcast their Western swing radio show from here during the '40s and '50s. By 1978, Cain's had become a concert hall—and the fifth stop on the Sex Pistols' infamous American tour.

The Midwest

DETROIT

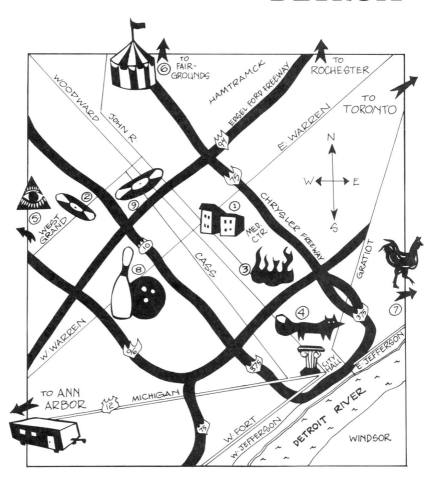

B erry Gordy's Motown empire dominates this city's pop music history, but many Detroit performers have found success before, during, and after Motown's reign. Before Smokey Robinson and Diana Ross had even stepped into the studio, LaVern Baker had R&B hits with Atlantic Records, Jackie Wilson had reached the charts with "That Is Why" and "Lonely Teardrops," and Wilson Pickett had toured extensively with the Falcons. But Gordy provided the city with its first substantial record company, giving many performers, songwriters, and producers in Detroit's large black community the chance to reach beyond amateur status. Aretha Franklin, though not a Motown affiliate, is also a product of Detroit. Her influential father, the Reverend C.L. Franklin, counted 4,500 in his congregation at the New Bethel Baptist Church, and Aretha's first recordings were made there when she was fourteen.

The local rock scene began to flourish in the late '60s, nurtured by unlikely allies like high school teacher/disc jockey Russ Gibb and White Panther Party revolutionary John Sinclair. The center of the scene was the Grande (pronounced Grandee) Ballroom, and it hosted shows by all of the legendary local bands: Mitch Ryder and the Detroit Wheels, the MC5 (for Motor City Five), Iggy and the Stooges, the Bob Seger System, Ted Nugent's Amboy Dukes, the Rationals, and SRC. The pioneers of space-age funk, George Clinton's Parliament-Funkadelic (evolving from the doo-wop group called the Parliaments), often played on rock and roll bills around town.

By 1972, the Grande had closed and the entire Motown operation had moved to Los Angeles. Detroit's musical output declined, and has kept declining. The city produces its share of musical talent—Marshall Crenshaw, producer Don Was, and (loosely speaking) Madonna—but rarely succeeds in keeping it. The '80s underground rock scene, galvanized by the Necros, L7, and Negative Approach, hasn't sustained itself. And it remains to be seen how long the rage for techno, a variant on house music developed in Detroit, will last.

MOTOWN SITES

❶ Brewster-Douglass Housing Project   *west of the Chrysler Freeway, just north of*
downtown

One of the nation's first experiments in public housing, Brewster-Douglass was home to the Supremes as they were growing up. After singing with classmates the Primes, a male vocal quartet that evolved into the Temptations, Florence Ballard recruited three neighbors, including Mary Wilson and Diana Ross, for her group, the Primettes. (And as one of Diana Ross's acquaintances told writer Nelson George, "When she was poor, living in the projects, she was just as snotty as she is now, so her fame didn't make her snotty.") The group visited Hitsville almost every day after school, and eventually got to help with handclaps and background singing for Motown sessions. Once their own hits started pouring in, the three Supremes each bought a house along a one-block stretch of Buena Vista Boulevard.

Most of the original structures of Brewster-Douglass—including the apartments where the Supremes lived—have been torn down and replaced.

Farnsworth and St. Antoine

This corner in Detroit was the center of activity for the Gordy family before the Motown enterprise took off. The family not only lived here, but Pops Gordy (Berry's revered father) owned the Booker T. Washington Grocery Store as well as a printing shop here, and the eight Gordy children were each put to work as soon as they were old enough to count. The first Gordy record label, Anna, was administered here by Gwen Gordy and her writing partner Billy Davis. And this was the site of Marvin Gaye and Anna Gordy's first apartment after they were married. The success of the Motown sound sent the family out to the suburbs in the mid-'60s; the buildings have since been razed to make way for the expansion of the city's medical center.

Gordy Mansion   *Boston Blvd.*

In 1967, Berry Gordy paid nearly $1 million for this three-story abode, complete with marble floors, a swimming pool, a bowling alley, and an underground tunnel that extended to a theater. Gordy sometimes conducted business here and he invited the Jackson Five to stay on the third floor when they were in town. In 1988, when Michael Jackson came to town to do a benefit for the Motown Museum, he requested that he and Gordy go back and have some fun there, like old times. As Gordy later recalled, "We had dinner alone, and we talked. He wanted to do some of the childlike things that he did before. And it was so much fun for me, too." Gordy still owns the mansion, but lives in Bel Air.

❷ Hitsville, USA   *2648 West Grand Blvd.*

This simple two-story structure is the original home of the Motown sound. Berry Gordy was a struggling songwriter when he purchased this building in 1959 (with an $800 loan from his family). He had co-written Jackie Wilson's "Reet Petite" and "That Is Why," but didn't see the royalties that were due him. This inspired him to start his own record company.

The building's upstairs rooms were turned into offices, one of which Gordy also used for a short time as his bedroom. The basement photographer's studio was turned into Studio A, while a tiny bathroom doubled as an echo chamber. The recording studio was often referred to as "the snake pit"—it was small, claustrophobic, and laced with competition. (Gordy often put several producers to work on the same song and then picked the best version—or told them to start over.) His method and the snake pit's set-up obviously worked. Gordy later recalled: "It was a little studio that had real wonderful acoustics and magical sound."

In the early '60s, the building was a bustling place, with auditions, rehearsals, recording sessions, and company business all going on. Aspiring artists like the Primettes (later the Supremes) and Norman Whitfield would hang around waiting for a chance to help out. Secretaries—most notably Martha Reeves and Syreeta Wright—were often recruited for sessions and then recognized for their talent. Stevie Wonder would wan-

Hitsville, the museum. (Courtesy of the Motown Museum.)

der around, sometimes barging into recording sessions in progress. Gordy eventually bought seven houses on the block to accommodate all of the activity. One of these was used for the grooming lessons that painstakingly prepared Motown artists for the stage and for the press.

In 1967, Motown operations were moved to 2457 Woodward Avenue, a bland office building that had better security but no atmosphere. Recording sessions continued here until 1972, when the entire company moved to Hollywood—Gordy apparently wanted to get into the movie biz. Since 1988, the site has served as the Motown Museum, and is open for tours.

King Solomon Baptist Church Gym   *6125 14th*
After Marvin Gaye was foiled in his plan to become a professional football player, he worked out here with the city's professional fighters. He brought journalists along to impress them.

Northland Inn   *Northland Center, Southfield*
Florence Ballard was brought here by Motown execs in 1967 and informed that she was no longer a member of the Supremes. The inn is now defunct.

OTHER DETROIT LANDMARKS

Bookie's Club 870   *870 West McNichols*
This punk club, now defunct, booked early shows by underground legends like Bauhaus, Killing Joke, the Damned, and the Necros. Iggy Pop

performed here once for a week. It closed in the early '80s, after other venues like Clutch Cargoes and St. Andrew's Hall took over its territory.

The Chit Chat Lounge   *8235 12th St.*
Motown employed some of the best musicians in town for their sessions. Most had jazz backgrounds and supplemented their Motown income with regular work at this club and the Twenty Grand. Legendary players Benny Benjamin, James Jamerson, and Earl Van Dyke were all mainstays.

Cobo Arena   *600 Civic Center Dr.*
Before, during, and after the Grande Ballroom's reign, many luminaries performed here. Jimi Hendrix brought the Experience here in 1969 and the Doors played in 1968. In addition, Bob Seger recorded *Live Bullet* here, Ted Nugent played here when he was fourteen, and the *Kiss Alive!* album was recorded here.

Creem Headquarters   *3729 Cass Ave.*
Founded here in 1969, *Creem* was the only major rock magazine to join the Underground Press Syndicate and to use the underground spelling of "Amerika." Dave Marsh, who was editor from 1971 to 1973, attracted many of the writers who had become disenchanted with *Rolling Stone*. *Creem* has since been sold—more than once—and is now a slick rock monthly based in southern California.

❸ The Flame Show Bar   *4264 John R. St.*
This was one of Detroit's best nightclubs in the '50s and '60s—lively, friendly, and comfortable. Singers like LaVern Baker, Johnnie Ray, and Della Reese made their reputations here, and plenty of Motown performers used the place to polish their acts. The club was opened in April 1950 with a show featuring Maurice King and his Wolverines. They continued as the house band for eleven years (and King went on to be an integral part of Motown's artist development program). In the late '50s, Anna and Gwen Gordy acquired the photography and cigarette concession here; they were as attracted to the music world as their little brother Berry was. In the fall of 1957, he got his big break here when he found out that a fellow named Al Greene (Jackie Wilson's manager, not the singer) was looking for new material for his client.

❹ The Fox Theater   *2211 Woodward Ave.*
Built in 1928, this incredibly lavish theater was restored to its former glory in 1988. Since then, hundreds of concerts have been given, by everyone from Public Image Ltd. to the old Motown stars (Diana Ross, Smokey Robinson, Stevie Wonder). But the theater has had glory days before: Jackie Wilson passed an audition here in 1953 to replace Clyde McPhatter in Billy Ward and the Dominoes. And '50s stars like Elvis and Buddy Holly performed here.

Motown's annual Christmas shows were legendary: a week of five shows a day in which the label's top acts would compete for the best

The Flame Show Bar. (Courtesy of the Burton Historical Society, Detroit Public Library.)

time slots. The groups would be moved to a better, later slot if, in Gordy's estimation, "their act was so good that their applause drowned out the name of the following act."

⑤ The Grande Ballroom   *on Grand River at Beverly, two blocks south of Joy Rd.*
This big hall, located in a rough neighborhood, became the center of the Detroit rock scene in the late '60s. It not only showcased the top local acts, it also brought in major touring stars like Cream, the Who, and Janis Joplin.

The hall was opened as a rock palace in October 1966 and was run by disc jockey/high school teacher Russ Gibb, or "Uncle Russ," as he was called. Gibb had visited Bill Graham's Fillmore operation in San Francisco and asked for the entrepreneur's advice on how to start a psychedelic ballroom in the Midwest. Because Detroit was 2,200 miles away, Graham was happy to oblige with details of strobe lights and light shows. Through his students, Gibb met John Sinclair, who promptly offered the services of the band he "sponsored": the MC5. The Grande thus started out with local acts but soon featured the likes of the Fugs, the Byrds, Sly and the Family Stone, and Pink Floyd. Iggy Pop and the Stooges played their first professional gig here in 1967, opening up for Blood, Sweat and Tears. And the classic MC5 album, *Kick Out The Jams*, was recorded here on October 30 and 31, 1968, marking the start of the "New Year of the revolutionary Zenta calendar." In liner notes written shortly before his death in 1991, Tyner tried to recreate the Grande atmosphere for listeners: "Close your eyes and you shall hear earth-shattering sound waves and see panoramic light beams. Can you smell the fragrance of patchouli incense and strawberry cigarette papers?" The MC5 was also, of course, present at the "Free John Sinclair" concert on January 24 and 25, 1970. So were the Stooges, the Bob Seger System, the Rationals, the Amboy Dukes, and many others.

The psychedelic posters for the Grande, created by Gary Grimshaw, rivalled those made for the San Francisco ballrooms. Grimshaw also handled the light show every weekend.

The Graystone Ballroom   *4237 Woodward Ave.*

This building was built in the '20s and torn down in 1980, much to the community's despair. In the intervening years, its ballroom featured jazz and R&B performers. For Motown buffs, this is the place where songwriter Eddie Holland (of Holland-Dozier-Holland fame) met Berry Gordy. Motown apparently owned the building when it was demolished.

This building should not be mistaken for another "Graystone" venue, which was used in the mid-'80s for landmark punk and hardcore shows. Located at 7816 Michigan Avenue and operated by Corey Rusk and his wife Lisa (with the financial backing of Russ Gibb), the club featured

The MC5 at the Grande Ballroom, recording the album Kick Out The Jams. *(Photo by Leni Sinclair.)*

shows by the Butthole Surfers, Scratch Acid, Big Black, Black Flag, and the Minutemen. "Anybody who was worth a shit came there," says Rusk. The club proved to be too much work for the Rusks, who were also running the Touch & Go record label at the same time, and it closed in 1986.

Lili's 21   *2930 Jacob St., Hamtramck*
Lili Karwoski, the warm-hearted proprietor of this Polish-style dive, has made loyal fans of the underground stars who have played in town. Lene Lovich (who was born in Detroit) still keeps in touch and the Clash often visited to drink Polish whiskey with Karwoski after their shows. The club has also served as a training ground for local bands since 1978.

The Michigan Palace   *Bagley and Grand River*
Now a parking garage, this is the hallowed ground of the last concert by Iggy and the Stooges. At that February 1974 show, Iggy tried to bait some biker types in the audience and ended up being pelted with eggs and bottles. The profanity and delirium can be heard in all its splendor on *Metallic K.O.* and numerous bootlegs.

❻ Michigan State Fairgrounds   *8 Mile Rd. and Woodward Ave.*
The first annual "Detroit Rock & Roll Revival" was hosted here by *Creem* magazine on May 30 and 31, 1969. On the bill were all the local faves—including the MC5, the SRC, the Amboy Dukes, the Bob Seger System, the Frost, and the Psychedelic Stooges—as well as Chuck Berry, Sun Ra, and the James Gang. This was the first place Iggy's parents saw him onstage with the Stooges. His father apparently climbed a girder in the grandstand for a better view.

The New Bethel Baptist Church   *8450 C. L. Franklin Blvd.*
This was the church of Aretha Franklin's father, the Reverend C. L. Franklin.

Olympia Stadium   *5920 Grand River*
Now a parking lot, this was the big concert venue in the '60s. The Beatles and the Rolling Stones both played here, despite the fact that the place had terrible acoustics.

❼ The Roostertail   *100 Marquette Dr.*
This riverside site was opened in 1958, and named for the spray left by the hydroplanes that raced by on the river. In 1964, it became a music venue, booking artists like Tony Bennett and Bobby Darin, as well as all of the Motown acts that were over twenty-one—i.e., Stevie Wonder couldn't appear. Several of them recorded live albums here. Thomas Schoenith, whose father opened the club, remembers that when it was announced that the Supremes would be appearing on December 28, 1964—the day after they had been on the Ed Sullivan show—eager ticket

The Roostertail, from above. (Courtesy of Thomas Schoenith.)

buyers blew out phone lines all over the surrounding area. Much of the Motown footage that's available now was filmed here during a mid-'60s taping of Dick Clark's "Where It's At."

Roseland Park   *Woodward and 12 Mile Road, Berkley, MI*
Rob Tyner, lead singer of the MC5, died of a heart attack in September 1991. He was buried here, reportedly wearing an MC5 T-shirt.

❽ The Twenty Grand   *14th St. and West Warren*
This was one of the city's top nightclubs in the '50s and '60s. It had a top-notch house band, which had included Thomas "Beans" Bowles since the early '50s. (Bowles met Berry Gordy through his brother and sisters, who used to frequent the club, and became an important part of the Motown organization, supervising the first Motortown revue.) The Twenty Grand also featured bowling alleys.

Motown's performers often played here. One night, Marvin Gaye was scheduled to perform—he had even been announced—but didn't show on stage. Berry Gordy, who was in the audience with a contingent of Motown's finest, went backstage, slapped his stage-shy brother-in-law and convinced Gaye to begin his show. George Clinton, at one point a Motown staff writer, performed here with both the doo-wop-styled Parliaments and his influential funk outfit, Parliament.

Perhaps inspired by Motown's success, club owner Ed Wingate decided to open a recording studio and form a record label, both called Golden World. For a time, he became a real competitor, luring Motown's session men to clandestine sessions with more money. The result was hits such as "(I Just Wanna) Testify" and "Stop Her On Sight." But Gordy eventually won out—he bought it and turned it into Motown Studio B.

⑨ United Sound *5840 Second Blvd. in the New Center Area*
Aretha Franklin has said this is her favorite studio; and outside of Hitsville's Studio A, it's certainly Detroit's most historic recording facility. John Lee Hooker recorded his first Modern Records singles here in 1948. Berry Gordy brought Smokey Robinson and the Miracles here in November 1957 for their first recording session—"Got A Job" was the result. In the '70s, producer Don Was spent days and nights here learning his craft, and George Clinton and his P-Funk protogés created many of their masterpieces in this bright blue building. As Clinton once explained, "This particular room has that sound that hits you right *on* your primal button."

Don Davis, the producer of hits like Johnny Taylor's "Disco Lady" and Marilyn McCoo and Billy Davis's "You Don't Have To Be A Star," has owned the studio since the early 1970s.

The Village *Woodward and Alexandrine*
This R&B club gave Mitch Ryder his first opportunity to perform on stage. As a sixteen year old named Billy Levise, he hung out there waiting for a chance to audition. As he told writer Susan Whitall, "I learned most of my music through gospel and rhythm and blues, and that's where I cut my teeth. Being the only white artist down there for a while, it was pretty scary. Then I got a job there, singing, for gas money. Then I worked at getting my name on the marquee! I became a member of a black vocal group down there, the Peps." The Village is now an adult bookstore.

The Walled Lake Casino *1904 Novi Rd., Walled Lake, MI*
This was a popular out-of-the-way spot for rock and rollers. Chuck Berry and the Four Seasons were some of the headliners at this big ballroom. The real attraction for local kids like Bob Seger was a homegrown group, Billy Lee and the Rivieras. In 1965, they were the Casino's house band and it was here that New York writer-producer Bob Crewe saw their performance. He signed them up and changed their name to Mitch Ryder and the Detroit Wheels.

The Westlawn Cemetery *31472 Michigan Ave., Wayne, MI*
The late, great Jackie Wilson is buried here in a large rose-colored marble mausoleum alongside his mother.

The Walled Lake Casino, from the inside and out. (Courtesy of the Detroit News.)

Schools

Cass Technical High   *2421 2nd*
> Diana Ross and Berry Gordy's second wife, Raynoma Liles, both gradu-
> ated from this prestigious, integrated arts school.

Lincoln Park High   *701 Champaign, Lincoln Park*
> Alma mater of the MC5 (except Michael Davis) and poster artist Gary
> Grimshaw. The band formed in 1976 while still in school.

Northwestern High School   *2200 West Grand Blvd.*
> Berry Gordy quit school in eleventh grade to become a professional feath-
> erweight boxer.

Oak Park High School   *Oak Park Blvd., Oak Park*
> Doug (The Knack) Feiger, producers Don and David Was, and songwriter/
> singer Marcy Levy all graduated from this school.

↳ DETOURS

Ann Arbor/Ypsilanti, MI   *38 miles west of Detroit*
Coachville Gardens   *3423 Carpenter Rd., Ypsilanti*
> Born in Muskegon, Michigan, James Newell Osterberg grew up in a small
> mobile home in this trailer camp near Ann Arbor. He gradually trans-
> formed himself into the self-destructive, punk prototype of Iggy Pop, who
> would later memorialize his childhood days in songs like "Head On." By
> the age of fifteen, Osterberg had picked up drumming and the nickname
> of Iggy, and joined his first band, the Iguanas. As lead singer for the
> Stooges and then as a solo performer, he provided plenty of gruesome
> anecdotes—throwing up during a show at New York City's Electric Cir-
> cus after shooting some heroin, rolling around on broken glass at De-
> troit's Michigan Palace—and, of course, intense rock and roll.

Crisler Arena   *333 East Stadium, Ann Arbor*
> This was the site of the "John Sinclair Freedom Rally," a benefit for the
> White Panther leader, who had been given a ten-year prison sentence for
> possession of two joints of marijuana. John and Yoko made an appearance
> as did Commander Cody, Phil Ochs, and Joy of Cooking. Speakers in-
> cluded Jerry Rubin, Ed Sanders, Bobby Seale, and Allen Ginsberg.

Discount Records   *300 South State St., Ann Arbor*
> This downtown record store employed both Jeep Holland (who went on
> to manage the Rationals and other Detroit heavyweights) and James
> Osterberg (later Iggy Pop).

The Fifth Dimension   *216 Huron St., Ann Arbor*
> This converted bowling alley hosted the first Michigan performances by
> Jimi Hendrix and the Who in 1967. Hendrix attracted about fifty people,
> and the Who attracted half of the Ann Arbor fire department when they
> blew off smoke bombs on stage. Pink Floyd and the Yardbirds also played

here. After being turned into a restaurant, the building burned down in the late '80s.

The Stooges Wax Museum   *1520 Hill St., Ann Arbor*

According to the myth propounded by Detroit fanzine *Motorbooty*, this building houses an impressive collection of memorabilia related to Iggy and the Stooges, including wax replicas and Iggy salt shakers. The spot's only *real* claim to fame is that it was the headquarters of the White Panther Party.

Ann Arbor Schools

Pioneer High School   *601 West Stadium Blvd.*

Alma mater of Bob Seger and Iggy Pop. Iggy was on the debate team.

University of Michigan

Attendees include Iggy Pop (one year), Madonna (one year), and Scott Morgan of the Rationals (one year). George Frayne was a graduate student in art here when he decided to go professional with Commander Cody and His Lost Planet Airmen.

Flint, MI   *57 miles NE of Detroit*

Grand Funk Railroad and ? and the Mysterians both formed in this Michigan city. Flint also contained an infamous **Holiday Inn** (2207 West Bristol Road), which has since become a Days Inn. It was here in August 1967 that Keith Moon threw himself a 20th birthday party that involved loud music, a food fight, room-wreckage, and—perhaps—driving a Lincoln Continental into the hotel pool.

The Stooges Wax Museum, 1990. (Fabricated photo by Mike Rubin.)

Rochester, MI   *20 miles north of Detroit*

This small Michigan city is the hometown of Madonna Louise Veronica Ciccone, who was born in Bay City, Michigan on August 16, 1959. Some Madonna landmarks:

Holy Family Regional School   *1240 Inglewood*

At the age of ten, Madonna received her first kiss at this Catholic school.

The Oklahoma   *Old Perch Rd.*

The large Ciccone family lived in a two-story colonial house in this little court of homes. Madonna was the third of eight kids.

St. Andrews Church   *1400 Inglewood*

The Ciccone family parish. When she was in seventh grade, Madonna caused a scandal at a St. Andrews talent show: she did a wild little dance in a skimpy costume to the Who's "Baba O'Riley." Her father grounded her for two weeks.

Toronto, Canada   *250 miles NE of Detroit*

The hometown of Robbie Robertson, Neil Young, and the Cowboy Junkies, this city had a particularly active folk music scene—centered around the Yorkville neighborhood—in the mid-'60s. It was here that Neil Young met Stephen Stills, Richie Furay, and Joni Mitchell.

The Church of the Holy Trinity   *10 Trinity Sq.*

The Cowboy Junkies' 1988 album, *The Trinity Session*, was recorded here on November 27, 1987.

The Concord Tavern   *923 Bloor St. West*

It was at this club, in 1964, that John Hammond Jr. first heard the Hawks, the former backing band for Ronnie Hawkins. He lured them to New York City for live shows and recording (*So Many Roads*), and then Bob Dylan hired them away from him. In 1967, they became the Band, one of the best ever.

Harbour Castle Hilton   *1 Harbour Sq.*

On February 27, 1977, the Royal Canadian Mounted Police entered Suite 2223 and discovered, among other things, five grams of cocaine and twenty-two grams of heroin. The suite's occupant, Keith Richards, was charged with possession of heroin for the purpose of trafficking. A six-month court battle ensued and—much to everyone's surprise—he got off scot-free. (The hotel is now called the Harbour Castle Westin.)

El Mocambo   *464 Spadina*

While embroiled in Keith Richards's heroin hassle, the Rolling Stones put on some legendary shows at this 300-seat club. In 1983, Stevie Ray Vaughn and Double Trouble recorded a live album here. The club is still going strong.

The Rivoli   *332 Queen St. West*

This site, which has been used as everything from a Communist bookshop to a bowling alley, has been called The Rivoli since 1982. The club has helped to launch Canadian bands like Cowboy Junkies, the Parachute Club, Bootsauce, and Jane Siberry, as well as the comedy troupe, the Kids in the Hall, who performed here regularly for five years.

The Rivoli in Toronto.

Varsity Stadium   *277 Bloor West*

The Rock & Roll Revival show, held here on September 13, 1969, featured revived pioneers like Little Richard, Jerry Lee Lewis, and Gene Vincent, as well as Alice Cooper and the debut of the Plastic Ono Band. Other than the Beatles' impromptu set on the roof of Apple headquarters in London, this show was John Lennon's first live performance since 1966. And it was Yoko's rock and roll debut. The backing band was under-rehearsed but undaunted, featuring Eric Clapton, Klaus Voormann on bass, and future Yes drummer Alan White, who was hired the day before the show. The slapdash but powerful set included covers of "Dizzy Miss Lizzy," "Blue Suede Shoes," and "Money," as well as signs of John and Yoko's future ventures in music making: "Cold Turkey" and "John John (Let's Hope for Peace)." The show was later released as *Live Peace in Toronto, 1969.*

CHICAGO

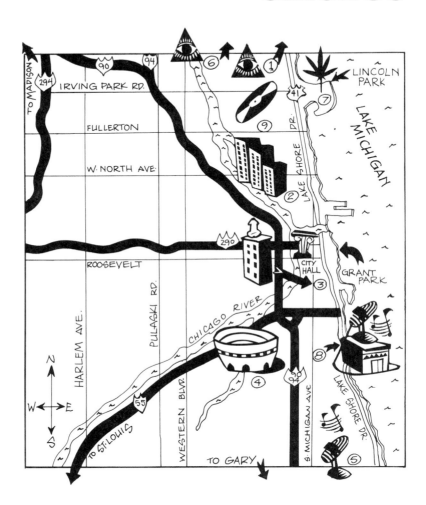

The nation's center of urban blues, Chicago has often fared badly when its pop music scene was compared to that of its Midwest rival, Detroit. It never produced a power label like Motown—partly because there were so many small companies competing for the same artists and material. And until the '80s, its rock scene faltered next to Detroit's, which had produced groundbreakers like the MC5 and Iggy Pop and the Stooges, and crowd pleasers like Bob Seger and Ted Nugent. But with the so-called industrial music revolution coming from Chicago's Wax Trax label and house music emerging from its underground nightspots, the Chicago music scene regained a pioneering spirit.

The city is best known for the pure blues and proto-rock styles recorded by Chess and other, smaller labels. Muddy Waters, Willie Dixon, and Chuck Berry are just three of the Chess Records figures that have influenced rock and rollers from Elvis and the Rolling Stones on down. Chicago has also produced strong R&B singers like Sam Cooke, Jerry Butler, Curtis Mayfield, and Lou Rawls. And one of the city's most enduring musical styles is the soulful pop created in the early '60s by the Dells, the Impressions and, later, by ex-Impressions Mayfield and Butler. The hits of the era—such as "For Your Precious Love" and "He Will Break Your Heart"—were gospel-influenced and smoothly crafted. But most of the independent labels that nurtured this sound had folded by the late '60s.

Chicago's '60s rock and roll bands didn't generate many hits, but the scene did have variety; the bands ranged from pop (the Buckinghams and the American Breed) to proto punk (the Cryan' Shames, the Trolls, the Shadows of Knight) to quasi-psychedelic (H.P. Lovecraft) to jazz-rock (the Chicago Transit Authority). The jazz-rock outfit shortened its name to Chicago, moved to Los Angeles, and hit it big with souped-up orchestral pop songs.

The city had plenty of nightclubs up until the '70s—when dance clubs became de rigueur—but never a hall like the Grande in Detroit or the ballrooms in San Francisco to bring together the city's young music fans. Attempts were made, but the Aragon Ballroom and Kinetic Playground were short-lived rock and roll ventures.

Today though the rock scene is healthy, featuring such bands as Eleventh Dream Day, Material Issue, and Smashing Pumpkins, as well as two of the most in-demand indie producers, Steve Albini and Iain Burgess. Its dance clubs are also respected, acknowledged as the birthplace of house music.

❶ The Aragon Ballroom   *1106 West Lawrence Ave.*

This imposing, sturdy structure was built in 1926, and for thirty years it was an extremely popular home for the big band sound. It was also used occasionally for touring rock and roll revues. In the mid-'60s, it became, in quick succession, a roller rink, a boxing arena, a wrestling venue and, for a year and a half, a link in the Cheetah mod-disco chain. Its most notorious incarnation was as a rock and roll palace. It hosted shows by big-name acts but a series of unfortunate incidents kept shutting the Aragon's doors. In 1972, for instance, a young patron took 250 milligrams of LSD, thought he was Batman and jumped from a second-story window, cracking his skull. In 1973, a young woman was shot when a fight between rival street gangs broke out on the dance floor. These days, the venue hosts a mix of rock and roll concerts and Spanish dance shows.

The Aragon, 1968. (Photo by Sigmund Osty. Courtesy of the Chicago Historical Society.)

Cabaret Metro   *3730 North Clark*

Built in 1926 as a Swedish men's club, it was also a theatrical venue and a gay bar before becoming the Cabaret Metro in 1982. Much admired for its layout and acoustics, it has hosted big names like James Brown, Faith No More, Iggy Pop (who says it is his favorite club), and Living Colour. One night a week, three bands without major label deals are featured. Downstairs is the Smart Bar, a dance club that recently became a Guns N' Roses hangout. Another rock nightspot of the moment is **Lounge Ax** (2438 Lincoln).

❷ Cabrini-Green Projects   *around Division and Larabie*

One of the few black areas on the near North Side, this sprawling public housing project was home to a good portion of the city's R&B talent in the '50s: Jerry Butler, Curtis Mayfield, Major Lance, Otis Leavall, and Billy Butler and the Chanters. As Jerry Butler told author Robert Pruter, "We were all into trying to sing. That was about the only thing to do really . . . the area didn't have street gangs at the time. Everyone would form a group and go into Seward Park, which had a recreation building and club rooms, in which everyone would practice." He and Mayfield formed the Impressions, who scored big with their first song, "For Your Precious Love." (*See* **Vee Jay.**) These days, Cabrini-Green is plagued with gang violence.

The Cellar   *Arlington Heights*

This club hosted the early performances by Chicago's pioneering garage band, The Shadows of Knight, still the Shadows back then. They played at this old warehouse while going to Prospect High School in nearby Mount Prospect. In 1966, their cleaned-up cover version of Them's "Gloria" became the city's first rock and roll song to become a national hit. Unfortunately for them, it was also the group's last national hit.

Chess Records   *2120 South Michigan Ave. from 1957; 4750 Cottage Ave., 1950–1957*

This world-famous label was founded in 1950 by Leonard and Philip Chess, Polish-Jewish immigrant brothers who owned several clubs on the South Side and wanted to record the bluesmen they booked. Over the next twenty years they recorded blues legends like Muddy Waters, Howlin' Wolf, and Willie Dixon, as well as rock and roll pioneers like Bo Diddley and Chuck Berry, who recorded on their Checkers label. Chess also signed up female performers like Etta James and Fontella Bass, whose "Rescue Me" was developed here in a rehearsal.

Willie Dixon was a key figure in the label's development. He started working there full time in 1951, writing songs such as Muddy Waters's "Hoochie Koochie Man" and Howlin' Wolf's "Back Door Man." He worked with vocal groups and played bass for Chuck Berry and Bo Diddley sessions. And he was there when the Rolling Stones came to pay a visit in 1965. He once recalled: I couldn't let 'em in my house because they had too many fans with them. They had maybe nine or ten limousines, plus God knows how many other people." The Stones recorded their 12 × 5 album here, naming one instrumental after the building's address, as well as part of *The Rolling Stones, Now!*

The Cabrini-Green housing project, 1959. (Photo by Betty Hulett. Courtesy of the Chicago Historical Society.)

The Chess building is now owned by Gerald Sims, a former Chess studio musician who is trying to convert it into a "living music museum where artists can record, where the public can hear lectures on the blues, and where tourists can visit."

❸ Chicago Hilton   *720 South Michigan Ave.*
In the late '60s, Chicago was home to an interesting band of groupies who called themselves the Plaster Casters: They documented their meetings with rock stars by making plastic molds of their penises. (Ringleader Cynthia Plaster Caster developed the idea as well as the molding technique.) In February 1968, they struck gold when Jimi Hendrix came to town. They did the deed here in Room 1628, and came up with their largest sculpture yet. "He was very much a sport," Cynthia once recalled. (A footnote: In a recent dispute over rights to her casts, Cynthia's attorney has been Santiago Durango, the former guitarist in Big Black and Naked Raygun.)

Chicago Trax   *3347 North Halsted*
This was a key recording studio in the '80s for the Wax Trax label, and particularly for the company's main producer, Alain Jourgenson (also a key member of Ministry and Revolting Cocks). He once described his mode of operation: "Our studio techniques are legendary. We make a studio our own little living room. Five-day sessions with strobe lights and psychedelic drugs. We just try to take the fear out of technology. I'm a technological idiot. I wing it. But I fake it better than anybody."

❹ Comiskey Park   *324 West 35th*
The former homebase for the White Sox was the site of many concerts, including one by the Beatles in August 1965. The park's most notorious event, a "disco demolition" rally, occurred in July 1979. DJ Steve Dahl arranged for fans bearing a disco disc to be admitted for only 98 cents. After the game between the Sox and the Tigers, the 10,000 records collected were blown up to the cheers of 70,000 people (including 20,000 who had been locked out). Thirty-four people were arrested at the mini-riot that ensued, and park officials canceled the second half of the doubleheader. A new ballpark was built just across the street in 1990.

Demon Dogs   *944 West Fullerton Ave.*
This diner makes a specialty of hot dogs, French fries, and the band Chicago. The walls are covered with Chicago's gold records and memorabilia, and the music consists of gems like "Saturday in the Park" and "Color My World." The owner of the place is a longtime friend, so keep your snide comments to yourself.

Earl of Old Town   *1615 North Wells*
This folk club, run by Earl Pionke in the late '60s and '70s, was the launching pad for Steve Goodman, John Prine, and Bonnie Koloc. In fact, Goodman and Prine were discovered the same night—by the unlikely

Earl of Old Town, 1973. (Photo by Joseph Domin. Courtesy of the Chicago Historical Society.)

team of Paul Anka and Kris Kristofferson—and brought to New York City for (separate) record deals.

Gate of Horn   *753 North Dearborn*

This was Chicago's first true folk music club. It also marked controversial manager Albert Grossman's first involvement with the music business. He persuaded a college friend to help him open this club in 1957. It became a magnet for the local literati—Nelson Algren, Saul Bellow, William Styron; it was also an inexpensive place at $2 to hear leading performers like Josh White, Big Bill Broonzy, and Bob Gibson. In 1961, Grossman abandoned the nightclub business to manage Peter, Paul and Mary and Bob Dylan, whom he called "the greatest folksinger in the world."

Highway Baptist Church   *2326 West Roosevelt Blvd.*

At the age of twelve, Sam Cooke joined this church's teenage singing group, the Highway QC's. They performed on programs with all the leading gospel groups as they passed through the city. He sang lead with the group until he was nineteen, when he was recruited into the nationally prominent Soul Stirrers. His funeral in December 1964 drew 200,000 mourners.

⑤ The High Chaparral   *77th and Stoney Island Ave.*

This was the top nightclub of black Chicago during the '60s. It featured the top stars of the day. This is the spot where, in 1968, a Motown performer and talent scout named Bobby Taylor first saw the Jackson Five. He got them an audition at Motown and they were soon signed up.

⑥ Kinetic Playground   *4812 North Clark*

When it opened on April 3, 1968, this building was called the Electric Theater. It featured eight sound towers, about fifty automated film and slide projectors, a kaleidoscope of full-length mirrors, an amoeba-shaped stage and—perhaps best of all—meditation booths which were serviced by a resident guru. The impresario behind this "serious theatrical adventure" was a twenty-five year old named Aaron Russo.

One of his first problems was a threatened lawsuit from New York City's Electric Circus—thus the name change to Kinetic Playground. But for over a year, this was the local scene's brightest hope. Russo brought in rising rock groups like Led Zeppelin, Spirit, and the Kinks; at last the city was connected to the trends developing in England and on the West Coast. Russo also followed the lead of San Francisco promoter Bill Graham and presented concerts by local bands on Tuesday nights.

But the venue was closed in 1970 because of a fire and, after two years

O'Banion's, 1980. (Photo by Linda Matlow, Pix International.)

of inactivity, it was taken over by New York promoter Howard Stein. Stein's representatives had it painted all black and presented straightforward rock concerts. (Russo eventually moved to New York and became Bette Midler's manager.)

❼ Lincoln Park   *bordering Lake Michigan, between LaSalle Dr. and Hollywood Ave.*
This was the site of the aborted "Youth International Party Festival of Life," assembled by Ed Sanders of the Fugs to coincide with the 1968 Democratic national convention. Six days of music and speeches were scheduled, along with exhortations to smoke dope and fuck in the streets. When the infamous Chicago riots broke out instead, only the MC5 had gotten a chance to perform.

Nate's Delicatessen   *807 West Maxwell*
The Blues Brothers was filmed in and around Chicago, and this was the spot where Aretha Franklin sang about getting some consideration. In the old days, Maxwell Street was a prime thoroughfare for the blues.

O'Banion's   *661 North Clark St.*
Set in a strip of gay bars, this club became the center of Chicago's punk scene after a club called La Mere Vipere burned down. Bands like Silver Abuse and Naked Raygun started out here. Another significant club was Oz, where a 1981 compilation featuring live tracks by Naked Raygun, Effigies, and Strike Under (pre-Breaking Circus), was recorded. That album was called *Busted At Oz*.

❽ The Regal   *47th St. and South Parkway—later King Dr.*
This majestic theater was Chicago's stop on the nationwide chitlin circuit. Its forty-five-year history is full of landmark events. In 1962, for instance, Stevie Wonder recorded his first hit, "Fingertips Pt. 2" during a Motown Revue concert here. Five years later, the Jackson Five won the theater's amateur night contest for three consecutive weeks. (Sufficiently encouraged, they went later to the Apollo and won its amateur contest, too.) The Regal was torn down in 1973, but the theater's name and tradition have been "adopted" by the Avalon Theatre (1645 East 79th St.), now renamed the New Regal Theater. It hosts a weekly amateur contest and books the biggest names in black music.

Universal Recording   *47 East Walton*
This was the city's main recording studio throughout the '50s and '60s. Vee Jay did most of its sessions there. Quincy Jones met engineer Bruce Swedien here in 1957 during a session for Dinah Washington. They have been working together ever since—on everything from films to *Thriller* to *Back on the Block*.

Vee Jay Records   *1449 South Michigan Ave.*
Vee Jay, run by the husband-and-wife team of Jimmy Bracken and Vivian Carter, was a key independent record company in the late '50s and '60s.

The Regal Theater, 1973, on the verge of being demolished. (Photo by Jim O'Neal. Courtesy of the Blues Archive, University of Mississippi.)

Before Motown exploded, it was the largest black-owned record label, with artists like Jimmy Reed and the Spaniels, and such pop classics as "Goodnight Sweetheart, Goodnight," Gene Chandler's "Duke of Earl," and the Impressions' "For Your Precious Love." (The latter group was signed to the label after they had come by hoping for an audition. Vee Jay's A&R man signed them up and had them record their gospel-tinged ballad, "For Your Precious Love." It sold over 900,000 copies on its first issue.) The label had a few white acts, too, most notably the Four Seasons and, for a few months, the Beatles—EMI/Capitol soon forced the little company to hand over the Fab Four. Unfortunately, by May 1966, bad management had forced the label to close; the Brackens were divorced soon after. (Writer/producer Carl Davis subsequently moved the Brunswick label into the building.)

The Warehouse   *1800 block of South Michigan Ave.*
This now-defunct club has been deemed the birthplace of house music; the proof is in the name. In 1977, New York City DJ Frankie Knuckles was asked to work at this club's opening night. The audience response was so overwhelming that he decided to stay. Over the next decade, Knuckles developed a fast and furious mix of music that borrowed from MFSB, Kraftwerk, and high-tempo R&B records. He attracted blacks and whites, gays and straights. And as Knuckles once recalled, "It was like a pagan party with people screaming and shouting. It was sort of scary and joyous at the same time."

Local club DJs picked up on the style but, strangely enough, the music wasn't heard on local radio. It still isn't, but it finally broke through internationally in 1986, and since then every pop star from Natalie Cole to Madonna has seen their hits remixed for dance clubs in the house style. Its various offshoots include hip house, acid house, deep house, and Hispanic house. Knuckles moved back to New York in 1987 after closing his other club, the Power Plant.

⑨ Wax Trax Records   *2449 North Lincoln Ave.*

Jim Nash and Dannie Flesher opened the first Wax Trax record store in Denver in 1974. They moved the operation to Chicago in 1978 and, two years later, started the Wax Trax label, the city's most prominent record company. The roster has included the Revolting Cocks, Front 242, Ministry, and My Life With The Thrill Kill Kult. And it all started right here. In fact, quite a few of the label's artists were employed here at some point. Groovie Mann (aka Frank Nardiello) of Thrill Kill Kult worked here as a buyer until the band went on tour. "Then I guess I got fired."

 # Schools

Cooley Vocational High School   *4046 North Leavitt*

Jerry Butler attended the school when it was Washburn Trade. Unfortunately, *Cooley High*, the classic coming-of-age movie, didn't feature any of Butler's music.

Hyde Park Career Academy   *6220 Stoney Island Ave.*

Minnie Riperton was discovered in 1963 by a Chess songwriter while in this high school's a cappella choir. She was recruited to be in the Gems, a Chess girl group. When the Gems broke up in 1966, she became a member of the Rotary Connection, Chess's only progressive rock group.

↜ DETOURS

Gary, IN   *borders on Chicago*

This grim, impoverished city has produced two notable R&B groups. The first was the doo-wop vocal group, the Spaniels, who sang "Goodnight Sweetheart, Goodnight." Then there was the Jackson 5.

Home of the Jackson 5   *2300 Jackson St.*

Joseph and Katherine Jackson and their nine children lived in this two-bedroom clapboard house.

Garnett Elementary School   *2131 Jackson St.*

All of the Jackson 5 attended this school. In 1963, five-year-old Michael performed "Climb Every Mountain" from *The Sound of Music* for his classmates, who gave him a standing ovation. The adults in attendance got teary-eyed.

Kingdom Hall   *3435 West 21st Ave.*

As Jehovah's Witnesses, the Jackson family attended services here.

Mr. Lucky's   *1100 Grant*
This was one of the local clubs the Jacksons played while entering talent contests in Chicago. In 1966, Joe Jackson started his boys on the chitlin circuit, and in August 1967, they entered the Apollo's amateur contest. They won.

East Troy, WI   *85 miles NW of Chicago*
On August 27, 1990, Stevie Ray Vaughan and three members of Eric Clapton's entourage were killed when their helicopter slammed into a ski slope here. Vaughan, Clapton, and Robert Cray had just performed at the Alpine Valley Music Theater a mile away.

Madison, WI   *144 miles NW of Chicago*
On December 10, 1967, Otis Redding's chartered plane went down in Lake Monona, just outside of Madison. Redding and four members of the Stax session band, the Bar-Kays, were killed. Ben Cauley, the group's trumpet player, managed to survive the crash. The group had been en route to a show at the Factory, a Madison, Wisconsin, nightclub. More recently, Smart Studios (1254 East Washington Ave.) has become an alternative rock landmark, recording local bands, Sub Pop bands like Tad, and a host of others. Butch Vig, producer of Nirvana's *Nevermind*, is a co-owner.

St. Louis, MO   *290 miles SW of Chicago*
This city has produced some of the country's best jazz and rock and roll artists, including trumpeters Miles Davis and Lester Bowie, and rock pioneer Chuck Berry. It was also an important launching pad for Ike and Tina Turner; the combustible pair met and honed their act in clubs here and in East St. Louis, Illinois, right across the Mississippi River.

Chuck Berry Birthplace   *2520 Goode Ave.*
Charles Edward Anderson Berry was born in this three-room house on October 18, 1926. The house was filled with Baptist hymns, and little Charles soon was picking out melodies on the family piano. The family moved down the street when he was three.

Sumner High   *4248 Cottage*
The alma mater of both Chuck Berry and Tina Turner. Berry made his first public musical appearance at a class show here; he sang the naughty "Confessin' the Blues," without realizing it might offend.

Cosmopolitan Club   *17th St. and Bond Ave., East St. Louis*
Chuck Berry's musical career hit its stride at this nightspot, one of the area's top R&B joints. In 1953, he was playing in Johnnie Johnson's Sir John's trio but Berry became more popular than Mr. Johnson himself. The band was rechristened as Chuck Berry's Combo. In 1955, Berry went to Chicago and got his recording contract with Chess. As for the Cosmopolitan Club, it was featured in the Chuck Berry film tribute, *Hail, Hail, Rock and Roll*, and now looks run-down and depressing.

The feud between Guns N' Roses and the city of St. Louis was sparked by the 1991 riot at Riverport Amphitheater. Here, St. Louis music fans show their feelings. (Photo by Tim Parker.)

Riverport Amphitheatre   *14141 Riverport Dr., Maryland Heights suburb*
On July 2, 1991, a full-blown riot started here after the abrupt close of a Guns N' Roses concert. Sixty people were hurt, sixteen were arrested, and the damages to the amphitheatre and equipment exceeded $200,000. The band blamed the melee on inadequate security, and the Riverport authorities say Axl Rose behaved improperly by venturing out into the audience to stop a fan from taking photos. In April 1992, the band had to cancel some Midwest concert dates in order to avoid arrest for Axl Rose, who had been charged with a misdemeanor.

CLEVELAND

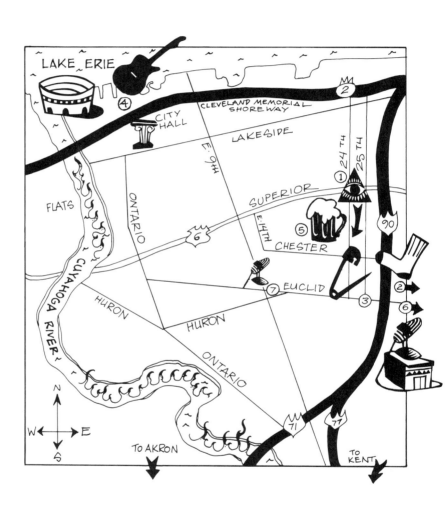

O hio's biggest city has plenty of rock and roll credits—even aside from the questionably located Rock and Roll Hall of Fame. (Why isn't it in Memphis?) Its most famous contribution may have been its first: the Moondog Coronation Ball in March 1952. The huge numbers of R&B fans it drew to the Cleveland Arena sent a signal to the record industry that R&B might indeed be a viable, profitable form of music. Alan Freed was one of three promoters of that event, and he went on to wider fame (and infamy) when he moved to New York City. (Freed's touring shows often featured Cleveland native, Screamin' Jay Hawkins, whose coffin-bound stage show was dreamed up by the disc jockey/entrepreneur.)

Since the '60s, Cleveland-area bands have been plentiful. A few—most notably the Raspberries—have gained commercial success. Others, such as Electric Eels and the Pagans, have acquired cult status. In the '70s, Pere Ubu and the Dead Boys broke out of the underground, without landing on the charts. (Not that they tried.)

These days, Clevelanders lament the local club scene but point to bands like Nine Inch Nails, Death of Samantha, Prisonshake, The Walk-Ins, and The Twist-Offs as proof of vitality.

① The Agora Ballroom   *1730 E. 24th St.; now 5000 Euclid Ave.*

This club opened in February 1966 as a private dance club for college students; nobody over twenty-five was allowed to join. By 1970, when the owners noticed that antiestablishment college students of the day didn't want to belong to anything—not even their own club—the Agora opened at the East 24th St. location and let in anyone over eighteen. The Buckinghams were the first act, followed soon by the likes of Ted Nugent, Rufus, Argent, Peter Frampton, and Robin Trower. Sunday nights featured local bands, several of whom later signed to major labels. The most famous of these is the Raspberries, who had a year-and-a-half residency here.

Blackfoot performing at the old Agora—the last show before a fire closed the club. (Photo by Anastasia Pantsios.)

The first Moondog Ball at the Cleveland Arena. (Photo by Hastings and Willinger. Courtesy of Cleveland State University.)

Before long, Agora owner Henry LoConti started opening up outposts all over the country, from Toledo to Atlanta. At the same time, the Agora had become a central venue of the Cleveland rock and roll scene, bringing in performers like David Bowie and Bruce Springsteen. (The building also housed a club called the Mistake, later known as the Pop Shop.) The original Agora had a fire in 1984 and has since been moved to a larger theater on Euclid.

❷ Cleveland Arena   *3717 Euclid Ave.*

This is the site of the famous Moondog Coronation Ball of March 21, 1952. Promoted by DJ Alan Freed, record store owner Leo Mintz and booking agent Lew Platt, the show featured R&B performers Paul Williams, Varetta Dillard, and the Dominoes. By the time the show began, 10,000 kids packed the venue, and at least 6,000 stood outside, trying to get in. Many eventually forced their way in, and the overcrowded show had to be canceled at 11:30. The "mob scene" was reported on by local papers as well as by the national music press. Music industry types were alerted that money could be made with R&B.

Freed promoted other shows here and around the state. On July 20, 1953, a revue called "the Biggest Show of '53" came to town. It featured Ruth Brown, the Clovers, and Wynonie Harris, and Freed helped promote it at this venue. And an August 1953 show featured Fats Domino, Joe

Turner, and the group that Freed managed, the Moonglows. Both shows went off smoothly, proving that R&B fans could be orderly if they wanted to be. The Arena has since been demolished.

Cleveland Cafe *11901 Berea*
This club is often cited in discussions on the sad state of the city's rock and roll audience. It books tribute bands, and tribute bands only, and packs 'em in. Recent attractions include homages to Aerosmith, the Eagles, and the Scorpions.

Cleveland Music Hall *1220 East 6th St.*
From the mid-'60s to the early '70s, all of the major rock shows were held here. The Doors played here immediately after the infamous Miami concert—and Morrison behaved. Davie Bowie's U.S. debut was held here on September 22, 1972. Soon after, the Richfield Coliseum was built between Cleveland and Akron, and started booking the big shows.

Cleveland Recording *5706 Vroman Rd., Painesville*
Now called Suma, this long-lived recording studio has been used by Grand Funk Railroad (from Flint, Michigan), the James Gang, Pere Ubu, the Outsiders, Joey and the Continentals, and many other Cleveland acts.

Cuyahoga River
This river, which flows from Lake Erie to Akron, became famous in 1974 when it caught on fire near Cleveland. The event inspired Randy Newman's song, "Burn On, Big River." It has since been all cleaned up.

The Drome *12th and Euclid Ave.*
This now-defunct hole-in-the-wall record store was owned by Johnny Dromette (aka John Thompson), an early supporter of the Cleveland underground. He booked bands here, and ran the Drome record label, which released the Pagans' classic punk 45s.

Hennessy's *11729 Detroit Ave., Lakewood*
This was one of Cleveland's great music bars. It closed in 1987, and was turned into a "green neon disco fern bar," according to one unhappy patron. David Bowie apparently called it "the home of the stars" when he was here in 1972. It launched local bands like the Adults, Snakerock, and the Action. The annual All-Star Cleveland Musicians' Jam, held each Thanksgiving Eve, was always an event. It's now called Wolf at the Door.

LaCave *Euclid and 107th St.*
This dimly lit basement featured local and national folk acts. The Velvet Underground also played here.

Otto's Grotto *in the Statler Building, Euclid and East 12th*
This mid-'60s club featured national acts and upcoming local groups. It was *the* hangout for Cleveland's radio and record promotion types.

Peabody's Down Under   *1059 Old River Rd.*
This club, which used to be called the Pirate's Cove, is located in a now-thriving downtown area called the Flats. As the Pirate's Cove, it booked punk shows in the late '70s and early '80s. Today it features some of the best local, national, and international bands.

Another memorable club in the Flats was **Pat's**, a tiny bar that nurtured a great scene in the late '80s with bands like Sosumi, The Pink Holes, the Floyd Band, and Home & Garden.

❸ The Piccadilly   *2901 Euclid Ave.*
This glam and glitter club, located in the penthouse of a hotel, saw the real start of the Dead Boys: On Halloween 1975, Cheetah Chrome, Johnny Blitz and Stiv Bators debuted here as a glitteresque group called Frankenstein. They played here again on New Year's Eve, and soon re-named themselves the Dead Boys.

The Record Rendezvous   *300 Prospect Ave. SE*
This big record shop was owned by Leo Mintz. After meeting WJW DJ Alan Freed in a downtown bar, he offered to buy him a radio show if he would play nothing but R&B. Freed agreed, and subsequently took most of the credit for introducing rock and roll to the world.

❹ Rock and Roll Hall of Fame and Museum   *proposed site: North Coast Harbor*
In 1983, the Rock and Roll Hall of Fame Foundation was created to honor rock and roll legends. In 1986, the Foundation chose Cleveland as the official site of this grand public project. That was the easy part. The hard part has been finding a suitable location and raising the $65 million needed to build the damn thing. City officials have also had a tough time fending off officials in other cities—San Francisco, Chicago, Philadelphia, and Memphis—who feel that their cities have had more of an impact on rock and roll. (You be the judge.) In any case, the groundbreaking is set for fall 1992 and the projected grand opening is scheduled for 1994. Among the items to be exhibited: Buddy Holly's 1955 high school diploma, the original lyrics to Jimi Hendrix's "Purple Haze" (which cost $20,000) and 317 pieces of Janis Joplin memorabilia (donated by Big Brother and the Holding Company).

Styrene Studios   *East 36th and Superior*
The Styrenes owned this rehearsal loft/makeshift recording facility, which was used for sessions by top underground acts such as the Pagans and Electric Eels.

❺ The Viking Saloon   *East 21st and Chester*
This bar has been called the Max's Kansas City of Cleveland. Like Max's, it is no longer around, but it did provide a launching pad for Pere Ubu and that band's precursors, Rocket From the Tombs and Cinderella Backstreet. After Stiv Bators of the Dead Boys exposed himself while per-

The old WHK Auditorium, now transformed into the new Agora. (Photo by Anastasia Pantsios.)

forming here in 1976, bars around town refused to book the band and they broke up. They re-formed to play in New York, at CBGB's 1976 summer festival, and went on to record two albums before breaking up (again) in 1980.

❻ WHK Auditorium   *5000 Euclid Ave.*
This crumbling radio theater was also known as Disastodome and hosted a series of major punk shows. Parts of Pere Ubu's live album were recorded at the second show, dubbed "Disasto2." At show number three, Pagans fans hurled a beautiful art deco couch off the balcony onto the audience below.

❼ WJW Radio   *1375 Euclid Ave.*
Alan Freed started out here as a classical music DJ but began his R&B show in July 1951. It was here that he acquired his "Moondog" persona, baying like a slightly crazed wolf while well primed with liquor. In 1952, local singer Al "Fats" Thomas brought a young R&B group called the Crazy Sounds to the studios to meet Freed. According to one story, Freed agreed to manage them and immediately renamed them the Moonglows. The DJ left for New York City's WINS in the fall of 1954, and continued to exploit Moondog mania with big shows and concert tours.

↳ DETOURS

Kent, OH *38 miles SE of Cleveland*

JB's *244 North Water St.*

In the '60s, this club was surrounded by other bars and clubs like the Kove and the Fifth Quarter. JB's is the only one to survive. It opened on March 27, 1966 with a show by the Majestics, who became the house band. The James Gang was the house band from 1969 to 1971. The Raspberries were signed to Capitol Records in 1971 after representatives of the label saw a show here.

Kent State University

This university has many rock and roll alumni, including Joe Walsh, two members of Devo, and Chrissie Hynde, who grew up in nearby Akron. The Crosby, Stills, Nash, and Young song "Ohio" was written in response to the brutal killings by National Guardsmen of four students at this campus in 1970.

Pittsburgh, PA *129 miles SE of Cleveland*

The hometown of Andy Warhol and a batch of great jazz players (Art Blakey, Kenny Clarke, et al.), this Pennsylvania city also has its share of rock and roll credits. In 1955, the Del-Vikings, one of the first racially integrated pop groups, was formed at a Pittsburgh Air Force base. Their classic song, "Come Go With Me," was recorded two years later in the game room of a local DJ named Barry Kaye. Since then, local bands like the Vogues, the Iron City House Rockers, and, most recently, the Cynics, have achieved varied degrees of fame.

JB's in Kent, Ohio.

MINNEAPOLIS/ST. PAUL

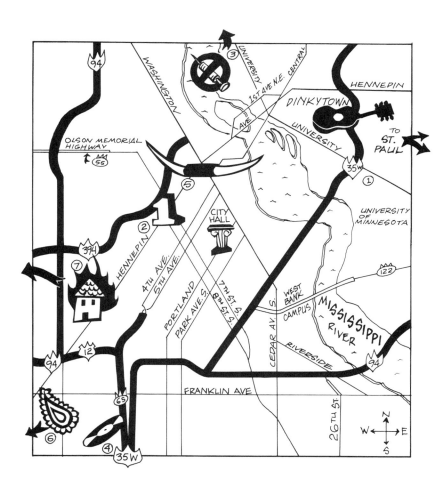

Now best known as the center of Prince's empire, this city has plenty of other pop music credits to its name. Some say it's the Mississippi River winding its way up from other legendary music cities like New Orleans and Memphis.

By the late '50s, a folk-music revival was gearing up here—as it was in many big college towns—and a young man named Robert Zimmerman registered at the University of Minnesota. He stayed for nearly three semesters, long enough to perform at places like the Ten O'Clock Scholar—and he left as "Bob Dylan."

Minneapolis's first pop hits are a varied lot: "Suzie Baby" by Bobby Vee, the Fendermen's "Mule Skinner Blues," and Dave Dudley's "Six Days On the Road," followed by rock and roll tunes like "Surfin' Bird" by the Trashmen and "Liar, Liar" by the Castaways. Bands like the Trashmen, the Castaways, the Litter, the Accents, and the Underbeats supported their mostly local hits by playing in the city (*see* Lake St.) and all over the Midwest ballroom circuit, which had been used for big band shows and polka parties a generation before.

Several noteworthy albums were recorded here by nonnatives, but it wasn't until the late 1970s that the homegrown stars began to emerge. Prince is the first and most famous of these but his former cohorts Jimmy Jam and Terry Lewis have also produced megahits (for Janet Jackson, Bell Biv Devoe, et al.). And rock bands such as the Replacements, Hüsker Dü, Soul Asylum, and Babes in Toyland have gained favor for their raucous live shows, proving the city is not just a great studio town. Remarkably, almost all of these recent luminaries have stayed in their hometown.

Big Trouble House   *1925 Colfax*

This two-story abode was a notorious party site during the '80s. A local band who lived there even named themselves after it. And Lori Barbero, the drummer for the female hard-rock trio Babes in Toyland, was also a recent tenant.

Blackberry Way   *606 13th Ave. SE*

This recording studio is located in a residential area in Dinkytown and, from the outside, it betrays no signs of being anything but a home. In fact, it was where many of the first Twin/Tone releases, including the Replacements' first LPs, were recorded. Soul Asylum's first EP, *Say What You Will*, was produced here by Bob Mould. In 1984, the three owners started a Blackberry Way record label.

The Blitz Bar   *507 Hennepin Ave.*

In 1976, this was one of the few places for local bands to play. Located under a strip club called the Roaring 20s, it was not a particularly safe place. In fact, someone had been shot and killed in the bathroom, so bands such as the Suicide Commandos would walk across the street to the Longhorn, then a jazz club, to use its facilities.

The Cabooze   *917 Cedar Ave. South*

This club with biker bar has been around for over twenty years; for nearly a decade, it was a top venue for electric blues shows. In the '80s, it was the site of early performances by Trip Shakespeare, the Gear Daddies, Run Westy Run, and Soul Asylum. Another top club is the Uptown Bar (3018 Hennepin).

Blackberry Way, studio in the snow. (Photo by Frank Lederle.)

Duffy's *2601 26th Ave. South*

This neighborhood bar opened as a rock and roll club in August 1979. One writer described the decor as reminiscent of "Uncle Ed's ornate Minnetonka billiard room." It was best known as a venue for national acts, ranging from Captain Beefheart to the Cramps. In the early '80s, it was turned into a bar called Norma Jean's.

❶ Dylan Haunts/Landmarks *all in Dinkytown*

Robert Zimmerman arrived in Minneapolis in September 1959. Bob Dylan left in October 1960.

Sigma Alpha Mu *925 University Ave. SE*

Bob Dylan spent his first few months of college staying at the University of Minnesota's Jewish frat. He didn't make many friends and left after Christmas break.

Gray's Drug Store *329 14th Ave. SE*

Dylan lived in a room above this store in early 1960. Last time I checked, the room was vacant.

The Ten O'Clock Scholar *416 14th Ave. SE*

Bob Dylan played his first solo shows here while a student at the University of Minnesota. He reportedly quit performing here when he demanded and was refused a raise to $5 from his usual $2 or $3 fee.

Enchanted Isle *Lake Minnetonka*

Produced by Dave and Sylvia Ray (he had been in the legendary folk group, Koerner, Ray and Glover), Bonnie Raitt's debut album was recorded at this site, an empty summer camp thirty miles west of Minneapolis. As Raitt wrote in her liner notes, "In between Ping-Pong and fishing, we recorded in a wood-frame garage with Dave and Sylvia working the equipment from a loft above us." It was recorded live on four tracks in order to capture "a more spontaneous and natural feeling in the music . . . It also reflects the differences between music made among friends living together in the country and the kind squeezed out trying to beat city traffic and studio clocks."

❷ First Avenue   *701 1st Ave.*

Minneapolis's top nightclub. In 1970, this building was transformed from a Greyhound bus depot into a rock and roll club called The Depot. Joe Cocker opened up the festivities, and acts such as Al Kooper, Rod Stewart, B. B. King, and Iggy and the Stooges also played during the club's short and troubled life. In 1972, the space became part of a disco franchise called Uncle Sam's. By the end of the '70s, though, it was a rock disco with occasional live shows by people like the Ramones and the Pretenders. Since 1982, when the name was changed to First Avenue, it has developed into the center of the Minneapolis music scene. It's featured Prince and all the players in his entourage as well as the local rock and roll royalty, from the Replacements on up. And the national acts booked here include everyone from Jesus Lizard to Toots and the Maytals. First Avenue is most famous, of course, for the central role it played in the film, *Purple Rain.* (*See also* **7th St. Entry.**)

First Avenue. (Photo by Daniel Corrigan.)

❸ The Hazelden Drug and Alcohol Rehabilitation Clinic *15245 Pleasant Valley Rd.*
in Center City

For almost a decade this has been a popular vacation spot for rock stars. Dethroned music mogul Walter Yetnikoff, who ruled CBS Records for over a decade, checked in for a stay in August 1989.

Heilicher Brothers *850 Decatur Ave. North*

From the late '40s to the late '70s, this record distributorship was one of the largest and most powerful in the United States. Run by Amos Heilicher with his brother Daniel, the company became a major record retailing chain. The Soma label was also a Heilicher enterprise (its name came from Amos, spelled backward). Soma's compilation LPs, *Big Hits of Mid-America*, Volumes 1 and 2, are collectors' items and revered by those who grew up with them.

❹ Kay Bank Studios *2541 Nicollet Ave. South*

The building was built in 1898 as a vaudeville theater and converted into a movie theater in 1932. In 1955, a man named Bruce Swedien transformed it into a recording studio; his clients included Art Tatum, Herbie Mann, and Swedish comedians. He moved to Chicago in 1957 (*see* **Universal Recording**), but he left behind what would remain the city's most popular recording studio over the next two decades. It went under seven different names but its most famous incarnation was as Kay Bank. The first pop song was recorded there in 1959 for Amos Heilicher's Soma label; that was Bobby Vee's big hit "Suzie Baby." From then on, all of the local labels like Soma and Metrobeat used it regularly, and came out with songs like "Surfin' Bird" and "Six Days On The Road."

In the '80s, it was called Nicollet Studios, and the Twin/Tone label and Hüsker Dü's label, Reflex Records, shared office and recording space here. Hüsker Dü's *New Day Rising* was just one of the underground classics recorded here. Today, the studio is called Creation Audio.

K-Tel International *15525 Medina Rd., Plymouth*

This building houses the record company that once gave us recycled hits in pseudo-psychedelic covers. Today it's a respectable outfit with jazz, new age, pop, and dance labels.

The Labor Temple *117 SE 4th St.*

Even Minneapolis had a psychedelic ballroom in the late '60s. Put on by local promoter David Anthony, shows at this hall—complete with wild light and slide shows, free flowers and cookies (that Anthony thinks were laced with something)—happened almost every Sunday night. (The big national acts would play in Chicago on Friday and Saturday, and then come here.) The Grateful Dead were the first to play. Anthony booked local bands such as the Litter, Crow, the South 40, and Joker's Wild as openers for acts like the Allman Brothers Band, Johnny and Edgar Winter, and the Illinois Speed Press. The Temple also holds the distinction of hosting the U.S. debut of Jethro Tull.

Teen hot spot, Mr. Lucky's, in 1964. (Courtesy of the Star Tribune/ Minneapolis-St. Paul.)

Lake Street

In the mid to late '60s, local bands played in ballrooms and VFW halls around Minnesota and the upper Midwest as well as in the clubs operating near the intersection of Lake and Nicollet Avenue. Lake Street was also "cruised" by the teenagers of the day. The main clubs were:

Mr. Lucky's   *2935 Nicollet Ave.*

This teen hangout served no alcohol but it could hold 2,000 kids. Local and national acts played here.

Magoo's   *2933 Nicollet Ave.*

Bands would play in the corner of this pizza place.

Across the street was George Garrett's **Nic-O-Lake Record Store** (2 West Lake St.). Garrett's independent record label released the Trashmen's "Surfin' Bird." After its national success, he was deluged with demos from aspiring stars. He had a basement studio there in which he'd record these bands. Unfortunately, all of this music history has been replaced with a large K-Mart.

❺ The Longhorn   *14 South 5th St.*

In mid 1976, a group of local music enthusiasts including Andy Schwartz, future–Twin/Tone founder Peter Jesperson, and guitarist Chris Osgood decided to convince area bar owners that there was a market for the music they were interested in—original, aggressive rock and roll. Jay Berini, the owner of this jazz club, which had once been a steakhouse, decided to give it a try. Before long, bands like the Wild Cats (later the Flamin' Os), the Suicide Commandos, the Boys, Curtiss A., and the Suburbs were packing the joint. Berini kept the tacky steakhouse decor, though, including lots of Frederick Remington fakes.

By 1981, Berini had been sent to prison (on a charge unrelated to the club), and the club's name had been changed to Zoogie's; the Longhorn's fake Wild West look was replaced with cheap tacky red wallpaper.

Macalaster College   *Summit Ave. at Snelling Ave. South, St. Paul*

Yes, this was Monkee Peter Tork's alma mater. Its more admirable distinction, however, lies in the college's black choir. Gary Hines was appointed the choir's director in 1971 and it has since evolved into The Sounds of Blackness. Their first album, *The Evolution of Gospel*, was produced by Jimmy Jam and Terry Lewis in 1991; it reached the national charts.

Moon Sound Studios   *2828 Dupont Ave. South*

This eight-track studio, a former hairdressing salon, was the lab for Prince's first experiments in recording. Owner Chris Moon, a British expatriate, had just opened the facility when, in the summer of 1976, Prince and his band, Champagne, shyly came in to record some songs. Moon charged the group his usual rate of $35 an hour, but in a matter of weeks he handed over the keys to the very impressive bandleader. As Moon told *Rolling Stone*, "He'd stay on the weekend, sleep on the studio floor. I wrote down directions on how to operate the equipment, so he would follow the little chart." Prince took advantage of the situation for a year and emerged with an impressive demo tape, on which he played all the instruments and handled all the vocals.

Mount Sinai Hospital   *2215 Park Ave. South*

Prince Rogers Nelson was born here on June 7, 1960.

Oak Folkjokeupus   *2557 Lyndale Ave. South*

This record store was a crucial rock and roll spot in the 1980s. Twin/Tone co-founder Peter Jesperson once managed it and the Replacements at the same time; thus the band got to practice in the basement. Another manager, Jim Peterson, later opened **Garage D'Or Records** (2548 Nicollet Ave.) And finally, independent producer Terry Katzman was a clerk here when he founded Reflex Records with Hüsker Dü's Bob Mould.

⑥ Paisley Park   *7801 Audubon Rd., Chanhassen*

Prince's $10-million studio was opened in 1987 and has since handled a lot more than the Purple One's own pet projects. George Clinton, Hammer, the Bodeans, Paula Abdul, the Fine Young Cannibals, R.E.M., and Madonna have all recorded here. (For a time, record companies sent artists to Paisley on the chance that Prince might wander by and share a song he'd written.) Prince's 1990 movie, *Graffiti Bridge*, and most of his videos have been shot here, as have commercials for Huggie's diapers and Comet cleanser.

Replacements' Birthplace   *2215 Bryant Ave. South*

This big house was home to guitarist Bob Stinson and his little brother Tommy, who played bass; the basement was the spot where their group, the Replacements, practiced and became a real band. Their public debut, in 1979, was scheduled at a halfway house for alcoholics in a South Minneapolis church. As the story goes, the band was fired for drunkenness before they had played a note. So they retreated to the studio and were almost immediately signed to Twin/Tone Records.

The Riverview Supper Club   *2319 NW River Rd.*

This venue opened in 1980 and has presented a great many top-notch black artists. For starters, the club's first house band was Flyte Tyme. When that group went on tour in 1981 as the Time, Alexander O'Neal took over. Mint Condition also played early shows here. Although today

The Replacements on the upper porch of the Stinson house, 1984. (Photo by Greg Helgeson.)

Hüsker Dü at the 7th Street Entry, 1980. (Photo by Greg Helgeson.)

it's more of a disco than a place for live music, the Friday jam sessions attract a number of local legends. Owner Jim Fuller had another famous club before this one—the **Cosey Bar and Lounge** (522 Plymouth Ave.). It featured legends like Muddy Waters and future legends like Prince and Andre Cymone, who performed in the mid-'70s as Grand Central.

Ron's Randolph Inn   *1217 Randolph Ave., St. Paul*
A week after first getting together in Greg Norton's basement and playing a bunch of Ramones covers, Hüsker Dü played their first show here on March 30, 1979. "We figured if the Ramones could do it, anybody could do it," Bob Mould once recalled. They were not asked back.

The Scholar Coffee House   *247 Cedar Ave., West Bank*
Although it's not the similarly named coffeehouse Dylan played in the early 60s—that one burned down—this establishment has its own claim to landmark status: guitarist Leo Kottke recorded *Twelve String Blues*, his first LP, here. The opening and closing of the Scholar's door can even be heard on it.

7th Street Entry   *29 North 7th St.*
This small room was originally the kitchen for the Minneapolis bus depot. In 1980, it was changed from the checkroom of First Avenue's predecessor, Sam's, into a club that booked decidedly uncommercial bands. As it happens, many of the bands booked here went on to considerable commercial success: the Replacements and R.E.M., to name two.

Hüsker Dü's first LP, *Landspeed Record*, was recorded here in 1981 without a sound check. The Pagans from Cleveland recorded their reunion show here in November 1986 for release as their second live album. And an upcoming local band called Rifle Sport titled its 1989 LP *Live at the Entry, Dead at the Exit*.

Sons of Norway   *1455 West Lake St.*
The hardcore band Loud Fast Rules made their debut at this hall, which they had rented for $150. The band soon changed its name to Soul Asylum and went on to inhabit the 7th Street Entry.

Sound 80   *2709 East 25th St.*
Founded in 1970 by two men who had worked at Kay Bank studio, this was the city's most technically advanced recording facility for over a decade. In December 1974, Bob Dylan returned to Minneapolis and recut four songs he had recorded in New York for his *Blood on the Tracks* album. It's also where the Lipps, Inc. smash called "Funkytown" was created. It took one hundred hours for the three producers/engineers to get the right combination of synthesized sound and raw, affecting vocals. Cynthia Johnson, a one-time member of Flyte Tyme, sang the lead, and the song became the first number-one record produced in Minneapolis. While doing demos for record companies, Prince met engineer David Rifkin; they ended up working together for ten years.

2541 Garfield
Hüsker Dü songwriter/drummer Grant Hart once lived at this address and wrote a song about it called "2541." The song, about the breakup of a romance, became the title track of his first solo album after the breakup of Hüsker Dü. Coincidentally, 2541 is also the address for Hüsker Dü's old office on Nicollet St. (*see* **Kay Bank Studios**). Next door to 2541 Garfield is the Modesto apartment house, which is mentioned on the back of the Replacements' *Hootenanny* LP.

❼ Utopia House   *14501 Minnetonka Blvd.*
Two of the three Suicide Commandos, Minneapolis's legendary punk group, lived in a Minnetonka farmhouse at this address. They paid $30 a month for rent, which allowed the group to get going. As guitarist Chris Osgood recalls, "We could afford to be starving musicians that way. We could practice there and play as loud as we wanted." In October 1977, the authorities gave notice they were going to demolish the house—supposedly as practice for the fire department—so Osgood wrote a song called "Burn It Down" and asked director Chuck Statler to film it. "It was really hot," says Osgood. This pioneering video may still be available from Twin/Tone records.

Way Community Center   *1913 Plymouth Ave. North*
In the early to mid '70s, Prince and his cohorts spent many hours here, practicing and composing.

👫 Schools

Central High   *3416 3rd Ave. South*
> Prince's alma mater. He apparently really shone in an extracurricular course called "The Business of Music."

North High School   *1500 James Ave. North*
> The alma mater of superproducers Terry Lewis and Andre Cymone.

Red Wing State Training School for Juveniles   *1079 Highway 292, Red Wing*
> After several incidents of arson and vandalism, Replacement Bob Stinson, then a ninth-grader, was pulled out of public school and sent to this academy, part of the Minnesota corrections system.

🦅 DETOUR

Mason City, IA   *150 miles south of Minneapolis*
> Buddy Holly, J.P. Richardson ("the Big Bopper"), and Ritchie Valens were all killed on February 3, 1959, minutes after their chartered Beechcraft Bonanza took off from the Mason City airport. The plane crashed five miles northwest of the airport on the Albert Juhl farm.
>
> They had just performed at the Surf Ballroom in Clear Lake, Iowa, as part of the Winter Dance Party revue, and were headed to the Armory in Moorhead, Minnesota. **The Surf Ballroom** (460 North Shore Dr.) survived the crash—you could even say it prospered. Aside from booking everyone from Sam the Sham to the Yardbirds to Joan Jett through the years, the ballroom hosts an annual Buddy Holly Tribute during the first week of February. Fans gather from all over the world to hear Buddy Holly "cover" bands.

The West Coast

SEATTLE

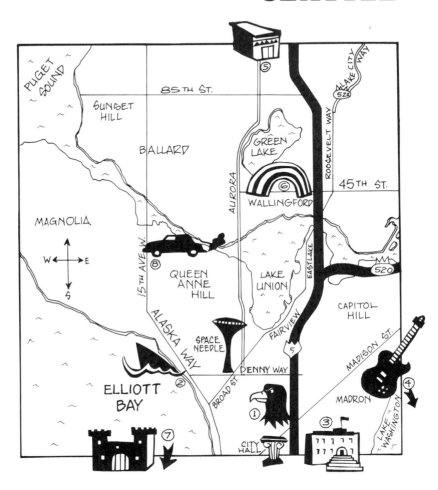

Jimi Hendrix may be Seattle's most famous rock and roll son, but he skipped town before graduating from high school, and returned just once before his death. Still, this city has other stars to call its own. Heading the list may be Bumps Blackwell, a legendary bandleader and record man, who produced sessions like Little Richard's "Tutti Frutti" and Sam Cooke's "You Send Me." He led a group here in the late '40s called the Junior Band, which at one point featured a teenaged trumpet player and arranger named Quincy Jones.

Jones had already worked with Ray Charles, who had come to town in 1948. By 1950, though, Blackwell and Charles had both left for Los Angeles, and Jones had entered Boston's Berklee College of Music.

Rock and roll gradually took hold of the region in the '50s. And by the late '50s, the Pacific Northwest was beginning to develop an impressive circuit of dance halls that booked local bands every weekend. Teenagers would pay a dollar or two to see several local bands at once; for the most part, these were instrumental combos and R&B–flavored cover bands who threw in more and more of their own songs. (A cover of "Louie, Louie" became a staple of nearly every band's repertoire.) Pat O'Day, the area's top disc jockey, was the acknowledged godfather of this scene. He even opened his own clubs and, later, a rock auditorium loosely modeled after San Francisco's Fillmore.

The Wailers and the Ventures were the first rock and roll bands to send a song to the national charts. In 1959, the Wailers made the Top 40 with an instrumental called "Tall Cool One." The next year, the Ventures hit number two with "Walk Don't Run." But while the Ventures continued with a stream of hits, the Wailers never saw much success outside of their devoted local following. (Their record company, Etiquette, released their own raw garage band music as well as the influential distortion of bands such as the Sonics.)

Few national acts emerged from Seattle in the '70s; Ann and Nancy Wilson's Heart did, but they had to go to Canada for their first record deal. The impressive dance club circuit had degenerated into a handful of "taverns" that booked original music. But somehow—some say because the bad weather and bad club scene kept bands in their garages rehearsing and finding new sounds—inventive bands have been exploding out of the region over the past decade. They range from the so-called "grunge" bands like Soundgarden, Mudhoney, Pearl Jam, and Nirvana to the eccentric pop of the Young Fresh Fellows and the Posies. With a boost from independent labels such as Sub Pop and PopLlama, these bands have found a national audience. Major labels have been quick to sign up the latest Seattle slew of new groups, and Hollywood has not been far behind. Cameron Crowe's movie *Singles* is set in the middle of the scene.

The Bird   *107 Spring St.*

> This club, which lasted from 1979 to 1981, is the birthplace of the Seattle punk scene. Because the extensive alternative club circuit had not yet been developed, the Bird relied heavily on San Francisco bands—Negative Trend, the Dils, the Avengers, the Zeros—and that was inspiration enough for many local kids. The owners tried two spaces—4th and

Spring, then on Capitol Hill—but ultimately couldn't beat the challenges of running an all-ages club. Especially because the core audience for such shows was still hovering at about one hundred people.

Birdland   *2203 East Madison*
In the '50s and '60s, this was the place to hear black performers. It also was where Jimi (then Jimmy) Hendrix was given notice by his high school band, the Rocking Kings, that his services would no longer be required. Apparently, Hendrix had been attracting the attention of another King's girlfriend. Hendrix ended up taking a beating in the men's room.

The Central Tavern   *207 1st Ave. South*
Until it changed ownership in November 1990, this was one of the few Seattle clubs that helped to introduce local bands to Northwest audiences; it featured groups like Green River, Mudhoney, Mother Love Bone, Soundgarden, Alice in Chains, and War Babies.

❶ Eagle's Auditorium   *Union and 7th*
In the late '60s, Pacific Northwest music kingpin Pat O'Day opened this venue with a fellow named Boyd Grathmeir. O'Day says now: "I was considered the crass commercial disc jockey so Boyd fronted it." It was supposed to be a counterculture hangout, after all, and featured bands like the Jefferson Airplane, Procul Harum, and the Doors. It's fondly remembered by some natives as the first place they did acid. It's still used occasionally for rock and roll shows.

❷ The Edgewater Inn   *2411 Alaskan Way*
This hotel, which sits on the edge of Puget Sound, is the site of the infamous 1969 Led Zeppelin "shark incident." As the story goes (and goes—it's been told repeatedly), drummer John Bonham and members of the band's entourage caught a sand shark (some say it was a red snapper) from the window of the hotel and proceeded to entertain a redheaded groupie with it (some say it was still alive). The hotel apparently doesn't mind the aura the Zeppelin legend has brought to it, but fishing from hotel windows is no longer allowed.

❸ Garfield High School   *400 23rd Ave.*
Jimi Hendrix's alma mater. In his sophomore year, he joined the Rocking Kings, a cover band started by an older classmate. They played the hits of the day (including "Yakety Yak" and "At The Hop") at local dances and Vancouver clubs. Hendrix never finished his studies—he dropped out, eventually enlisting in the army—but in 1968, Garfield invited him back to receive an honorary diploma.

The Gorilla Room   *2nd Ave.*
This small, seedy club—where public bathrooms doubled as dressing rooms—was an important local punk venue. The club became **Gorilla**

Garfield High School, 1992. (Photo by Cam Garrett.)

Gardens, after moving to a twin movie theater in Chinatown. It hosted important all-ages shows in the mid-'80s: Sonic Youth, D.O.A., et al.

Graven Image *311 South Washington St.*
This art gallery/club was the regular venue for an influential local band called the U-Men, which broke up while the Seattle scene was still just an underground phenomenon.

❹ Greenwood Memorial Park *4th and Monroe, Renton*
Jimi Hendrix, who died in London in September 1970, is buried here. An electric guitar is etched in his gravestone.

Muzak Headquarters *915 Yale Ave. North*
Since 1987, Seattle has been the base of operation for Muzak, the infamous creator of souped-up string and synthesizer versions of pop hits. Several Sub Pop employees, as well as members of some Sub Pop bands, worked here at one time or another. In fact, this was the record company's first (unofficial) headquarters. Sub Pop co-founder Bruce Pavitt remembers the surprise of distributors who called up the main line.

The Paramount *901 Pine St.*
Since 1968, this theater has hosted shows by hundreds of notable touring bands, including T. Rex, Funkadelic, and Bob Marley and the Wailers. In March 1990, it hosted a memorial service for Andrew Wood, the lead singer of Mother Love Bone, who overdosed on heroin.

❺ Parker's *17001 Aurora Ave. North*
This Seattle hall and restaurant was opened in 1932 for big band dances. During the '60s, local bands like the Wailers and the Sonics packed the

Parker's, 1992. (Photo by Cam Garrett.)

place with screaming teens; and in the '70s, when it was called Aquarius, Heart played regularly. It's now called Parker's again, and books a wide range of music, but mostly Top 40.

Pat O'Day's Party Line   *707 1st Ave.*

In the '60s, this club was a teen hangout that provided telephones at each table so that the boy at table 25 could speak with the girl at table 31. Pat O'Day was the Northwest's top DJ and he put on shows at the Spanish Castle and other dance halls around the Northwest. The Beach Boys played here early on, but didn't go over well because they weren't dressed all alike. O'Day recalls: "The kids just didn't go for their denims, Pendleton shirts, and scraggly hair." The Party Line has since been transformed into a bank.

⑥ The Rainbow Tavern   *722 NE 45th*

During the mid-'80s, this was one of the best places to find acts that didn't want to play Top-40 covers. Jonathan Poneman, who eventually co-founded Sub Pop, handled the booking and remembers it as "a herd-'em-in, get-'em-drunk, herd-'em-out sort of tavern." Sounds unlikely because he was able to book all sorts of people, including Henry Kaiser, the Neville Brothers, and Sun Ra. The Rainbow also gave two legendary local groups, Green River and the Young Fresh Fellows, their first shows. It is now a strip joint.

Ray Charles Haunts

After a five-day bus ride from Jacksonville, Florida, seventeen-year-old Ray Charles slept for twenty-four hours at a hotel and then headed over to the **Rocking Chair** (12th St., now 12th Ave.) for something to eat. He ended up entering the talent contest the club was holding, and that led to a regular gig at the **Elks Club** down the street. He later returned to the more prestigious Rocking Chair and worked with a very young Quincy Jones. It was in Seattle that Charles was introduced to marijuana and heroin, for which he developed a sixteen-year habit.

Reciprocal Recording   *4230 Leary Way NW*

This studio was used for most of Sub Pop's recordings through 1990. Engineer/producer/Skin Yard guitarist Jack Endino was the producer on most of these releases.

The Rainbow Tavern, 1986. (Photo by Cam Garrett.)

Doug Hollis' Sound Garden sculpture. (Photo by Cam Garrett.)

The Showbox   *1426 1st Ave.*

This sorely missed alternative venue booked original, local bands as well as eccentric pop purveyors such as Devo, the Ramones, and XTC. It is currently Seattle Improvisation, a comedy club.

Sound Garden Sculpture   *7600 Sand Point Way*

This giant environmental art piece was, obviously, the inspiration for the name of the Seattle band, Soundgarden.

❼ The Spanish Castle   *Midway, WA, between Seattle and Tacoma*

This dancehall is undoubtedly the most famous in the Pacific Northwest circuit. And not *only* because Jimi Hendrix named a song after it.

It opened on Thanksgiving night 1959 with a show featuring Conway

Twitty. With the next weekend's show—featuring pioneering garage band the Wailers—the hall's prospects improved considerably. From there on, it became headquarters for local rock and roll. National acts like Dorsey and Johnny Burnette, Jerry Lee Lewis, Bobby Vee, Jan and Dean, Lloyd Price, and Roy Orbison played there, as did local legends like the Dynamics (featuring Jimmy Hannah), the Frantics (who moved to San Francisco and became Moby Grape), and Little Bill and the Blue Notes. The Ventures, the premier instrumental group of the day, played their first show with their permanent lineup here. The Wailers recorded a live album here.

A local teenager named Jimi Hendrix attended many shows at the

The Spanish Castle, circa 1981. (Courtesy of The Seattle Times.*)*

Castle. He regularly brought his Fender amplifier in case the band on stage blew its amp out; he told O'Day he would lend the band his if they would let him jam with them. That apparently only happened once, but Hendrix went ahead and included "Spanish Castle Magic" on *Axis: Bold As Love*, his second album.

The Castle closed after two awful accidents occurred in the space of one week. Three girls ran across the highway to join a line for a Jan and Dean concert; they were hit and killed by a truck in full view of hundreds of people in line. A few days later, a car pulling out of the Castle's driveway was hit by a car driving by. The site is now a parking lot.

⑧ Ventures' Start-Up Story
In 1958, Don Wilson was working, unhappily, at his father's used car lot (15th and NW Dravus, Ballard) when a young bricklayer named Bob Bogle came by to inspect the merchandise. Wilson dissuaded Bogle from a purchase, and asked if there were any openings at Bogle's place of employment. There was indeed a job available, and Wilson became a hodcarrier. After finding that they both played guitar, the two men began practicing together. They soon were playing at the Blue Moon Inn and the Britannia, both in Tacoma. By 1960, their first recording, "Walk Don't Run" had become a big national hit; they were the area's first rock and roll stars.

↖ DETOURS

Olympia, WA   *58 miles SW of Seattle*
The Northshore Surf Club and the Capitol Theater
These were the main venues of the 1991 International Underground Pop Festival. Organized by Calvin Johnson and Candice Pedersen, who run K Records, the five-day fete featured acts like Bikini Kill, Fugazi, the Fastbacks, L7, Scrawl and Johnson's band, Beat Happening.
Olympia High School   *1302 North St.*
This is the alma mater of the Fleetwoods, who started writing the song "Come Softly To Me" while standing on a street corner. The trio performed it twice at Olympia High, and their fellow students begged them to record it. After hearing a tape of it, a Seattle record promoter named Bob Reisdorff started Dolphin (later Dolton) Records so that he could release it himself. The song became a number-one hit in 1959.
Timberline High School   *6120 Mullen Rd. SE*
Rickie Lee Jones was expelled from here when she was sixteen.

Aberdeen, WA   *108 miles SW of Seattle*
The hometown of Nirvana's Kurt Cobain and Chris Novoselic, as well as the Melvins, once described as "legendary quaalude-metal titans." Cobain once summed up the town as "Twin Peaks without the excitement."

Portland, OR   *174 miles SW of Seattle*

The Kingsmen and Paul Revere and the Raiders were the first two local bands to hit it big nationally. Out of all the Northwest bands covering "Louie Louie," the Kingsmen version was the one to break nationally. Paul Revere and the Raiders, famous for their pseudo-Revolutionary War costumes, had moved to Los Angeles by the time of their first national hit. In the '70s and '80s, bands ranged from the unlistenable (Quarterflash) to the great but unheralded (the Surf Trio, the Wipers). The current local music scene is as healthy as it's ever been, with reigning bands such as Sweaty Nipples, Dharma Bums, and Hitting Birth. The Mayor's Ball, which featured seventy-five bands in 1992, has become a big annual event.

Locals Only   *61 SW 2nd*

Dan Sause says Portland has one of the best music scenes in the U.S.— and he's got this record store to prove it. Opened in 1989 by Sause and his partner, Arden Thomas, Locals Only stocks 1000 different releases by Portland-area acts (with just a few Seattle discs thrown in for good measure).

The Satyricon   *125 NW 6th Ave.*

This club has become a key Northwest setting for underground rock; it booked bands such as Nirvana, Sweaty Nipples, and Dharma Bums when they were just starting out. Its smaller counterpart, **The X-Ray Cafe** (214 West Burnside St.), features many of the same bands.

SAN FRANCISCO

S an Francisco has long been a pioneering music town—in 1899, for instance, it got the country's first jukebox—but until the mid-'60s, it hadn't made any particular inroads in rock and roll. Up until then, the only homegrown group with any national success was the fairly forgettable Beau Brummels. And the live entertainment scene was dominated by two DJs, Tom Donahue and Bobby Mitchell, who booked Top-

The Grateful Dead perform in the middle of Haight Street, 1968. (Photo by Jim Marshall.)

40 package shows at the Cow Palace, and had the only rock and roll record label in town.

That all changed of course with the advent of the free-love, psychedelic Haight-Ashbury scene and the birth of the flower children. Pop concerts became "happenings," and pop tunes grew into lengthy jam sessions, spiked with folk, jazz, blues, Indian ragas, and psychedelic drugs. Musicians and ordinary folks looking for something different flocked here from all over the country to be part of the scene.

The first important venue in this new age was actually 150 miles away, in Virginia City, Nevada. In June 1965, the Red Dog Saloon (North C St.), hosted the debut of a San Francisco band called the Charlatans, who had perfected their impressive Wild West costuming before having a single rehearsal. The engagement lasted nearly all summer, becoming an all-involving experience for the band and for their artist friends—a Wild West entourage—who contributed lighting, posters, and a festive atmosphere. These witnesses brought back the strange excitement of the event to San Francisco, and tried to recreate it at a rock and roll dance at the Longshoremen's Hall. It was a huge success.

By 1966, places like the Fillmore, the Longshoremen's Hall, and the Avalon were all hosting rock and roll events, with promoters like Bill

Graham and Chet Helms competing for the ever-growing contingent of young music fans. At the same time, the number of local bands multiplied wildly, with musicians like Steve Miller and Boz Scaggs coming by to investigate the scene—and staying forever.

San Francisco's influence on the music of the day was undeniable—from free outdoor concerts nationwide to the many psychedelic bands sprouting up. Even the Beatles—with their Sgt. Pepper guise—were inspired by the surrealistic San Francisco scene.

But the area's music was never limited to psychedelic sounds. Even at the height of flower power, Creedence Clearwater Revival and Sly and the Family Stone were drawing avid followings. The Doobie Brothers and Journey carried their straightforward rock formulas to the charts in the '70s.

In the mid-'70s, San Francisco generated another distinctive music scene. The Dead Kennedys, Flipper, and Romeo Void were perhaps the most visible members of a hyperactive underground. (The Kennedys' lead singer, Jello Biafra, ran for mayor in 1979 and finished fourth in a field of ten.)

More recently, an emerging rap and hip-hop scene has asserted itself with artists like Hammer, Digital Underground, Too Short, and the Disposable Heroes of Hiphoprisy. And today's thriving rock scene includes acts as dissimilar as Sister Double Happiness, Metallica, American Music Club, Chris Isaak, Faith No More, Primus, and Voice Farm.

❶ The Airplane House   *2400 Fulton St.*
> In the late '60s, this big colonial mansion was the headquarters—and living quarters—of the Jefferson Airplane, who, along with the Grateful Dead, were the standard-bearers of the Haight-Ashbury music scene. The rooms were wired so that the all-night jams in the basement could be heard from anywhere in the house. Record-release parties featured the best drugs around.

❷ The Avalon Ballroom   *1268 Sutter St.*
> In 1964, a transplanted Texan named Chet Helms started a crucial weekly jam session (*see* **Big Brother Birthplace**). By 1965, he was putting on dance concerts at big halls like the Fillmore. But when Bill Graham took control of the Fillmore in April 1966, Helms started booking shows at this upstairs auditorium. Janis Joplin, Helms's friend from Austin, Texas, had her first show with Big Brother and the Holding Company here, on June 10, 1966.
>
> Like Graham, Helms booked local stars like the Jefferson Airplane, Country Joe and the Fish, and the Steve Miller Blues Band as well as nationally rising groups like the Doors. But Helms viewed the Avalon as a place for more than mere music events; it was a sanctuary where music

and drugs such as LSD and pot could be used to alter one's state of consciousness. As he recently explained, "We provided a safe environment where people could let go their egos. It had a religious aspect rather than being an entertainment event. I never at any time saw myself as being in the music business." Ultimately, Bill Graham's better organized outfit drove Helms out of San Francisco music promotion. The ballroom was closed in September 1968, and has since been remodeled into the Regency II movie theater.

Big Brother Birthplace   *1090 Page St.*

This site is now occupied by two modern apartment buildings, but the rooming house that used to stand here was a bona fide rock and roll landmark. The house was operated by Peter Albin and his brother Rodney, who rented out the twenty rooms to students, musicians, and artistic types. In late 1964, Chet Helms, a young tenant from Austin, Texas, began to organize jam sessions in the basement ballroom. Because the city offered so little entertainment for teenagers, these sessions turned into underground dance parties. Helms started charging fifty cents admission, but that only increased the draw. Big Brother and the Holding Company emerged from the jam sessions, with Peter Albin as the band's bass guitarist. In 1966, Helms introduced Janis Joplin, his friend from Austin, to the band, and she became the group's vocalist and driving force.

Helms went on to promote regular dance concerts at the Avalon Ballroom with the Family Dog collective/commune. He also organized the first Human Be-In (*see* **Golden Gate Park**).

The Boarding House   *960 Bush St.*

This former recording studio became an important local showcase in the '70s. It witnessed early performances by the Tubes and the Pointer Sisters; and, in 1978, Neil Young chose to introduce his *Rust Never Sleeps* material here in a legendary five-night solo stint. The Boarding House was also a key comedy club, and helped to launch Steve Martin. Owner David Allen relocated to Columbus Avenue in 1980 but that version lasted only until 1982.

Candlestick Park   *off Highway 101, Paul St. exit*

This ballpark was the site of the last announced Beatles concert on August 29, 1966. The group played twelve songs in thirty-three minutes, protected from 25,000 fans by a six-foot fence and 200 policemen. No wonder they didn't want to tour again. (They did, of course, perform before an audience once more—on the roof of Apple Records in London.)

❸ The Carousel   *Market and Van Ness*

In late 1967, the Grateful Dead and the Jefferson Airplane decided to take over this ballroom, a popular big band hall in the '30s and '40s. The idea was to put on their own rock and roll dances in their own fair-minded and artistic style—as opposed to the style of the suspiciously pragmatic Bill Graham. (One night, people seeking admission had the choice of paying five dollars or throwing a dollar into a fire.) As Dead drummer Mickey Hart once recalled, "The Carousel was our own place, and the familiarity of it was an asset musically. It was *home*. Doing one-nighters, you're exposed to various elements, and there's an uncertainty to your existence." By the end of June 1968, however, the enterprise had gone bankrupt. Bill Graham obligingly took it over, renaming it the Fillmore West.

❹ The Cow Palace   *Geneva and Santos*
In 1963, local music kingpins Tom Donahue and Bobby Mitchell promoted a popular series of shows at this huge hall, which has also served time as a convention center and cattle exhibition space. In 1964, Barry Goldwater was nominated for president here. Phil Spector conducted an orchestra of L.A. session musicians; the Ronettes, the Four Seasons, Marvin Gaye, Martha and the Vandellas, and the Beach Boys were just a few of the featured acts.

Even better, the Beatles started their first full tour of the U.S. here on August 19, 1964. They returned a year later, too. The Cow Palace continues to be used as a music palace—recent attractions include the Red Hot Chili Peppers and Metallica.

❺ The Fillmore Auditorium   *1805 Geary St.*
From 1965 to 1968, this old second-story ballroom was a true mecca for the young and restless. Bill Graham first leased it in December 1965 for

The Cow Palace, booking everything from cattle to Metallica.

a benefit for the San Francisco Mime Troupe, which he managed. The show featured the Gentlemen's Band, the Mystery Trend, the Great Society, and the Jefferson Airplane, and about 3,500 people paid $1.50 each to get in.

The hall's virtues—including much better acoustics than the octagonal Longshoremen's Hall—became apparent to a host of other promoters (most notably Ken Kesey and Chet Helms) and to the owners of the hall, who promptly tripled the rental price.

On January 8, Kesey threw his first Acid Test in San Francisco here. And the Warlocks (later called the Grateful Dead) were the house band for this event, as they were for all of Kesey's other Acid Tests. Chet Helms's first dance concert was held the next month, and was called Tribal Stomp. He had even more success a few weeks later with the Paul Butterfield Blues Band. But by April 1966, Bill Graham wasn't willing to share the space anymore; for the next two years, he put on shows every weekend (and during the week in the summer). Many of these performances are legendary, including Jimi Hendrix's triumphant six-day run after the Monterey Pop Festival and Otis Redding's three-night stay in late 1966.

Graham made a point of presenting black artists to his predominantly white audiences—from Aretha Franklin and Sam and Dave to then lesser known blues and jazz artists like B.B. King, Muddy Waters, and Roland Kirk. The hall was also famous for its surreal, full-color posters, its light shows and the many benefit shows Graham brought in.

In 1968, Graham moved his shows out of the increasingly hostile Fillmore area, and into the more spacious Carousel Ballroom, which he renamed the Fillmore West. For a time, the Flamin' Groovies used it as a rehearsal hall and held dances there. Graham reopened the Fillmore Auditorium in 1988 but damage from the October 1989 earthquake forced it to close again.

③ Fillmore West   *Market and Van Ness*
Bill Graham took over this big ballroom's lease in July 1968, and continued the powerful booking strategy he had begun over at the Fillmore Auditorium. He then opened the Fillmore East in New York City—and closed them both in mid 1971. By then, he was the most important concert promoter in town, and his stature only grew as time went on.

At the two Fillmores, Graham booked the major touring acts of the day—stadiums had not yet become the only choice for rock stars. Legendary nights include the Who in June 1969 (booked with Woody Herman's Herd), the Led Zeppelin/Isaac Hayes/Roland Kirk bill in November 1969, and the New Year's Eve shows that lasted from 9 P.M. to 9 A.M. and included breakfast. This hall also saw the big-city debuts of Tower of Power and Santana.

The week-long series of concerts that closed up the hall featured nearly all of the big local groups, and Graham made quite sure the historic events were recorded and filmed for future consumption. The building was torn down and replaced with a Honda dealership.

The Carousel becomes the Fillmore West, 1968. (Photo by Jim Marshall.)

Golden Gate Park

Situated right beside "the Haight" (as the Haight-Ashbury neighborhood was fondly referred to), this was the site of many free concerts by the Grateful Dead and other local legends. The park's stadium was the site for the first Human Be-In on January 14th, 1967. The event attracted 20,000 people—who in turn attracted all of the major record companies to San Francisco. In late 1991, it was the site of a memorial concert for Bill Graham. Santana, Los Lobos, Crosby, Stills, Nash & Young, and John Fogerty all performed, and the Grateful Dead played a Graham favorite, "Sugar Magnolia".

The Grateful Dead house   *710 Ashbury*

The members of the Grateful Dead lived here communally from 1966 to 1968. Jerry Garcia once described the atmosphere: "People trying to start various spiritual movements would be in and out. Friends trying to organize benefits would be in and out. There would be a lot of energy exchanged. It was a real high in those days because Haight-Ashbury was a community." Most of the band subsequently moved to suburban Marin County, where the group's headquarters is now located.

the Hungry i   *546 Broadway*

Now a strip club, this was the site of some of Lenny Bruce's notorious performances. This is also where John Phillips met Michelle Gilliam, "the quintessential California girl," in 1961. Phillips soon separated from his wife, and he and Michelle were married the next year. (Their daughter Chynna is a member of Wilson Phillips.) In 1965, they formed the Mamas and the Papas with Dennis Doherty and Cass Elliot.

Hunter's Point   *south of Candlestick Park*

Michael Franti and Rono Tse, the masterminds behind the Beatnigs and then the Disposable Heroes of Hiphoprisy, met in the San Francisco club scene in the mid-'80s. When they decided to create music together, they had no money to buy instruments. So they went out to the shipyards here and made music with scrap metal.

The I-Beam   *1748 Haight St.*

This building once was a masonic hall in which Harry Truman and Dwight D. Eisenhower gave speeches. Since 1978, it's been a dance club that hosts live bands several nights a week. Local stars such as Negativland, the Avengers, Chris Isaak, Voice Farm, Faith No More, Sister Double Happiness, and Limbo Maniacs have all played important early shows here.

KSAN   *211 Sutter, then 345 Sansome*

After leaving the Top-40 radio station KYA, where he had reigned since 1961, disc jockey Tom Donahue formed KSAN in 1968. It became the

The first Human-Be-In at Golden Gate Park. (Photo by Jim Marshall.)

Dancing at the I-Beam. (Photo by Mick Hicks. Courtesy of Cathy Cohn.)

most powerful station in the area with its free-form progressive format, featuring songs that lasted over the usual three-and-a-half-minute limit and disc jockeys who played what they wanted. In 1976, Howie Klein helped pioneer punk music on Bay Area radio when he joined Chris Knab to produce a show called the "Outcast Hour," later known as "The Heretics." (Klein, Knab, and Butch Bridges formed 415 Records, which put out records by the Mutants, Nuns, SVT, and Pearl Harbor and the Explosions.) This station has the additional distinction of having received all of the Patti Hearst letters. In 1980, a country station took over the call letters.

⑥ Longshoremen's Hall   *400 North Point*

On October 16, 1965, this union auditorium was the site of San Francisco's first rock and roll dance for hippies. It wasn't billed as that, of course—those proto-hippies were much more imaginative. It was "A Tribute to Dr. Strange." The event was presented by a collective called the Family Dog, whose members had summered at the Red Dog Saloon.

Not surprisingly, the Charlatans—including Mike Wilhelm, later of the Flamin' Groovies, and Dan Hicks, later of Dan Hicks and His Hot Licks—were a prime attraction. Also featured were veritable unknowns such as the Jefferson Airplane, the Great Society (featuring Grace Slick) and the Marbles (who remain unknown to this day). And as Ralph Gleason recalled, everyone looked like they were at a costume party, many dressed as Buffalo Bill or bonnie Prince Charlie. It was the beginning of a frenzied era of festive experimentation.

A week later came another event, this one called "A Tribute To Sparkle Plenty" and featuring the Lovin' Spoonful. On November 6 came "A Tribute to Ming the Magnificent," starring Frank Zappa and the Airplane. Mind-boggling light shows accompanied the music.

Before being abandoned because of its strange, echoey acoustics, this hall was also the site of a three-day "Trips Festival," which Tom Wolfe described as a "hulking, crazed whirlpool." The newly christened Grateful Dead were a prime attraction. Today the Longshoremen's Hall presents the occasional concert.

❼ Mabuhay Gardens   *443 Broadway*

In 1976, this nightclub's main draw was a supper show of dancing Filipino girls and a Filipino Elvis impersonator. Since these acts were not too lucrative, owner Ness Aquino was open to suggestions. A Canadian

The Dead Boys hang out in front of the Mabuhay Gardens, 1977. (Photo by Chester Simpson.)

The Dead Kennedys performing at On Broadway, 1982. (Photo by Erich Muller.)

named Mary Monday persuaded him to book her band, the Britches, on a Monday night. Because tickets sold well, Aquino agreed when the Nuns asked to rent out the place in late 1976. That show sold out, and signaled the start of the all-punk/underground booking policy at the "Fab Mab," as it had become known. In the spring and summer of that year, bands like Devo, Blondie, the Dead Boys, the Ramones, and the Damned made their San Francisco debuts here.

The Mab gave local bands such as the Avengers, Negative Trend, and The Mutants a training ground and much needed exposure. And on July 19, 1978, the Dead Kennedys made their debut, after a week's rehearsal.

Booking agent Dirk Dirksen became the Bill Graham of the new San Francisco underground. He was widely mistrusted but he brought attention to the local scene and was willing to find booking slots for new bands. In the early '80s, Dirksen opened another club, **On Broadway**, in the theater upstairs from the Mab. He had had a falling-out with Aquino over his resistance to booking the then-popular hardcore bands.

⑧ The Matrix   *3138 Fillmore St.*

In August 1965, Marty Balin opened this club with partner Matthew Katz and formed a band that would play there regularly: the Jefferson Airplane. It was here that Grace Slick and her husband Jerry saw the band and decided to form their own group, the Great Society; Slick ended up replacing vocalist Signe Anderson in the Airplane in 1966. The cover of Jefferson Airplane's first album, "Surrealistic Pillow," was shot here. It's now a small bar called the Pierce St. Annex Drinking Establishment.

The Pit

This short-lived punk club was located south of Market in a residential warehouse called Project One, a so-called hippie artist commune. A promoter named Paul Backovitch, but more popularly known as "Rat," put on several shows here, including one legendary gig with KGB, the Mutants, and the Dead Kennedys. A new dance called "the Biafra" was born that night when audience members climbed on stage to copy Jello Biafra's moves. The crowds for the show brought community protests—and the end of punk at the Pit. The LP series *Rat Music For Rat People* documented the bands that played here and at a place called 330 Grove—and their offspring: the Dead Kennedys, the Avengers, Flipper, Black Flag, Butthole Surfers.

Rolling Stone's First Offices   *746 Brannan*

It was at this address, in a huge second-floor rent-free loft, that Jann Wenner assembled his first staff and the first issues of *Rolling Stone*—a pioneering counterculture magazine—up until the early '70s.

San Francisco Club of the Deaf Inc.   *530 Valencia St.*

Some of the most memorable San Francisco punk shows were held at this social club for the hearing impaired. The first was held on December 2, 1978 and featured the Offs and Mutants. The room, on the second floor, was dark, small, and smoky. It also was dangerous; one clubgoer recalls thinking "If there's a fire, I'm sure to die." But the venue was an immediate hit, and became known as the Deaf Club. All of the emerging local bands performed there, including the Units, Pearl Harbor and the Explosions, and the Humans, and L.A. bands like X, the Germs, and the Alley Cats also made visits.

In the summer of 1979, however, fire codes and maximum occupancy rules closed the Deaf Club to punk promoters. A compilation album called *Can You Hear Me?* was produced by Robert Hanrahan, the manager of the Offs and Dead Kennedys; he had found the space and booked the first gig.

Slim's   *333 11th St.*

Boz Scaggs owns this club—along with five partners. It's known for its food, drink, and top-notch booking. Rickie Lee Jones has described it as "the perfect atmosphere."

The Temple Beautiful   *1839 Geary St.*

This Jewish synagogue, which survived the 1906 earthquake, was used for rock shows in the early '70s, but its notoriety stemmed from a series of punk shows later that decade. On February 8, 1979, 1,500 punks descended on a benefit—featuring the Clash—for a nonprofit group called New Youth, who were raising money for a permanent punk clubhouse. (The clubhouse never materialized but a "punk directory" was published instead.) The Avengers' jam-packed farewell concert was also held here. Some San Franciscans claim that slam dancing was developed at this venue.

⑨ Winterland   *corner of Post and Steiner*

Before it was a famous rock palace, the Winterland was a skating rink. It became Bill Graham's main venue after he closed the Fillmore West in 1971. Winterland had more space and less atmosphere but it hosted a number of landmark shows: it was the site of the first and final performances of the Band. Martin Scorsese's *The Last Waltz* captured the legendary last show, which had guest appearances by Van Morrison, Neil Young, Bob Dylan, and Eric Clapton. A year and half later, on January 14, 1978, the Sex Pistols played their own swan song here, capping off an an absurdly eventful seven-city American tour. The Winterland closed at the end of 1978—after, of course, a series of triumphant shows, including performances by the Grateful Dead and Bruce Springsteen. The building was torn down in the early 1980s to make way for an apartment building.

Quicksilver Messenger Service performing at Winterland. (Photo by Jim Marshall.)

↳ DETOURS

THE BAY AREA

The Peninsula

The Morocco Room   *2010 South El Camino Real, San Mateo*

Two early '60s rock and roll bands, the Beau Brummels and the Vejitables, were both discovered by Tom Donahue and Bobby Mitchell while performing here. Sly Stone produced their hits.

Dana Morgan Music   *534 Bryant, Palo Alto*

This musical instruments store was the birthplace of the Warlocks, which soon evolved into the Grateful Dead. The first in the magical chain of events occurred on New Year's Eve of 1963. Bob Weir and a friend were wandering by this store when they heard Jerry Garcia inside playing the banjo, waiting for his banjo students to come by. Weir and friend introduced themselves, and convinced Garcia that his banjo students were probably not going to show up on New Year's Eve. Before long, the three musicians were deep into a lengthy jam session (using, of course, the instruments in the store). That night they decided to form a jug band.

Inspired by the Beatles, Weir and Garcia decided they wanted their jug band to become more of a rock and roll band. Pigpen, who worked at the store, was recruited to sing lead and play the harmonica. Bill Kreutzmann, who often visited the store, was asked to play drums. The son of the owner of the shop became the bass player. Now dubbed the Warlocks, the band practiced in a small room at the music shop.

Magoo's   *639 Santa Cruz Ave., Menlo Park*

Before hooking up with Ken Kesey and his acid tests, the Warlocks were regular attractions at this pizza parlor. When Dana Morgan, Jr., dropped out of the band because he couldn't keep up with its busy schedule, their new bassist walked right in. As Phil Lesh once recalled: "My friends and I took acid and went to see Garcia's band play . . . We came boppin' in there, and Pigpen ate my mind with the harp, singing the blues. They wouldn't let you dance, but I did anyway. We were so stoned!"

Alta Mesa Cemetery   *695 Arastradero Rd., Palo Alto*

Grateful Dead legend Ron McKernan—aka Pigpen—died in March 1973 at the age of 27. He's buried here under a marker that reads "Pigpen was and is now forever one of the Grateful Dead."

Berkeley   *12 miles east of San Francisco*

Beserkley Records   *1199 Spruce St.*

This independent record label, run by a fellow named Matthew King Kaufman, was home to such local faves as Earth Quake, Greg Kihn, the Rubinoos, and Jonathan Richman. Legend has it that Richman actually lived in the offices for two years.

Gilman Street Project   *924 Gilman St.*

This hall has been around since 1987, putting on impressive all-ages shows of all types. This is where Jello Biafra first saw the Beatnigs play;

he then signed them to his Alternative Tentacles label. Gilman Street's main rival in the hardcore days was a place called the Farm.

Keystone Berkeley   *2119 University Ave.*

In the 1970s, this was a regular showcase for Tower of Power, Mike Bloomfield, and Jerry Garcia's offshoot groups.

The Longbranch   *2504 San Pablo Ave.*

Before it closed in 1977, Eddie Money and Earth Quake had been mainstays of this well-loved club.

UC Berkeley

Its famous rock and roll attendees include drummer/composer Stewart Copeland and Greil Marcus, who began writing about music while a political science major here.

Greek Theatre

In 1978, Chet Helms staged "The Tribal Stomp," a Family Dog reunion featuring Country Joe and the Fish, the Butterfield Blues Band, Canned Heat, and Big Brother. It was also the site—in September 1982—of the Doobie Brothers' last show. The Bread and Roses Festivals have been a tradition here since the 1970s.

Oakland   *10 miles east of San Francisco across the S.F.-Oakland Bay Bridge*

This city's impressive list of homegrown R&B and rap artists includes Tower of Power, Larry Graham, the Pointer Sisters, Digital Underground, Hammer, Pebbles, Sheila E., and Tony! Toni! Tone!

Oakland Coliseum

Entrepreneur/dancer/rapper Hammer was an eleven-year-old named Stanley Kirk Burrell when he became a bat boy at this stadium. He was a fixture of the ballpark throughout his teens, and got his nickname from his resemblance to Hank Aaron. Hefty loans from two of the players helped him start his first record company.

Sausalito   *8 miles north of San Francisco*

This town, reachable by ferry or bridge from San Francisco, has several pop music claims to fame. During his engagement at the Fillmore West, Otis Redding stayed on a houseboat here and wrote "(Sittin' On) The Dock Of The Bay," his last song and biggest hit. John Cipollina and his beatnik housemates from Quicksilver Messenger Service lived here before they recorded their first album. And the **Record Plant** recording studio (2200 Bridgeway) has been used by many neighborhood stars, including Sly Stone, John Fogerty, and Huey Lewis. It got off to a good start on Halloween night 1972, when John Lennon and Yoko Ono came to the Plant's opening party in tree costumes.

Mill Valley   *20 miles north of San Francisco*

The Sweetwater   *153 Throckmorton Ave.*

Since the early '70s, this club has been the area's prime gathering point for its famous musicians. Different configurations of the Dead and the Airplane have played here, and jam sessions have featured the likes of

Village Music of Mill Valley. (Photo by Mush Emmons.)

Van Morrison, Elvis Costello, Huey Lewis. Note: this sort of activity is usually kept private, i.e. no paying customers allowed.

Village Music   *9 East Blithedale*
This world-famous, memorabilia-crammed record store has been around since 1970, catering to famous residents nearby and to their fans.

Altamont Speedway   *40 miles SE of San Francisco; on Interstate 589 between Livermore and Tracy*

The "festival" put on here in December 1969 stands today as one of rock and roll's most disastrous moments. At the end of their triumphant 1969 American tour, the Rolling Stones scheduled a free concert for the Bay Area. Although its location was changed several times, about 300,000 gathered at this site, which proved to be terribly inadequate in size and facilities. "Security" was provided by the Hell's Angels, who knifed one young black man in full view of a camera. The nightmarish festival—and all of the events surrounding it—was captured in the 1970 documentary, *Gimme Shelter*, produced and directed by the princes of cinema verité, the Maysles brothers, with Charlotte Zwerin.

Monterey   *140 miles south of San Francisco*

The Monterey Pop Festival was the first of the great rock and roll festivals. In mid-June 1967, thousands of people converged on the town's fairgrounds and heard the top pop and rock artists of the day—Simon and

Garfunkel, the Grateful Dead, the Byrds, Otis Redding—as well as a number of acts that would soon be superstars: Jimi Hendrix and Janis Joplin, to name two.

The three-day event was engineered by John Phillips (of the Mamas and the Papas) and Lou Adler, then the president of Dunhill Records. They were based in Los Angeles but were well aware of the revolutions taking place in San Francisco; seven of the city's best bands made appearances. Phillips even composed a tune for the occasion, "San Francisco (Be Sure to Wear Flowers in Your Hair)".

Along with landmark performances by the Who, the Jimi Hendrix Experience (their U.S. debut) and Otis Redding, Monterey also featured drugs, many of them courtesy of the infamous druggist, Augustus Owsley Stanley. As one festival participant told *Rolling Stone*, "Owsley and his people had big gallon jars full of purple pills. People were invited to take handfuls."

The event raised $250,000 for charity and spawned countless rock and roll festivals, none of which matched Monterey for the music produced or the sense of community fostered. The town of Monterey remains the site of an annual jazz festival, the oldest continous one in the nation.

Salt Lake City, UT   *750 miles NE of San Francisco*

This bastion of Mormonism has never claimed to be a breeding ground for rock and roll. Nor should it; the Osmonds are Utah's biggest pop stars, and they're originally from Ogden. Nevertheless, the city has more rock history to its name than the tragic 1991 AC/DC concert, during which several fans were crushed to death.

The Shilo Inn   *206 SW Temple, formerly the Royal Inn*

Greg Lake of Emerson, Lake, and Palmer was arrested here for swimming naked in the pool.

The Zephyr Club   *301 SW Temple*

Run by a fellow named Sam Callis, the Zephyr is considered to be the best nightclub in the area. It books a mix of local acts and touring blues and rock bands.

Denver, CO   *1,234 miles NE of San Francisco*

Though no real superstars have emerged from this city—John Denver (aka John Henry Deutschendorf) made Aspen his home—it does have an active live music scene. The top bands today include Big Head Todd and the Monsters, the Fluid, the Samples, and the Subdudes. Denver has also been the site of several landmark concerts, including the U.S. debut of Led Zeppelin.

Herman's Hideaway   *1578 South Broadway*

The Subdudes and Big Head Todd and the Monsters are the top local bands to emerge from this long-standing nightclub. The Hideaway's competitors include the **Mercury Cafe** (2199 California St.) and the **Garage** (2301 Blake St.).

Red Rocks Amphitheatre, outside of Denver. (Photo by Jim Krebs.)

Red Rocks Amphitheatre   *South of Interstate 70, Morrison*
This gorgeous open-air amphitheater, built in 1941, has staged memorable shows by the likes of the Grateful Dead, Neil Young, and Stevie Ray Vaughan. (When the Beatles played here in 1964, they had to halt their 35-minute set a few times because of the effects of the altitude.) Its most famous concert took place in June 1983 in the pouring rain, when U2 came to town. The Irish band had planned to film the show. The only problem was, as guitarist Edge once explained, "the day we were doing it, it was pissing with rain and had been for two days. So we had a choice—we either cut our losses and move to a nearby indoor stadium, or we take a chance and just do it in the rain." Fortunately, they stayed. The video, "Live At Red Rocks—Under A Blood Red Sky" was released the next year, to much acclaim.

LOS ANGELES

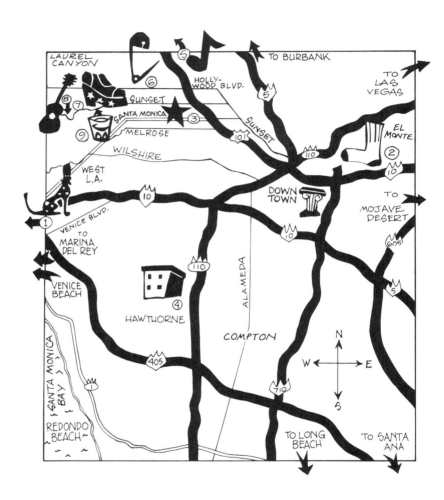

This sprawling metropolis rivals any other American city for rock and roll landmarks. Starting with the early doo-wop hits by the Platters and the Coasters, L.A.'s pop music history is as long as it is deep, ranging from the relentlessly upbeat surf music of Jan and Dean and the Beach Boys to the brutal strain of hip-hop called "gangsta rap."

Each era had its own favored nightclubs, studios, and hangouts, but L.A.'s Sunset Strip in the mid-'60s is often celebrated as the most exciting scene of all. The Byrds' sudden success with "Mr. Tambourine Man" gave rise to a new type of pop music—folk rock—and the Mamas and the Papas, Sonny and Cher, and the Turtles quickly followed. By 1966, clubs like the Whisky-A-Go-Go, the Trip, and the Cheetah were packed with teenage music fans and aspiring musicians of all stripes. Legendary bands like the Buffalo Springfield, the Doors, Love, and Frank Zappa's Mothers of Invention all got their start here. "It was a twenty-four-hour party," recalls one nostalgic participant.

In the next decades, Los Angeles nurtured both the singer/songwriter movement (*see* **The Troubadour**) and its antithesis, the punk-rock explosion (*see* **The Masque**). Kids in the surrounding suburbs then created hardcore, a more violent, alienated strain of punk rock. (The local police force became infamous for its harsh treatment of both the fans and the bands in the early '80s; matters had not improved since the infamous Sunset Strip "riots" in 1966.)

These days, while gangsta rappers such as Ice-T, Eazy-E, Yo Yo, and N.W.A. work out of Compton and South Central L.A., the Sunset Strip is dominated by hard rock clubs like Gazzarri's and the Troubadour, where bands such as Poison made their reputations. The Cathouse, another hard rock landmark, has launched bands such as Guns N' Roses and Warrant. Meanwhile, rock bands as varied as Mary's Danish, Concrete Blonde, Hole, and Rage Against the Machine play around town—at a variety of clubs rather than one particular spot.

Bel Air

This exclusive neighborhood is home to many pop music moguls, including Berry Gordy. The Beatles also stayed here—at 356 St. Pierre Road—in August 1964, when the Ambassador Hotel canceled their reservation. Hotel officials wisely feared an onslaught of Beatlemaniacs. In 1965, the group stayed at 2850 Benedict Canyon.

The Beyond Baroque Foundation   *681 Venice Blvd., Venice*

Since 1968, this establishment has hosted Friday night poetry readings and Wednesday night workshops. John Doe and Exene Cervenka met here in 1977, and soon formed the band X.

The Canterbury   *1746 Cherokee, Hollywood*

In the late '70s, members of the Germs, the Extremes, the Weirdos, the Bags, and the Screamers all made this run-down, infested building their home. It was run by a Rastafarian "minister," who probably didn't approve of all the heroin use going on.

Capitol Records   *1750 North Vine, Hollywood*

This rock and roll landmark which looks like a stack of records, has had a big effect on some aspiring stars. Native Texan Don Henley, for instance, once recalled driving into town for the first time: "I had never

seen the Capitol Records tower—I was freaking out. It was like there
was this big metal and concrete symbol of the record industry. I had so
many Capitol records when I was a kid—45s, you know, when they had
that purple label with the Capitol dome. I believe the writing was in
silver. It was a manifestation of all my childhood records. I was awe-
struck."

The Cathouse   *836 North Highland, Hollywood*
This sleazy hard-rock hangout opened in October 1986, and almost every
L.A. band in the genre has performed here. Founded by Taime Downe
and Riki Rachtman (an MTV veejay since the late '80s), the club has been
proud of its female clientele, whose get-ups consist of ripped fishnets,
metal-studded bustiers, garter belts and other bits of lingerie. As one
owner has said, "We have this policy of never really leaving the air
conditioning on too long so it gets really hot, so they show a lot of flesh
here." Rachtman also runs a Thursday night club called the **Bordello**
(7969 Santa Monica, West Hollywood). The Cathouse was featured in
Penelope Spheeris's documentary, *The Decline of Western Civilization,
Part II.*

Central Avenue
In the late '40s and early '50s, this street was filled with clubs and tiny
juke joints. Louis Jordan was a regular here, as was Johnny Otis, who led
the house band at the Club Alabam. Right next door was the **Dunbar
Hotel** (4225 South Central), which catered to all of the major black figures
of the day, from Duke Ellington and Ella Fitzgerald to Paul Robeson and
W.E.B. DuBois.

Chateau Marmont Hotel   *8221 Sunset Blvd., Hollywood*
A favorite of music and movie makers. John Belushi died in bungalow 3,
and Barry Mann and Cynthia Weil wrote "You've Lost That Lovin' Fee-
lin' " in room 2H.

❶ The Cheetah   *at the foot of the old Pacific Ocean Park pier, Venice*
This was one of the top nightspots in the late '60s. It was housed in the
huge old Aragon Ballroom, and though its light show was substandard,
it attracted crowds on weekends. The Paul Butterfield Blues Band, Love,
Jefferson Airplane, and the Doors were some of the acts featured. (Ray
Manzarek remembers one Doors concert here as "a transcendental moment. The music attained its proper place.") It has since been torn down
and replaced by condominiums.

Club 88   *11784 Pico, West Los Angeles*
In the 1980s, this was the West Coast equivalent of CBGBs: It was
dilapidated and booked good bands on their way up. The Go-Gos, the
Bangles, the Blasters, and X are a few of the groups that played here.

The Cheetah. (Courtesy of the Department of Special Collections, University Research Library, UCLA.)

Club Lingerie   *6507 Sunset Blvd., Hollywood*
This venue has had many incarnations. It was the KRLA Teen Night Club in 1960 and the Red Velvet throughout the '60s, featuring acts like the Kinks, Sonny and Cher, and the Righteous Brothers. In the '70s, when Motown's offices were nearby at 6255 Sunset, Stevie Wonder and others hung out here. Since the early 1980s, the site has been booked by former Masque man, Brendan Mullen; he's brought in everything from "the first hip-hop event west of the Rockies" to bands like the Cramps and the Replacements to jazz and blues acts.

Continental Hyatt House   *8401 Sunset Blvd., West Hollywood*
This hotel was nicknamed "the Riot House" by touring rock stars who had fairly free reign here in the '70s. Led Zeppelin and Keith Moon

were the most notorious players. (Some locals claim that Zeppelin was required to put down a $50,000 deposit each time they stayed there.) It's now called Hyatt on Sunset.

East L.A.

This Chicano section of L.A.—broadly speaking, the area east of Indiana Street—has nurtured doo-wop groups (Ruben and the Jets), a rock and roll pioneer (Ritchie Valens) and roots rockers (most notably Los Lobos). Whittier has long been the main drag, suitable for cruising on weekend nights, and it was immortalized by Thee Midnighters' 1964 hit, "Whittier Boulevard." One of the top venues in the '60s was the **Montebello Ballroom**, on Atlantic Boulevard, in Montebello. It featured Chicano and soul acts, including the Jaguars, Li'l Julian, and the Johnsons Three Plus One (later called the Brothers Johnson). On Atlantic and Whittier stands the **Golden Gate Theater**, which also presented the area's top bands.

Elks Lodge   *607 South Parkview*

A major punk rock benefit was held for the Masque in February 1978. It lasted for two days and featured the Dickies, Weirdos, Flesheaters, X, and half a dozen others. The event ended in a food fight, and raised $4,500. The following year, at an Alleycats/Plugz/Go-Gos show, the first major confrontation between the police and punks occurred here. Near the end of the show, cops marched into the lodge in full riot gear, looked around, and then marched out. Then, without warning, they charged back inside, swinging nightsticks at bewildered punks and touching off a small riot. The victims of what became known as the St. Patrick's Day Massacre retreated to the old Masque for treatment and commiseration. From then on, the police presence at concerts became increasingly heavy, especially at hardcore shows. The Elks Lodge later became an "event club" called Power Tools, and then The Scream, a rather wild dance club. It is now the Park Plaza Hotel.

② El Monte Legion Stadium   *11151 Valley Blvd., El Monte*

This big pink building was the top dance hall for the Hispanic community in the late '50s and early '60s. Johnny Otis put on shows here, including one that introduced Li'l Julian Herrera to the scene. Herrera's "Lonely Lonely Nights" became a big local hit. The kids here developed dances such as the Pachuco Hop, the Hully Gully, and the Corrido Rock, sort of an early version of slam-dancing. Big stars like James Brown, Chuck Berry, and Fats Domino also packed the place with teenagers. A post office replaced the stadium in 1974.

Gazzarri's   *9039 Sunset Blvd., West Hollywood*

Bill Gazzarri opened this club in the mid-'60s and presented quintessential L.A. acts like the Byrds and the Buffalo Springfield. In the early '80s, this was one of the glam-rock palaces: the musicians in leather and heavy makeup were nearly as pretty as the barely dressed females in the audience. Mr. Gazzarri's sleazy dance contests are featured in Penelope Sheeris's *The Decline of Western Civilization, Part II.*

Marvin Gaye's Last Home   *2101 South Gramercy*
On April 1, 1984—one day before his forty-fifth birthday—the great soul singer Marvin Gaye was shot here by his father, Marvin Gay, Sr. The two had been having one of their countless arguments, and Gaye's father claimed self-defense.

❸ Gold Star Recording Studios   *6252 Santa Monica, Hollywood*
Los Angeles studios have produced as many hit songs as any other city's, and Gold Star is the most famous facility of all. Producer Phil Spector created his famed "Wall of Sound" here—and with it such richly textured hit singles as "He's A Rebel," "Da Doo Ron Ron," "Be My Baby," and "River Deep, Mountain High." With the aid of engineer Larry Levine, arranger Jack Nitzsche, and the virtuosic West Coast session players, Spector lavished huge amounts of time and money on any given single ("River Deep, Mountain High" cost the then-staggering sum of $20,000), and proved that even in rock and roll, the producer could be far more important than the artist. His "Wall of Sound" method included a crowded room of musicians (up to 25 players, including two rhythm sections) and the greatest echo chambers in the world—concrete rectangles about three feet high and four feet wide. Gold Star had its share of non-Spector hits as well, starting with such early classics as "Summertime Blues" by Eddie Cochran and "Tequila" by the Champs and moving on to the Beach Boys' *Pet Sounds* and Iron Butterfly's *In-A-Gadda-Da-Vida*. Sold in the mid-'80s, the property is now a minimall.

❹ Hacienda Motel   *9137 South Figueroa St.*
Sam Cooke was the country's top soul star when he was fatally shot here on December 10, 1964. As the story goes, Cooke had picked up a woman at a nightclub and brought her back to his room. She ran out for some reason and he ran after her, bursting in on the motel's manager, who shot him out of fear.

❺ The Hollywood Bowl   *Highland Ave. and Cahuenga Terrace, Hollywood*
This outdoor arena has witnessed many legendary shows. The Beatles' 1964 and 1965 concerts here were recorded for a live album. Another highlight was Jimi Hendrix's opening show for the Monkees in 1967. Since then, acts such as Elton John, Bob Dylan, and Santana, have all played here.

Hong Kong Cafe   *425 Gin Ling Way*
From the summer of 1979 to the end of 1980, this club was a hotbed of imaginative punk and art bands. It started booking bands after Madame Wong's banned the more volatile new bands from its stage. The ensuing rivalry between the two clubs was dubbed the Won Ton Wars, but both

The Hong Kong, 1980. (Photo by Al Flipside.)

did well for several years. Among the bands that started out here are the Human Hands and Nervous Gender (which featured Phranc, the self-described "Jewish lesbian folksinger").

The Landmark Motel   *7047 Franklin, Hollywood*
Now called the Highland Gardens Hotel, this was the site of Janis Joplin's heroin overdose on October 3, 1970. She died in room 105.

Eugene Landy Offices   *8383 Wilshire Blvd.*
In search of someone who could get her husband, Brian Wilson, out of bed and into the real world, Marilyn Wilson visited these offices in 1975. At the time, the Beach Boy weighed about 240 pounds and had some serious drug problems. Landy, a psychologist, was happy to oblige. He took complete control of Brian Wilson's life, making sure he got paid for this effort. (By the next year, monthly fees—including charges for additional staff—had escalated to $20,000.) Over the next decade and a half there were fallings out between the two. And others have tried to intervene, claiming that Landy has brainwashed Wilson. But Landy and Wilson always seem to reconcile. Most recently, Wilson dedicated his autobiography, *Wouldn't It Be Nice*, to the doctor.

Laurel Canyon

In his *Song Cycles* album, Van Dyke Parks called Laurel Canyon "the seat of the beat." In the '60s, this was certainly the area for hip pop stars and rock and rollers.

Carole King House   *8815 Appian Way*

The New York–born songwriter moved here in the late '60s, after her divorce from Gerry Goffin, her songwriting partner. She lived here while recording *Tapestry*, at one time the best selling album in history.

Joni Mitchell House   *Lookout Mountain Rd.*

Graham Nash wrote "Our House" while living here with Ms. Mitchell, who wrote *Clouds* and *Ladies of the Canyon* while here.

Frank Zappa House   *NW corner of Laurel Canyon and Lookout Mountain*

The famous Tom Mix log cabin has since burned down, but from 1966 to 1968 it was the residence of Frank Zappa.

The London Fog   *8909 Sunset Blvd., West Hollywood*

The Doors had their first club date here in December 1965. After they passed an audition (which was packed with UCLA friends), they were contracted to do four sets a night for six days a week. They were paid $5 each on weekdays, $10 on weekends. This difficult schedule continued for four months, allowing them to work on their songs and stage manner (Morrison lost his reserve), but not gaining them much of a following from the sailors, pimps, and hookers that frequented the Fog. In the summer of 1965, they were asked to be the house band at the Whisky-A-Go-Go down the block, and they went. The club has since been transformed into Duke's Coffee Shop.

Madame Wong's   *949 Sun Mun Way*

After the Masque was closed down, the L.A. punk scene moved north, to Chinatown—initally to this restaurant. Esther Wong was convinced to allow a few power pop bands such as 20/20 and the Zippers onto her bamboo-festooned stage. Those shows went well, but gradually the groups and the crowd grew more threatening, and Wong threw them out. Punk rock moved over to the Hong Kong Cafe, and power pop reigned supreme here. In 1979, **Madame Wong's West** was opened in Santa Monica (2900 Wilshire); the original was closed four years later.

Maharishi's Meditation Center   *3465 West Sixth St.*

This is the mid-'60s hotspot where John Densmore, Robbie Krieger, and Ray Manzarek all met.

❻ The Masque   *Cherokee and Hollywood Blvd., Hollywood*

This legendary club, located in the basement of the Hollywood Center building, was the first real gathering spot for L.A.'s punk rock community—musicians, artists, and fans, several of whom started up fanzines to chronicle the scene.

The site was initially opened as rehearsal spaces by a transplanted

Scotsman named Brendan Mullen. After a few BYO parties—featuring bands like the Controllers and the Skulls—Mullen discovered he had a rock and roll club on his hands. Fans would pack the place, even after he started charging admission, for early shows by X, the Germs, the Skulls, the Screamers, Wall of Voodoo, Needles and Pins, and the Go-Go's. Mullen remembers his initial refusal to let the Germs onstage—he had heard that they were terrible musicians and that they threw food around. Undaunted, the Germs snuck in and used other people's equipment, and Mullen was won over.

Mullen recently had this to say of the Masque: "It was about one hundred children from totally dismembered families stalking a creepy Hollywood basement during a five-minute hallucinatory funhouse-in-hell of self-mutilated anti-beauty."

Unfortunately, the Masque didn't have the requisite fire exits and permits, and police closed it down in January 1978. After a benefit for

Arthur J. and the Gold Cups—the Masque's house band—featuring Geza X on guitar, Pat Delaney on alto sax, Marc Moreland on guitar, and Brendan Mullen on drums. (Photo by Gabi.)

the Masque (*see* **Elks Lodge**), Mullen and Slash Records' Bob Biggs opened "the Other Masque" at Santa Monica and Vine. It flourished for several months but closed in mid-'79. Mullen then promoted punk shows all over town; he now books Club Lingerie.

McCabe's Guitar Shop   *3101 Pico Blvd., Santa Monica*
This has been a top acoustic music venue for over two decades. It's an intimate place—seating about one hundred—but luminaries like Jackson Browne, Tom Waits, and Linda Ronstadt showed up in the '70s and bands like fIREHOSE, R.E.M., and Dream Syndicate have played here more recently.

The Music Machine   *12220 Pico Blvd., West Los Angeles*
For most of the '80s, this club booked all sorts of music, especially rockabilly and roots music. Clifton Chenier, Los Lobos, Otis Rush, and Bo Diddley have all played here, as have X, Jane's Addiction, and the Violent Femmes. It's also featured hard rock: On one memorable night, the rivalry between the glam crowd and the underground sleazy types came to a head when a fight broke out between members of Guns N' Roses and Poison.

NBC Studios   *3000 West Alameda Ave., Burbank*
Elvis's famous 1968 Christmas special, sponsored by the Singer sewing-machine company, was filmed here. The highlight of the show was his deceptively low-key jam session with old Memphis bandmates Scotty Moore, Charlie Hodge, Alan Fortas, and D.J. Fontana. It reminded the world of his charmed musical roots and charisma. The audience, oddly enough, was drawn from a nearby hamburger stand because Col. Parker hadn't given out the tickets he had demanded. But that apparently didn't faze Presley, who hadn't performed in front of a live audience in seven years. Less entrancing were the special's production numbers, including a hokey tale of the King's journey from country boy to superstar. From here, Elvis kept up his comeback attempt with mesmerizing shows in Las Vegas.

The Palomino   *6907 Lankershim, North Hollywood*
From the '50s through the '80s, this club was L.A.'s best country music showcase. In the last decade, it's been the center of a new circle of country singers like Jim Lauderdale, Dwight Yoakam, Divine Horsemen, and Candye Kane. And the booking policy was widened to include bands like Junkyard and the Red Hot Chili Peppers.

Pandora's Box   *Sunset Blvd. and Crescent Heights, West Hollywood*
It's been replaced with a scenic traffic island, but in the mid-'60s it was a popular teenage nightclub. DJ Jimmy O'Neill ran it and booked bands like Love and the Beach Boys. The house band included Leon Russell and David Gates. It was closed and torn down soon after the 1966 Sunset

Teens get ready to riot in front of Pandora's Box. (Courtesy of the Department of Special Collections, University Research Library, UCLA.)

Strip riots, which were sparked off when the L.A.P.D. started enforcing curfew violations. The Buffalo Springfield song, "For What It's Worth," was inspired by the riots.

The Rainbow Bar & Grill   *9015 Sunset Blvd., West Hollywood*
This hangout, strategically placed next to the Roxy, was opened in the early '70s by a bunch of music execs. It's since been overrun by musicians and groupies—most recently, of the hard-rock variety. Anthony Kiedis of the Red Hot Chili Peppers cruised for chicks here as a preteen. The Rainbow's interior can be seen in the Guns N' Roses video of "November Rain."

Rodney Bingenheimer's English Disco   *7561 Sunset Blvd., Hollywood*

This early-'70s glitter-rock, multi-mirrored hangout was run by an L.A. fixture who had been deemed "Mayor of Sunset Strip" by Sal Mineo. It featured live music on special occasions—a Sean Cassidy/Iggy Pop double bill, for instance. Otherwise, it was a gathering spot for folks like David Bowie, Queen, Suzi Quatro, Marc Bolan of T. Rex and their assorted underage groupies. (Joan Jett started visiting when she was 13.) As Kim Fowley recently told Lance Loud, "In 1972, David Bowie was Jesus Christ and Rodney's was the Sistine Chapel." At the end of the '70s, Bingenheimer hosted a new wave show on the influential KROQ radio station, later turning out a series of compilations ("Rodney on the ROQ"). Although he was the first in the area to broadcast bands like the Ramones and Blondie, some local punks despised him: witness the Angry Samoans' "Get Off The Air."

❼ The Roxy   *9009 Sunset Blvd., West Hollywood*

Founded by four music-biz honchos including Elmer Valentine and Lou Adler, this was L.A.'s top showcase club in the '70s, often featuring big names such as David Bowie and Bruce Springsteen. Its most famous show may have been Bob Marley and the Wailers' performance on May 26, 1976. The audience was filled with stars, including Robbie Robertson, Bob Dylan, John Bonham, Carole King, and even Warren Beatty. The show apparently stunned everyone, and the twenty-minute encore medley ("Get Up, Stand Up," "No More Trouble," and "War") was reggae bliss.

Another, quite different, performance also stands out. In 1979, the Germs performed here and lead singer Bobby Pyn (born Paul Beahm, later known as Darby Crash) threw peanut butter at horrified members of the audience.

After a short stint as a theater, the club is now rented out to independent promoters.

Sound City Studio   *15456 Cabrito Rd., Van Nuys*

This studio has witnessed some historic partnerships. In 1968, Beach Boy Dennis Wilson helped a charismatic young man named Charles Manson record some demos. For some reason, Manson never got a contract. Six years later, Mick Fleetwood was in the studio and heard a tape that Lindsay Buckingham and Stevie Nicks had just made. He promptly recruited the duo into Fleetwood Mac and superstardom. And in 1991, Nirvana and Butch Vig teamed up to record *Nevermind* here.

The Starwood   *NW corner of Crescent Heights and Santa Monica Blvd., West Hollywood*

This revered '70s nightspot started out as PJ's in the '60s; the Standells, of "Dirty Water" fame, played here regularly, as did Trini Lopez. The next decade saw performances by everyone from Bachman-Turner Overdrive and Quiet Riot to Devo and Peter Tosh. Van Halen was seen here by Warner Brothers staff producer Ted Templeman in 1976, and they were soon signed to the label. In early 1981, the club attracted the L.A. punks with Tuesday-night performances by bands like Fear and Black Flag. The Germs played their last show here, before Darby Crash killed himself. But legal troubles forced the club to close in 1981, and it's since been converted into a mall.

Tropicana Motel   *8585 Santa Monica Blvd., West Hollywood*
This was a favorite crash pad for rock stars, from the decadent days of Jim Morrison to the time it was demolished in 1988. Morrison stayed there when rooms were $10 a night, and folks like the Clash, Iggy Pop, the Ramones, and Bruce Springsteen all followed his lead. Tom Waits, Rickie Lee Jones, and Chuck E. Weiss were regulars in the early '80s.

⑧ The Troubadour   *9081 Santa Monica Blvd., West Hollywood*
In the early '60s, the club was a hangout for the bohemian folk scene; performers like Odetta, Phil Ochs, and Peter, Paul and Mary played acoustic sets here. The club's Hootenannies, or Hoot Nights, served as open auditions for musicians—it's also how Roger McGuinn met David Crosby. But it wasn't until 1967 that owner Doug Weston allowed rock and roll into the Troubadour. The first amplified band was the Buffalo Springfield, then came the Byrds, the Nitty Gritty Dirt Band, and Poco. But the most influential trend generated here was that of the sensitive, self-conscious singer/songwriter. Would-be genius types like Joni Mitchell, Jackson Browne, and Neil Young gathered here, initially at Hoot Nights and then gradually as headliners. Members of the Eagles hung out here, and eventually got together as Linda Ronstadt's backing band.

There have been other landmark events: In August 1970, Elton John made his world-shaking U.S. debut here, astounding sold-out audiences with his frenzied staged antics (like playing the piano with his feet in the air). In 1974, John Lennon got drunk on brandy alexanders here and heckled a Smothers Brothers performance. He was physically removed from the club. And a huge number of L.A. power-pop bands were signed after the Knack was signed out of here in 1978. The Knack and almost all of the rest rapidly faded into obscurity.

L.A.'s punk rock bands were not welcome here. After the Bags played a set, during which tables were overturned, the Troubadour's waitresses signed a petition against the genre and its violent purveyors. In the 1980s, Weston switched the club over to a hard-rock format; it was instrumental in the signing of Guns N' Roses. Geffen A&R man Tom Zutaut once recalled the night he saw the band there: "Axl Rose was the most charismatic, electrifying performer I'd ever seen. The musicians were amazing . . . Everything about the band was right." He walked out after two songs, hiding his enthusiasm for the band from other music execs, and offered them a contract the next day.

Venice Beach

This hippie/bohemian spot has been the site of several key meetings in rock and roll history. In July 1965, Ray Manzarek ran into Jim Morrison, whom he had vaguely known at UCLA film school. Sitting on the beach talking, Morrison sang something he'd written called "Moonlight Drive." Manzarek loved the lyrics, and they soon decided to, in Manzarek's words, "get together and make a million dollars." In the summer of 1981, two Texans named Gibby Haynes and Paul Leary were selling Son of Sam silk-screened T-shirts here and met a fellow named Bruce Licher, who turned them on to music like Black Flag, X, and the Circle Jerks. They formed the Butthole Surfers soon after. The '80s hardcore band Suicidal Tendencies was also formed from this locale.

The Whisky-A-Go-Go, circa 1964. (Courtesy of the Department of Special Collections, University Research Library, UCLA.)

⑨ The Whisky-A-Go-Go   *8901 Sunset Blvd., West Hollywood*
This club opened in 1964, taking over the site of a converted bank. The Whisky has since booked everything from Johnny Rivers (who played the first show) to hardcore and heavy metal. It's also been the site of frequent police harassment—most notably during the infamous Sunset Strip riots of 1966 and fifteen years later when the hardcore bands took hold.

The Whisky first gained notice when its female DJ started dancing during Johnny Rivers's set. She was suspended in a cage at the right of the stage, and the audience assumed it was part of the act. The "go-go girl" was born. The Whisky's bookers had a knack for choosing house bands; the Buffalo Springfield, the Doors, and Chicago are just the most prominent. It also brought in upcoming acts like the Who, Otis Redding, Led Zeppelin, and Elvis Costello (in his L.A. debut). Probably the most infamous performance here was by the Doors. After a four-month run, the band performed an incendiary version of "The End," and got themselves kicked out of the place. But by then, they had been signed to Elektra Records and been booked around the country.

Punk and hardcore bands were booked here in the early '80s. One good night, July 4, 1982, featured the Dead Kennedys, TSOL, and the club debut of the Butthole Surfers. But hardcore groups were effectively banned after a series of police-punk confrontations involving the L.A.P.D.'s army of helicopters and squad cars. These days the Whisky mainly books hard-rock bands.

Dennis Wilson Death Site   *13929 Bellagio Way, Basin C-1100, Marina Del Rey*
On December 28, 1982, Beach Boy Dennis Wilson fell overboard here and drowned.

🚶 Schools

Antelope Valley High School   *44900 Division Street, Lancaster*
Frank Zappa was a student here when he met Don Van Vliet (aka Captain Beefheart) and formed his first band, the Black Outs.

Fairfax High School   *7850 Melrose Ave.*
The city's top rock and roll high school, Fairfax counts as alumni Phil Spector, Jerry Leiber, Herb Alpert, three members of the Red Hot Chili Peppers, and Slash of Guns N' Roses.

Hale Junior High School   *23830 Califa St., Woodland Hills*
Five of the six original members of Fishbone first met on the daily bus ride from South Central L.A. to this predominantly white school in San Fernando Valley. The sixth lived in the Valley already.

Hawthorne High   *El Segundo and Inglewood, Hawthorne*
The alma mater of the Wilson brothers and Al Jardine of the Beach Boys, as well as the MacDonald Brothers of Redd Kross, and Greg Hetson of Circle Jerks and Bad Religion.

Pacoima Junior High School   *9919 Laurel Canyon Blvd.*
Ritchie Valens built an electric guitar in this school's wood shop while
he was a student. He used it to record his first hits, including "La Bamba."

Taft High School   *5461 Winnetka Ave., Woodland Hills*
The alma mater of, among others, Joan Jett, Jane Wiedlin (of the Go-
Go's), and Ice Cube.

UCLA

The alma mater of many rock and rollers. Jim Morrison and Ray Manzarek met in film school here.

Royce Hall

The Doors gave their first performance here—improvising a soundtrack
for one of Ray Manzarek's film projects. Robbie Krieger played guitar,
Manzarek played the flute, and John Densmore, Morrison, and some
young women worked with rattles, tambourines, and drums. They then
moved on to a club date at the London Fog.

Utility Tunnels

When Bruce Licher was an art student here in 1980, he had the bright
idea of making a film in the dark tunnels underneath the university. He
then realized it was a good space for music making, and soon the pioneering noise band Savage Republic was born. "The temperature was about
110 degrees, so we'd go down for about forty minutes at a time. The song
"Procession" grew out of a session when the percussionist was sitting at
the juncture of two tunnels and the two guitar players each started walk-
ing away down the tunnels."

USC

Young M.C. (aka Marvin Young) was still a student majoring in business
here when he co-wrote Tone Lōc's "Wild Thing," the biggest hit of 1989.

☠ Famous Graves in the Los Angeles Area

Roy Brown   *Eternal Valley Memorial Park, Newhall*
Johnny and Dorsey Burnette, Sam Cooke   *Forest Lawn Cemetery, Glendale*
Eddie Cochran, Karen Carpenter   *Forest Lawn, Cypress*
Darby Crash   *Holy Cross Cemetery, 5835 Slauson, Culver City*
Pee Wee Crayton, Big Mama Thornton   *Inglewood Park Cemetery, 720 East Flor-
ence, Inglewood*
Roy Orbison   *Pierce Brothers Cemetery, 1218 Glendon, Westwood*
Esther Phillips   *Forest Lawn Hollywood Hills, Burbank*
Randy Rhoads   *Mountain View Cemetery, Highland and Waterman, San Bernardino*
Minnie Riperton   *Pierce Brothers Cemetery, 1218 Glendon, Westwood*
Big Joe Turner   *Roosevelt Memorial Park, Gardena*
Ritchie Valens   *San Fernando Mission Cemetery, San Fernando*

↳ DETOURS

SOUTH BAY/LONG BEACH

Hawthorne
Beach Boys Home *3701 West 119th St.*
> The Wilson family, starring Brian, Carl, and Dennis, moved here in 1945 and stayed until the Beach Boys hit it big in the early '60s. From most accounts, the Wilson kids had traumatic childhoods; father Wilson, an aspiring songwriter, was the prime tormentor. But it was here that the boys honed their harmonies and wrote their first classic songs, including "My Room."

Long Beach
Long Beach Auditorium *Long Beach Blvd. and Ocean Blvd.*
> The Beach Boys made their first successful live appearance here on December 31, 1961. (Two nights before, they had opened for Dick Dale at a nearby ballroom, and had bombed.) The occasion was a Ritchie Valens Memorial dance, and the boys performed three songs, including their first single, a local hit called "Surfin'."

Redondo Beach
The Bel Air Club *312 Catalina*
> Along with the Rendezvous Ballroom in Costa Mesa, this was an early home of surf music. An instrumental group called the Bel Airs played here regularly after their song, "Mr. Moto," became a local hit.

The Fleetwood *300 North Harbor Dr.*
> In the early '80s, this was one of the key venues for hardcore, the violent punk music that was developed by kids in Orange County and the South Bay. The hall has been described as "something of an old supermarket," but it fit the bill, and featured bands like Vicious Circle, Agent Orange, and the Adolescents. A Holiday Inn now sits on its site.

Hermosa Beach
The Church *1225 Manhattan Ave.*
> Part of this "community craft center" was rented out by Black Flag as a rehearsal hall and performance space. It saw the debuts of Red Cross (later Redd Kross), the Last, and the Descendents. (SST Records started out in Hermosa Beach in 1978—its first headquarters were located at Monterey and Pier Avenue.)

MOJAVE DESERT *115 miles east of Los Angeles*

> Several legendary concerts were held in the Mojave in the early '80s. The first was the Mojave Exodus at Lake Lucerne, which featured Savage Republic and the Minutemen. The second was called Mojave Auszug, and it starred the "Berlin conceptual antiartists" Einsturzende Neubauten. The last show featured Redd Kross, the Meat Puppets, and Psi

Hardcore haven, The Church, in Hermosa Beach. (Photo by Al Flipside.)

The Minutemen at Mojave Exodus. (Photo by Matt Nudelman.)

Jamming at Mojave Exodus. (Photo by Scot Allen.)

Com, Perry Farrell's band before Jane's Addiction. And finally, U2 found the name of their *Joshua Tree* album when photographer Anton Corbijn took them out here for the cover shoot. Perhaps Corbijn had been inspired by the cover of the first Eagles album, which was also shot in the area. Perhaps not.

Joshua Tree Motel *61259 29 Palms Highway, Joshua Tree*

This is the spot where Gram Parsons died on September 19, 1973. It's now the Copper Sands Youth Camp.

Cap Rock

This 175-foot-high granite formation in the Joshua Tree National Forest is the spot where Parsons was cremated. Two of his friends stole his body from the Los Angeles Airport and took him to this site for cremation, as he had supposedly wanted.

Las Vegas, NV   *282 miles NE of Los Angeles*

Las Vegas has not been particularly conducive to the rock and roll spirit over the years. The city's tawdry glitz doesn't blend well with the rebel image rock and rollers try desperately to maintain. (The band Slaughter is a recent exception.) Nevertheless, the city has always had a few human-scale clubs—off the Strip—that catered to local rock fans. Unfortunately, one of the most durable, the Moby Grape, closed its doors in 1991.

The Frontier Hotel   *3120 Las Vegas Blvd. South*

Elvis's first show in Las Vegas was given here in 1956. He opened up for Shecky Green in the Venus Room—and made no new fans. He was a bigger hit thirteen years later (*see* **Las Vegas Hilton**). The Supremes' last show with Diana Ross was presented here on January 14, 1970. Oddly enough, their last song was "Someday We'll Be Together."

Graceland Wedding Chapel   *619 Las Vegas Blvd. South*

Many rock and roll weddings have been performed here—complete with an Elvis Presley impersonator as a witness. The chapel's most famous clients have been Jon Bon Jovi, who married his high school sweetheart here in May 1989, and Phil Joanou, the director of the U2 concert movie, *Rattle and Hum*. He was married here in March 1992; footage from the ceremony was featured in U2's 1992 U.S. tour—it was shown on a big screen above the stage. (By the way, Elvis and Priscilla were married in Las Vegas's **Aladdin Hotel**.)

Las Vegas Hilton   *3000 Paradise Rd.*

Elvis was the second act to play this hotel, then called the Las Vegas International, when it opened in 1969. Except for a television taping, the King hadn't performed in front of an audience in eight years. But he was scheduled for two shows a night for four weeks, and he apparently wowed his audience every time he stepped on stage. (Elvis stayed in a thirtieth-floor suite which is now, of course, named for him.)

The Graceland Chapel in Las Vegas.

Phoenix, AZ   *390 miles SE of Los Angeles*

This southwestern city is the hometown of a varied lot of rock and rollers, including Duane Eddy, Stevie Nicks, Vincent Furnier (later known as Alice Cooper), the Tubes, and the Meat Puppets. It's also been the subject of at least two classics, "Funky Broadway" and Jimmy Webb's "By the Time I Get To Phoenix."

Audio-Video Recorders of Arizona   *3830 North 7th St.*

Legendary guitarist Duane Eddy recorded twelve Top-40 hits at this studio (at its former location, 3703 North 7th St.), including "Ramrod" and "Rebel Rouser." Eddy's longtime engineer, Floyd Ramsey, sold the place and retired in 1991.

Cortez High   *8828 North 31st Ave.*

Vincent Furnier's alma mater. In 1964, Vince and four friends performed at a school sports award banquet as the Earwigs, a spoof/tribute to the Beatles and Stones. They couldn't play but managed to hit the local charts the next year—as the Spiders—with a tune called "Don't Blow Your Mind." By 1968, the band had changed its name to Alice Cooper, moved to Los Angeles and signed with Straight, Frank Zappa's label. (Their anthem "School's Out" was apparently inspired by the nurturing atmosphere at Cortez.)

The Sun Club   *1001 East 8th St., Tempe*

This rock and roll club has featured nearly all the major alternative acts, from the Feelies to fIREHOSE, as well as local pioneers like the Meat Puppets.

BIBLIOGRAPHY

Barth, Jack. *Roadside Elvis*. Chicago: Contemporary Books, 1991.

Belsito, Peter and Davis, Bob. *Hardcore California*. Berkeley: Last Gasp, 1983.

Berry, Chuck. *Chuck Berry: The Autobiography*. New York: Harmony Books, 1987.

Berry, Jason; Foose, Jonathan; and Jones, Tad. *Up From the Cradle of Jazz: New Orleans Music Since World War II*. Athens, Georgia: University of Georgia Press, 1986.

Bird, Christiane. *The Jazz and Blues Lover's Guide to the U.S.* Reading, Mass.: Addison-Wesley Publishing, 1991.

Bream, Jon. *Prince: Inside the Purple Reign*. New York: Macmillan, 1984.

Bronson, Fred. *The Billboard Book of Number One Hits: The Inside Story Behind the Top of the Charts*. New York: Billboard Publications, 1985.

Brown, James, and Tucker, Bruce. *James Brown: The Godfather of Soul*. New York: Thunder's Mouth Press, 1990.

Brown, Peter, and Gaines, Steven. *The Love You Make: An Insider's Story of the Beatles*, New York: McGraw Hill, 1983.

Brown, Rodger Lyle. *Party Out of Bounds: The B-52's, R.E.M. and the Kids Who Rocked Athens, Georgia*. New York: Plume, 1991.

Broven, John. *Rhythm & Blues in New Orleans*. Gretna, La.: Pelican Publishing Co., 1974.

Charles, Ray, and Ritz, David. *Brother Ray*. New York: Dial Press, 1978.

Clark, Dick, and Robinson, Richard. *Rock, Roll & Remember*. New York: Thomas Y. Crowell, 1976.

Connelly, Cynthia; Clague, Leslie; and Cheslow, Sharon. *Banned in D.C.* Washington, D.C.: Sun Dog Propaganda, 1988.

Cross, Charles R. *Backstreets: Springsteen, the Man and His Music*. New York: Harmony Books, 1989.

Dannen, Fredric. *Hit Men: Power Brokers and Fast Money Inside the Music Business*. New York: Vintage Books, 1991.

Davis, Sharon. *Motown: The History*. Middlesex, England: Guiness Publishing, 1988.

Davis, Stephen. *Hammer of the Gods: The Led Zeppelin Saga*. New York: Ballantine Books, 1989.

Escott, Colin, and Hawkins, Martin. *Good Rockin' Tonight: Sun Records and the Birth of Rock'n'Roll*. New York: St. Martin's Press, 1991.

Fein, Art. *The L.A. Musical History Tour: A Guide to the Rock and Roll Landmarks of Los Angeles*. Winchester, Mass.: Faber and Faber, 1990.

Fletcher, Tony. *Remarks: The Story of R.E.M.* New York: Bantam Books, 1990.

Fong-Torres, Ben. *Hickory Wind: The Life and Times of Gram Parsons*. New York: Pocket Books, 1991.

Gaines, Steven. *Heroes and Villains: The True Story of the Beach Boys*. New York: NAL Books, 1986.

Gans, David, and Simon, Peter. *Playing in the Band: An Oral and Visual History of the Grateful Dead*. New York: St. Martin's Press, 1992.

George, Nelson. *Where Did Our Love Go? The Rise and Fall of the Motown Sound*. New York: St. Martin's Press, 1985.

Gillett, Charlie. *The Sound of the City: The Rise of Rock and Roll*. New York: Pantheon Books, 1983.

Goldrosen, John, and Beecher, John. *Remembering Buddy: The Definitive Biography.* New York: Penguin Books, 1987.

Guralnick, Peter. *Sweet Soul Music: Rhythm and Blues and the Southern Dream of Freedom.* New York: Harper & Row, 1986.

Hager, Steven. *Hip Hop.* New York: St. Martin's Press, 1984.

Hannusch, Jeff. *I Hear You Knockin'.* Athens, Ohio: Swallow Publications, Inc., 1985.

Hirshey, Gerri. *Nowhere to Run: The Story of Soul Music.* New York: Penguin Books, 1985.

Hopkins, Jerry, and Sugerman, Danny. *No One Here Gets Out Alive.* New York: Warner Books, 1980.

Kozak, Roman. *This Ain't No Disco: The Story of CBGB.* Winchester, Mass.: Faber and Faber, 1988.

Lemlich, Jeffrey M. *Savage Lost.* Miami: Distinctive Publishing Corp., 1992.

Lewisohn, Mark. *The Beatles Day-by-Day: A Chronology 1962–1989.* New York: Harmony Books, 1989.

Marsh, Dave. *Before I Get Old: The Story of the Who.* New York: St. Martin's Press, 1983.

———. *Born to Run.* Dolphin Books, 1979.

McDonough, Jack. *San Francisco Rock.* San Francisco: Chronicle Books, 1985.

Miller, Jim, ed. *The Rolling Stone Illustrated History of Rock & Roll.* New York: Rolling Stone Press, 1980.

Monk, Noel E., and Guterman, Jimmy. *Twelve Days on the Road: The Sex Pistols and America.* New York: William Morrow and Co., 1990.

Palmer, Robert. *Deep Blues.* New York: Penguin Books, 1981.

Pareles, Jon, and Romanowski, Patricia, eds. *The Rolling Stone Encyclopedia of Rock & Roll.* New York: Rolling Stone Press, 1983.

Presley, Priscilla Beaulieu, and Harmon, Sandra. *Elvis and Me.* New York: G.P. Putnam's Sons, 1985.

Pruter, Robert. *Chicago Soul.* Chicago: University of Illinois Press, 1990.

Rayl, A.J.S. *Beatles '64: A Hard Day's Night in America.* New York: Doubleday, 1989.

Robbins, Ira A., ed. *The Trouser Press Record Guide.* New York: Collier Books, 1991.

Shannon, Bob, and Javna, John. *Behind the Hits.* New York: Warner Books, 1986.

Simon, Clea, and Milano, Brett. *Boston Rock Trivia.* Boston: Quinlan Press, 1985.

Spector, Ronnie, and Waldron, Vince. *Be My Baby.* New York: Harmony Books, 1990.

Stambler, Irwin. *The Encyclopedia of Pop, Rock & Soul.* New York: St. Martin's Press, 1989.

Tosches, Nick. *Hellfire: The Jerry Lee Lewis Story.* New York: Dell Publishing Co., 1982.

Turner, Tina, and Loder, Kurt. *I, Tina.* New York: William Morrow and Co., 1986.

Wilson, Brian, and Gold, Todd. *Wouldn't It Be Nice: My Own Story.* New York: Harper-Collins, 1991.

And countless issues of *Billboard, Creem, Pulse, Rolling Stone, Spin, Details, Option, Musician,* and *The Village Voice.*

INDEX